RATED RX

RATED RX

SHEREE ROSE
WITH AND AFTER BOB FLANAGAN

EDITED BY YETTA HOWARD

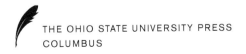

THE OHIO STATE UNIVERSITY PRESS
COLUMBUS

Library of Congress Cataloging-in-Publication Data
Names: Howard, Yetta, editor.
Title: Rated RX : Sheree Rose with and after Bob Flanagan / edited by Yetta Howard.
Description: Columbus : The Ohio State University Press, [2020] | Summary: "A collection of photographs, archival materials, creative works, and essays exploring BDSM, sexuality, disability, temporality, and artistic legacies in the career of Sheree Rose, late partner of supermasochist Bob Flanagan"—Provided by publisher.
Identifiers: LCCN 2020017685 | ISBN 9780814214480 (cloth) | ISBN 0814214487 (cloth) | ISBN 9780814256039 (ebook) | ISBN 0814256031 (ebook)
Subjects: LCSH: Rose, Sheree, 1941– | Flanagan, Bob, 1952–1996. | Performance artists. | Performance art. | Sadomasochism. | Bondage (Sexual behavior) | Masochism in art. | Art, Modern—20th century.
Classification: LCC HQ79 .R273 2020 | DDC 306.77/5—dc23
LC record available at https://lccn.loc.gov/2020017685

Cover photo: Judy Ornelas Sisneros, from *100 Reasons* performance at Coagula Curatorial, 2014

Cover design by Angela Moody
Text design by Juliet Williams
Type set in Palatino Linotype

♾ The paper used in this publication meets the minimum requirements of the American National Standard for Information Sciences—Permanence of Paper for Printed Library Materials. ANSI Z39.48-1992.

For Jenn

CONTENTS

PART 2: 1999–2018

SECTION 3: APPENDICES
OUT-OF-PRINT PUBLICATIONS ABOUT
SHEREE ROSE BY BOB FLANAGAN

ACKNOWLEDGMENTS

I first heard about Sheree Rose and Bob Flanagan in 1997 when, while undergraduates in Boston, my fellow queer punk pal Marco Repola and I went to see *Sick: The Life and Death of Bob Flanagan, Supermasochist* at a local arthouse movie theater. Fast forward to 2012 and Zarah Ersoff, my lover at the time, met Sheree at a kinky brunch in Highland Park, Los Angeles, and, not too long after that, Zarah introduced us over happy hour drinks. This book would never have materialized if Zarah did not have the subcultural wherewithal to make this connection. The idea for this book began around 2013, when Sheree did a memorable talk at San Diego State University—I collaborated with Meagan Marshall to bring Sheree to SDSU as part of the Living Writers series that spring. Now, at forty-three, I am finished with what is a long-overdue collection on Sheree's legacy in underground culture and performance art history. If we take cues from what the synchronicities that our existences and worlds communicate, I do not think it is a coincidence that, as I submit the final version of this *Rated RX* manuscript, I am the same age that Bob Flanagan was when he died. It goes without saying that my gratitude first and foremost goes to Sheree—the wisdom, experience, and life narratives that she shared with me over the years have changed my life and my thinking about the ways to experience existence in resisting the sexism of the heteronormative world. The intimate value of her friendship is immeasurable, and I hope this book helps to give her the recognition she deserves for living fiercely, independently, and creatively.

This project would not be possible without the ONE National Gay and Lesbian Archives at the University of Southern California Libraries. The Sheree Rose and Bob Flanagan Papers, from which much of the material reproduced in this collection is sourced, are a goldmine of materials—photographic and otherwise—that Sheree donated to the ONE in 2014. It was at that point, while consulting with Sheree, that the possibilities for an archive-book were on the horizon and when I began the archival research. At ONE, archivist Loni Shibuyama was indispensable in my research, selections, and processing of materials from the Rose/Flanagan Papers. I would also like to thank former ONE archivist Cooper T. Moll, who cataloged the Rose/Flanagan Papers; ONE director Joseph Hawkins; and ONE staff members Bud Thomas and David Evans Frantz, who also helped make this project possible at many stages during my years of research. I am also grateful to the ONE Archives Foundation, Inc., for the honor of being one of the 2018 ONE Archives LGBTQ Research Fellows.

I would especially like to acknowledge producer and artist Luka Fisher: in addition to contributing an essay and materials to *Rated RX*, Luka's involvement with this project extended in many directions that were not limited to locating materials included in this collection that were not in the Rose/Flanagan Papers at ONE. Luka also helped with some of the crucial connections, documentation, and circulation associated with this project during many stages of its completion. I also wish to acknowledge Tanya Augsburg, whose contributions to *Rated RX* go beyond her essay and her *Nailed, Again!* documentation; conversations with Tanya about her friendship and history with Sheree in the context of her experience with the feminist politics of performance art cultures cannot be overestimated in their value to this project.

In addition to the support from the ONE Archives Foundation, Inc., support for this project came from SDSU College of Arts and Letters Dean Norma Bouchard and the SDSU Research Foundation. I would also like to thank the external committee for the SDSU Department of English and Comparative Literature Warner Innovation Award, which I received in 2018. I wish to acknowledge colleagues and friends at SDSU who attended my Warner Innovation Award talk, provided feedback on this project, and/or explicitly supported my efforts along the way, especially Quentin Bailey, Pablo Ben, Edee Benkov, Mike Borgstrom, Clarissa Clò, Chris Curtis, Edith Frampton, Mary Garcia, Emily Hicks, D. J. Hopkins, Paul

Kaplan, Eve Kornfeld, Jaime Lennox, Meagan Marshall, Angel Matos, Bill Nericcio, Arzu Ozcal, Walter Penrose, Jessica Pressman, Esther Rothblum, Phillip Serrato, Jenny Minniti-Shippey, Joseph Thomas, and Katie Waltman. Thanks go to Kim Navarro for her edgy design of the poster for my Warner Award talk on this project.

I am also thankful for the feedback I received when presenting portions of this project at the College Art Association conference in 2018, especially from fellow panelists Jessica Cooley and Keri Watson, and, in association, Lu Auz. I appreciate the support of Stef Snider and Aaminah Shakur: Stef and Aaminah chaired the 2020 College Art Association panel "Crip Solidarity and Access Intimacy in the Arts," where I presented some portions of this project. Thanks also to the other presenters on this panel, Jessica Cooley, Theo Ciccarelli Cornetta, and Alison Kopit. Special thanks to *F213* [one degree above the boiling point of blood] exhibit lead curator Tanya Augsburg and to all who attended the *F213* opening at the Arc Gallery and Studios in San Francisco, where Sheree and I, included as artist and writer in the exhibit, presented Sheree's *Blue Takes Washington* (1993) in spring 2019. Thanks also go to Chelsea Zeffiro for inviting me to discuss this project on "The Body as Archive and Movement as Archive" panel held at Art Produce Gallery in San Diego as part of the 40 North Dance Film Festival in fall 2018. I also wish to thank the other artists and scholars who participated on this panel, Jesse Keller, Karen Schaffman, and Terry Sprague, the audience members, and Art Produce Gallery Executive Director Lynn Susholtz.

Scholars of underground culture understand how important it is to get support from friends, artists, and other scholars who are also invested in and/or involved in some of these cultural contexts. These folx and others who have expressed support or enthusiasm for the project along the way include Christopher Smith Adair, Frederick Luis Aldama, Jen Ansley, Ron Athey, Daniel Babcock, Stacy Banas, Wonda Baugh, Ilona Berger, Andromeda Breeze, Ashley Capachione, Cassils, Amy Cimini, Kate Clyde, Gino Conti, Jih-Fei Cheng, Dino Dinco, Brit Donaldson, Laura Dunne, Zarah Ersoff, Nikki Eschen, Pony Lee Estrange, Ramzi Fawaz, Esteban Flores, Randy Focazio, Laura Fugikawa, Margaret Galvan, Nora Gilbert, Deanna Gold, Michael MP Griffin, Sarah Hankins, Sue "Spyke" Hirshon, Dominic Johnson, Peter Kalisch, Shayna Kessel, Rheytchul Kimmel, Paige Kirby, LE Legirl, Nick Lesley, Sam Lopez, Brian Mark, Marci McMahon, Cristy Michel, Tone Milazzo, Larry Monteleone, Justin Morrison, Hoang Nguyen, Cassie Pinner, Marco Repola, Sal Shabazz, M.J. Stevens, Jenny Stoever, Paul Tighe, Karen Tongson, Xavier Vasquez, Kirin Wachter-

Grene, and Mike Zimbouski. My twin sister, Nancy Howard, has been particularly supportive of this project from the moment I received the contract for it.

Immense gratitude goes to Tara Cyphers at The Ohio State University Press, especially for her patience as this project got closer to publication. Tara has tirelessly championed this project from the start. Her generous feedback, encouragement, and careful advice throughout the editorial process made *Rated RX* the book that I envisioned it to be. She helped transform what began as a bullet-point list of materials to my multiple spreadsheets and materials overview documents with complex numbering/lettering systems. Two anonymous reviewers provided extensive and extremely useful reports, and this project owes a great deal to their comments, suggestions, and recommendations. Becca Bostock at The Ohio State University Press helped to facilitate what could have been some nightmarish permissions scenarios.

Editing *Rated RX* has been the most labor-intensive project of my academic career thus far, even if in the spirit of a labor of love. Editing this collection—part of the time in the midst of heartache, emotional lows, illnesses/bodily betrayals, deaths, and a move—involved not only overseeing contributions by academics well versed in the academic publishing world (which is by itself a lot of work) but also many explanatory conversations and emails with those who were less familiar with academic publishing protocols. *Rated RX* is a comprehensive editorial endeavor whose result includes exceptional essays by scholars, artists, and writers spanning a range of genres and approaches to the project. Significantly, the editing, selection, and organization of the photographs and other materials proved to be an enormous amount of work, more than I ever imagined, well exceeding anything I have edited, especially since I did not bring in co-editors to help me with the workload. Needless to say, *Rated RX*'s many moving parts means that I exhale deeply now with relief that the book has come to fruition. I hope reader-experiencers of *Rated RX* take as much pleasure in their journeys through it as I did in the (sometimes masochistically inflected) journey to it.

Finally, thanks to my love, Jenn Tyburczy: you're everything to me.

Tina Takemoto's "Love Is Still Possible in This Junky Word" interview with Sheree Rose originally appeared in *Women and Performance: A Journal of Feminist Theory*, vol. 19, no. 1, 2009, pp. 95–111, copyright *Women & Performance* Project, Inc., reprinted with permission from Taylor & Francis, Ltd. My "Obliquely Chronophilic" interview with Sheree Rose and Martin O'Brien first appeared in *Fiction International* 47, 2014, pp. 73–84, special issue "Phobia / Philia" and reprinted with permission from *Fiction International* | Editor-in-Chief Harold Jaffe. Jane DeLynn's "The Duchess of LA" first appeared in her *Don Juan in the Village* (Pantheon, 1990), copyright Jane DeLynn, reprinted with permission.

Performing the Minority Body Archive across Time and Sheree Rose's Legacy in Underground Art History

YETTA HOWARD

> Often people say that Bob was a submissive but he dominated everything in terms of our work. The fact is, that's not true. In an SM relationship only the dominant is empowered to decide. That's my feminism. It certainly isn't everybody's definition of feminism, but it was my version of a feminist approach to SM.
>
> —Sheree Rose, from Dominic Johnson's "Slave to Love: An Interview with Sheree Rose"

> I wouldn't [have] gotten involved in all this art crap if it weren't for [Sheree]. I would have spent all my time as her slave, writing dopey little ditties in the back room. Would I have lived as long? Would we have stayed together? Would life have been so good? Probably not.
>
> —Bob Flanagan, from *The Pain Journal*

> The thing that people don't understand is that Bob was *my invention*.
>
> —Sheree Rose, from Tina Takemoto's "Love Is Still Possible in This Junky World"

As I prepare to revise this introduction, Sheree Rose is in Santa Monica, California, recovering from a heart attack. In June 2018 Rose essentially saved her own life by getting to the hospital when she detected unusual sensations and, fortunately, had the heart attack at the hospital, after

1

which she underwent surgery and a miraculous recovery. It is perhaps odd to think of Rose as the one being visited in a hospital, since she has had an entire lifetime on the other side of that. Rose is primarily known for blurring the boundaries between art practice and lived experience in

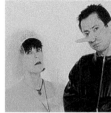

p. 199

the context of her full-time, Mistress-slave relationship with her late partner of sixteen years, Bob Flanagan. Flanagan, "supermasochist" performance artist, suffered from cystic fibrosis (CF) but, with Rose, translated his illness into extreme and revolutionary approaches to art practice before his death in 1996, what Linda Kauffman has called "Sadomedicine": "juxtapos[ing] the 'pathology' of CF with the 'pathology' of masochism" (21). But in the thinking about Rose's dominance and Flanagan's submission in the context of their sexual-performative-lived dynamics, something in underground art history has been amiss: the reduction of Rose as an assistant to Flanagan in performance practice or the inaccurate characterization of her as simply his caregiver. That Rose's art died with Flanagan's death is a misconception and, more importantly, undermines the parity between them in their collaborative work. An artist in her own right, Rose has been undervalued or mischaracterized as secondary to Flanagan and has therefore been less explored as an artist. Rose continues to be a cultural innovator in the present, and this book situates Rose's body of work in a multiply temporal dialogue among her solo art practices, her collaborative performances with Flanagan in the 1980s and 1990s, and her work spanning the period 1999–2017 that reimagines or "resurrects" some of her earlier work, collaborative or otherwise. While some of her recent performances embody or are inspired by ideas of theirs when Flanagan was alive but were never carried out because he ran out of time to live, Rose's work ultimately asks us to rethink lived, performed temporalities alongside inhabitations of ill, crip, and aging bodies as a presentation of a minority body archive across time.

I borrow "minority body" partially from Elizabeth Barnes's book of the same name, *The Minority Body: A Theory of Disability* (2016). Barnes's chapter on "bad-difference" versus "mere-difference" is particularly relevant to the minority discourse with which *Rated RX* is concerned. For Barnes, "bad-difference" is the notion that having a disability makes one "worse off" than nondisabled people whereas "mere-difference" characterizes those with disabilities as "non-standard" but not inferior to able-bodied individuals (55). When we consider what Barnes and many other crip theorists have posited, many narrow-minded perspectives that surround the crip body have more to do with dominant perspectives that fail to acknowledge, understand, accept, or accommodate difference. Difference is at the heart of Rose's body of work, whose constellation of crip difference, sexual difference, gender difference, and subcultural difference subversively wrenches itself away from normative sexuality and dominant views of the feminist body, which *Rated RX* traces across time by interrogating the perceived stasis of the archive and the illusory temporariness of performance. In such contexts, the queerness of Rose's archive is one that situates bodies in and out of time and aligns with what Alison Kafer theorizes as "the process of articulating other temporalities, other approaches to futurity beyond curative ones" (28). Here, Kafer's theory of crip time as "always already present in queer time" (28) and J. Jack Halberstam's theory of queer time that includes "nonnormative logics and organizations of community, sexual identity, embodiment, and activity in space and time" (6) become instructive for comprehending what it means to engage queerly with performed-lived time, whether functioning as duration, age, or illness in Rose's work.

Invested in the in/finite "timeless" possibilities of Rose's minority body archive, *Rated RX* does not attempt to be an exhaustive survey of Rose's work with and after Flanagan as its subtitle may suggest to some. Instead, this book seeks to resuscitate Rose's mortality-based and ritualistic creative practices in order to contemplate how collaboration moves between life and art—and how art may script and re-script itself in the lives of those who perform it as much as in being performed. Part of what is at stake in this project is how Rose's art addresses minoritarian embodiment and radical inhabitations of Dominant/submissive roles in the many forms that her feminist transgressions of power have taken. As a feminist project that critically reassesses artistic legacies through the lens of Rose's collaborative strategies, *Rated RX* considers what it means to decenter the male artist as the site of innovation and to reorient sexist approaches to curation and the politics of the archive through Rose's art practices. This project shows how her performances modify our understandings of the body in its varied modes of nondominant subjectivity. Primarily based on archival materials from the Rose/Flanagan Papers at ONE National Gay and Lesbian Archives at the University of Southern California Libraries, *Rated RX* is an edited collection of photography, archival materials, and essays that attempts to fill in the gaps of underground cultural and performance art histories where Rose has either been thought of as less worthy of attention than Flanagan or has been neglected as a self-sufficient feminist artist.

Carrying the potential risk of sounding sensationalistic, the title of this collection, *Rated RX*, has multiple significations. One of the central themes in Rose's life-work has been illness and the medical body; thus the title invokes the medical terminology of *Rx* as executed through Rose's performances. *Rx* is Latin for "recipe/mixture" — related to the mixing of medicinal compounds — but in this case, mixture becomes a way to think about Rose's collaborative strategies, the mixture of bodily dynamics in and out of normatively performed and lived time. Yet what is distinctively observable in the title is *Rx*'s miscapitalization. This intentional miscapitalization is meant to misappropriate and subvert medical terminology in the same way that Rose's collaborative work radically reworks propriety associated with medical practices, documentation strategies, and temporal frameworks in her approaches to performance, photography, and BDSM. Sonic Youth's *Dirty* (1992) album — included in this collection via an image of the rare, special edition compact disc — one of many postpunk, noise, and industrial music contexts associated with Rose and Flanagan, does something somewhat similar with capitalization. The album's title *Dirty* appears on the album cover and compact disc itself as *diRty*, which functions to accentuate the auditory roughness of the *R*. In turn, the *R* suggests onomatopoetic grunting as an articulation of BDSM pleasure/pain, as an embrace of being sexually "dirty." Combined with the letter *X* in *RX*, *R* brings out the marginality that often accompanies *X*. *X*, of course, has more than oblique associations with the concept of X-rated. It resonates with the prefix *ex-*: much of Rose's work reflects ex-plicit content, while signifying ex-treme performance and s-ex-ual practices, out-sider art, and being ex-cluded from feminist art histories and underground cultural histories. Indeed, performance art does not go by rating systems as with some film, but the title places pressure on the norms of expectation — a key strategy in much performance art, especially in its more extreme forms. The title therefore plays with what may sound familiar (Rx and Rated R) as it destabilizes assumptions about its denotations. Moreover, notions of rating speak to the classificatory systems in play when contemplating feminist art (Rose) as less worthy of art by men (Flanagan) and the gender politics that come with collaborative practices, and so *Rated RX* comes to stand for the need to create one's own systems of recognition uninvested in official forms of approval. Rose has often said that she never got into art for any form of official recognition even though, as this book shows, her work has been severely neglected and has more than earned a crucial place in radical histories of performance art, feminist art, and underground culture documentation. This collection, then, attempts to grapple with how minoritarian embodiment in Rose's work pushes up against allowable or acceptable forms of sexual-performative-lived expression and how putatively risky strategies of being in the world offer some of the most satisfactory ways to live in opposition to the doldrums of the normative.

Hence, the multiple significations of *RX* also correspond to the many ways that the letter *S* has functioned in Rose's performance practices. Rose's iconic mark of *S*, which she has carved with a razor on skin in sharp, elongated angles resembling a back-ward *Z* on Flanagan (including posthumously), herself, and many others in both performance and nonperfor-mance settings, symbolically marks a necessary insta-bility of its proliferating meanings for and about Rose, as Amelia Jones, Tanya Augsburg, and Martin O'Brien 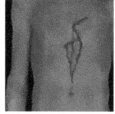 address in their essays in this collection. *S*, as these contributors write, is all at once but not reducible to "Supermasochist," "Sheree," "Slave," "Survival," "Sick." In *The Book of Medicine,* which remained unpublished for over twenty years until Rose's and Rhiannon Aarons's effort to pub-lish it in 2017, Flanagan writes, "Beneath her 'S' my lungs are a soupy, sloppy mess, like split pea, like shit, like sewage, and it's all stopped up inside, so on the surface I'm one sputtering, slobbering, sorry specimen, suffocating and spasming like someone put a sock in my esophagus—and she's supposed to feel sexy when I'm suffering?" (62). In Rose's sexual-performative dynamic to which Flanagan refers in this extensive render-ing of nondominant corporeality as antinormative model of desirability, the eroticization of the ill body operates as a queer-crip sign of contesting the neoliberal impulse to be collapsed into an assimilative model of het-erosexual and able-bodied inclusion. Rose as Mistress to slave Flanagan follows a trajectory of what David T. Mitchell with Sharon L. Snyder calls "peripheral embodiment" (14) in that BDSM sexuality co-signs the "exces-sive deviance from culturally inculcated norms" (14) in the commitment to denying heteronormative and ableist mandates of relationality and how it translates into field-changing practices of art-making.

Born in 1941, Rose is possibly one of the least likely people to have initiated a radical reassessment of art-world conventions through deep investments in queer sexualities that have fundamentally disrupted the status quo of art practice and lived experience as routed through per-formance and minority bodies. As an artist who fashioned the bridging of underground art practices and sexual subcultures with the art world, Rose directly contributed to the transformation of museum/gallery/

p. 285

hospital/domestic spaces and the confluence of BDSM, disability, and performance art. But her background may be what is the most surprising and unexpected part of all this. Growing up in Southern California in the mid-twentieth century, Rose was the typical Encino homemaker, married with two children, living a "nice" but dull and ultimately oppressive heteronormative life. Both she and her first husband were schoolteachers, and, after they divorced in the late 1970s, she got involved in the Los Angeles punk scene and feminist activism and received graduate degrees from California State University, Northridge, and University of California, Irvine. Rose and Flanagan helped initiate the BDSM scene in Los Angeles, which included starting the Los Angeles Branch of the Society of Janus (Vale and Juno, *Bob Flanagan* 105). Targeted by notoriously conservative and homophobic Senator Jesse Helms in a 1989 letter to the National Endowment for the Arts during the culture wars of the 1980s, Rose's photography and video work of genital piercing, tattooing, and other body-modification rituals was included in the same list with Flanagan, tattooist Don Ed Hardy, and photographer Bobby Neel Adams. In the letter, Helms was targeting those involved in Andrea Juno and V. Vale's *Modern Primitives* exhibit (also the name of one of their RE/Search volumes, discussed below). During this time, during the period 1989–1993, Rose was an integral part of Club FUCK! a queer, leathersex, BDSM, and body modification nightclub and performance space, which was raided by the Los Angeles Police Department in 1993.

Even though writing about Rose and Flanagan's art appeared in underground publications and subcultural contexts throughout the 1980s and 1990s, it was not until the late 1990s that scholarly work on Rose and Flanagan began to appear more prevalently. Amelia Jones and Linda Kauffman were among the first to write about Rose and Flanagan in their early academic monographs. These scholars opened the doors to understanding Rose and Flanagan through the queerness of their gendered dynamics and the exceedingly nonheteronormative qualities of their sexual lives that surfaced in approaches to performance practice. In discussing Rose as Dominatrix and Flanagan as a masochistic man in life and art, Jones writes that their collaborative work "is hardly recuperative of a privileged relationship to the father/phallus; it flamboyantly resurfaces this suppressed male body—which is enacted yet just as dramatically veiled behind the symbolic functions of artistic authority and art historical interpretation" (*Body Art* 234). For Kauffman, Rose and Flanagan's collaborative art "makes us realize how little theorizing has been devoted to *heterosexuality*, which for so long has been presumed to be 'natural'" (21; emphasis in original). In her work on masochism in performance art, also written in the late 1990s, Kathy O'Dell emphasizes Flanagan but situates his collaboration with Rose as central to "dealing more publicly with his masochism and performing at alternative art spaces" (76). With much less emphasis on Rose, Lynda Hart was also one of the first to write about Flanagan and Rose in a scholarly study and notably indicates that Flanagan "became a performance artist rather serendipitously, after he became involved with Sheree and her passion for documenting their relationship on video and through journals" (139). As Hart, Jones, Kauffman, and O'Dell suggest in their respective early writings on Rose and Flanagan's collaborative work—albeit in quite disparate ways—the importance of eschewing dominant perspectives of sexual, performance, and *exhibition* practices cannot be overestimated when contemplating the upturning of gender roles that Rose embodied in *being the Dominant* in her relationship with Flanagan.

Documenting the Underground

While the range of *Rated RX*'s archival materials addresses these numerous yet interconnected vectors of gendered, subcultural, and bodily difference in underground art history through Rose's performance and documentation practices, Rose's photography and video art is another less-explored feature of her artistic legacy that this book aims to highlight. In the 1980s and 1990s, Rose was the staff photographer for the legendary literary arts center Beyond Baroque in Venice, California, where independent art, poetry, and music scenes mixed and where subcultural and luminary figures such as Patti Smith, Tom Waits, and Henry Rollins read and/or performed their work; some of these rare photographs by Rose are included in this volume. But one of the earliest writing on Rose's pathbreaking photography of underground and sexual cultures appears in RE/Search #12 *Modern Primitives* (1989) volume, which includes a chapter on her photographs and videos from that era. *Modern Primitives* features Rose's photographs of genital, nipple, and play piercings at a time when piercing and tattooing were still very much markers of subcultural difference and reflections of inhabiting bodily autonomy outside the mainstream. In her interview with Andrea Juno in the volume, Rose discusses practices such as the queer pleasures of engaging in sex involving penis piercings: "it's like a steel dildo—it's incredible!" (Vale and Juno, *Modern* 109). Rose goes on to use feminist philosophy as a justification for identifying as Dominant (111) and discusses the overlaps between the piercing/

tattooing and BDSM communities and the ways that breaking down the pleasure/pain binary associated with both has spiritual and empowering effects. "We're interested in the imaginative possibilities of body modifications," remarks Rose, "the creativity that can be made manifest by pushing the body to its limits" (113). Ideally, Rose's documentation of the body modification underground would have a much more prominent place in the photographic and video vanguard of this subculture's history. Discussed in Luka Fisher's essay in this collection is *Needles and Pins* (1987), Rose's video documentary focusing on piercing pioneer Jim Ward's hands in action, which included a clitoral piercing, at the Gauntlet, his legendary Los Angeles–area piercing studio that was a key site of BDSM and queer world-mixing. Archival documentation of a *Needles and Pins* screening at a 1988 EZTV event is included in this collection. In 2015 the exhibit *Dress Codes: Chuck Arnett and Sheree Rose* at ONE National Gay and Lesbian Archives included the documentary and Rose's prints of women at BDSM events and fetish clubs. From 1983 to 1993 Rose shot a range of spanked and tortured asses from the BDSM underground; artist Mike Kelley named each of these photographs after conceivable names for paddles. Also based on spanking Flanagan one hundred times in a row, this series was titled *100 Reasons,* and, in collaboration with Kelley, Rose and Flanagan made a video piece of the spanking using the same name. Included in

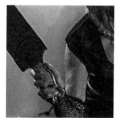

this book is Judy Ornelas Sisneros's photographs of Rose's re-performance of the spanking, which was part of Rose's *100 Reasons* exhibition at Coagula Curatorial in 2014. Also included in these pages is the pamphlet for the 1993 *TranceSex* video marathon festival at the Mondrian Hotel on the Sunset Strip in West Hollywood, California, where Rose's film was shown with films by

p. 275

Carolee Schneemann, Vito Acconci, Annie Sprinkle, Gran Fury, and Andy Warhol.

As is apparent, Rose's extensive involvement with queer, BDSM, and leather communities was bound up with her photographic and video documentation of these subcultures. Rose also, of course, continuously photographed Flanagan throughout their sixteen years together—whether in the midst of BDSM scenes at home, in spaces designated for performance, or while he was doing something mundane. Rose documented all of Flanagan's solo performances, and, in addition to how it has functioned for the archival conservation of her collaborations with Flanagan, Rose's photography should be understood as its own performance. With an unfortunate omission of mentioning Rose's photography, Rosemarie

Garland-Thomson writes that Flanagan "provokes his viewers by render-ing himself a contemporary freak figure" (358) and "aggressively enlists the exotic mode to counter unequivocally the rhetoric of sentimentality and renounce even the admiration of the wondrous" (358). Rose's docu-mentation practices are the vehicle for this mode of exotic display and give the performances their recollective and visual longevity. And it is Rose's photography that is almost exclusively included in V. Vale and Andrea Juno's *Bob Flanagan: Supermasochist* (1993), the first volume of the "People Series" in their RE/Search underground culture books, which maintain a wide cult following into the present. Moreover, in Rose and Flanagan's most well-known collaborative work, *Visiting Hours* (1992–95), Rose's *Wall of Pain* photographic collage of Flanagan's face in various expressions of pain (inflicted by her) took up an entire wall of the exhibit and, fashioned with hypodermic needles, the collage continues to be an explicit example of the performative aspects of her photographic vision.

In all my research trips to dig through the Rose/Flanagan Papers at ONE Archives, I uncovered unexpected and exciting materials. But in the context of Rose's photography, it is worth noting the discovery of letters to Rose and Flanagan from Tom Hallewell, a promoter and contact person for Psychic TV—one of the most influential groups in industrial and exper-imental music. The letter to Rose included in this book is one of many examples that places Rose's photography in a vital early part of the group's visual history. Rose's photograph to which the letter refers is of Genesis P-Orridge (founding member of Throbbing Gristle and member of Psychic TV) and Paula P-Orridge, which appears in *Modern Primitives,* and is reproduced in this collection. Materials such as these demonstrate how Rose's photography circulated within and lent to the visibility and image of these significant underground auditory-performance cultures. In addition to being the foremost figure in industrial music culture, P-Orridge, whose queerness and trans identities cannot be separated from the trans-gressive sounds that coextend with their corporeal forms of transgression, becomes a suitable point of departure for contemplating how Rose's pho-tography was ahead of its time when it came to LGBTQ politics.

Without the goal of subscribing to an assimilative form of queerness, Rose's involvement with queer sexual cultures operates in the same scope as her deep involve-ment in BDSM cultures. Rose's photograph *Blue Takes Washington* (1993) was taken at the March on Washing-ton, a landmark gay rights event that, in following the 1987 March, promoted queer visibility more than two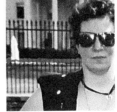

p. 246

and half decades before any sustained discourse on gay marriage. In the spring of 2019, *Blue Takes Washington* was selected to be in the *F213* [one degree above the boiling point of blood] exhibit at the Arc Gallery and Studios, San Francisco, an exhibition that lead curator (and contributor to this collection) Tanya Augsburg describes as a mobilization of feminist anger's boiling point in reaction to Donald Trump's presidency and the creative and necessary forms of rage that it continues to inspire (Augsburg 20). *F213* paired artists with writers, and statements by both appeared in the gallery alongside the works. Both Rose and I were in this exhibit and presented the work in San Francisco at the opening in April 2019 with Blue (Sue "Spyke" Hirshon, the subject of the photograph) in attendance. Rose writes, "Blue was my slave, and she proudly posed in all her butch glory in front of the White House. The photo has lost none of its power and is more relevant than ever in today's political climate" (Artist Statement 96). I write in my statement accompanying Rose's *Blue Takes Washington* that "the photographic subject is both personal and political: subversively clutching chains in defiance of the White House in the background, Blue, one of Rose's slaves, boldly displays butch gender while publicly proclaiming involvement in leather culture as a distinctly political act extending beyond the contexts of the 1993 March on Washington" (Howard 96).

Minority Bodies in Life-Performance

Contemporary classical composer Brian Mark's *Breathe* (2017) is a stunning, approximately ten-minute sonic meditation on CF, a piano duo written for musicians Isabelle O'Connell and Kathleen Supové and inspired by Mark's friend Alice Vogt, who lives with the illness and underwent her first double-lung transplant in 2008 and a second one in 2017 (the first recipient of a second double lung transplant in South African history). Beginning with insulated sounds of the slow struggle to breathe with an amplified sense of taking in the available air, we hear Vogt's voice discussing her experience with the illness, which is spliced throughout the piece and accompanies a slowly building tapestry of subdued yet spontaneous opposition between each player that develops into minor-key tonal torrents and gently discordant assemblages of notes that situate themselves outside the conventional piano scales. Weaved into the unexpected forays into the shifts in speed between the respective parts for each piano, Vogt's illness narrative punctuates the piece and describes the experience of CF as trying to breathe through a straw, a constant ordeal of gurgling mucus, the feeling of slowly drowning, and sometimes coughing up blood. The materiality of the body's blockages is reflected as cascading and dissonant piano notes fall into each other and leave no room to be discerned from each other, an auditory manifestation of struggling with the limitations engendered by amended corporeal encounters with oxygen. Vogt discusses the Romantic-era classical composer Frédéric Chopin—who is thought to have died from the illness—and, in turn, *Breathe* "incorporates elements of music quotation from Chopin's various works (*Nocturne Op. 9 No.1 in Bb Minor, Prelude No. 15 in Db Major,* and *Prelude Op. 28 No. 4 in E Minor*) juxtaposed with sounds of breathing and circulation" as well as "chord progressions from Pink Floyd's 'Breathe (In the Air)'" (brianjmark. com). We run into obliquely and explicitly cast crescendos that dramatically find their way to the end of the composition but not without some degree of tussle that comes through as a glorious framework of competing tonality.

Composed as a duo, *Breathe*'s experimentation with the spatiality of performer-body-sound is a useful way to link Flanagan with Martin O'Brien vis-à-vis their shared illness and shared collaborations with Rose. As Mark describes, "The use of two pianos in this work is a multi-sided canvas of both experiences" (brianjmark.com) but also becomes a way to consider the crip body's queerness as relational enactments of duration as well as of revised life-time in light of the non-able-body and illness in BDSM-based performance. Rose's recent work as a "multi-sided canvas," then, temporally straddles her collaborative work with Flanagan, who at the time of his death at forty-three in 1996 was the longest-living person with CF, and with London-based, queer performance artist O'Brien, who also has CF but, performing in his twenties and early thirties with Rose, who is in her seventies, is several decades younger and has been her most consistent collaborator in the 2013–2017 performances. These modes of survival that are wrapped up in misaligned age and life expectancy point back to Flanagan's "Fight Sickness with Sickness" CF/BDSM message, which, as Robert McRuer has observed, "might [be detected as a] seemingly incomprehensible way to survive, and survive well [. . . but also that] surviving well can paradoxically mean surviving sick" (183). In atemporal synchronicity, O'Brien describes himself as "the sick little baby that is somehow chosen by the ghost of a masochist artist" (57) and, as collaborative life-death transgressions that exceed their performative-mortal contexts, O'Brien writes, "Bob is living on, through Sheree, through me" (57).

Just as O'Brien, then, in collaboration with Rose recasts "survival of the fittest" as a dissident "survival of the sickest" (the fiercely anti-eugenicist title of O'Brien's 2018 artist monograph), Rose's twenty-first-century performances need to be considered in the context of age and how it is united with illness and disability studies discourse. In complicating the embrace of Eve Sedgwick's classic work on reparative strategies, Paul K. Saint-Amour's theorizing of "weak theory" encompasses moving past binaries such as paranoid versus reparative (440) and thus invites a consideration of minoritarian experience and forms of critique unbeholden to ameliorative logics. As Saint-Amour writes, "Weak theory is *descriptive*, seeking to know but not necessarily know better than its object" (444) and that it "finds the risk of bad surprises an acceptable price to pay for the prospect of good ones" (444). Questioning the impulse to move toward what is "strong," to hesitate with the need to fix things for what is considered "better," "weak theory" may very well fall in line with O'Brien's contention in his "Sermon on Sickness," included in his essay in this collection, that "the only way to survive is to join the unwell. Sickness is a desired state of being." We might then extend this to account for how age understands itself in light of disability and illness: in other words, being older becomes a noble state inasmuch as it parallels, if counterintuitively, what Alison Kafer has discussed as "a critique of longevity" (41) as intrinsic to disability studies. "The devaluation of disabled bodies," Kafer writes, "is due in no small part to those bodies' failure to adhere to norms of bodies as unchanging, impermeable, long-lasting, and stable" (41). Given that Rose is performing well into her seventies, her age as a vector of difference, along with some of her health challenges such as the heart attack mentioned at the start of this essay and a medical history that includes back surgery, which meant inhabiting differences in mobility, cannot be overlooked as coming into play when exploring the crucial ways that feminist considerations of minority embodiment in her recent performances entail how age intersects with illness and disability. Jane Gallop's *Sexuality, Disability, and Aging,* as its title suggests, brings these connections into relief and issues a theoretical call to action involving what it means to dwell in the productive possibilities of age-related negative configurations such as how "late-onset disability" can be thought of in terms of the "mid-life crisis": "The so-called mid-life crisis is indeed an identity crisis. But [. . .] what makes it a crisis is that our notion of identity is static rather than longitudinal" (109). Gallop continues to explain that "a queer longitudinal perspective is not individual but is rather emphatically embedded in a cultural context, in a queer counter-culture" (110) and invites a disengagement with normative temporality that rests on the "need to tell our alternative stories" (110). Rose's life in art and performance tells alternative stories about intimacy, about accessibility, and about collaboration.

In reflecting ill, aging, and disabled bodies through queer sexual, temporal, and spatial frameworks, Rose's collaborative and durational performances during the period 2013–2017 including with Martin O'Brien and Rhiannon Aarons such as *Do with Me As You Will / Make Martin Suffer for Art* (2013) and *Philosophy in the Bedroom* (2016), which marked the occasion of Rose's seventy-fifth birthday, have taken place in spaces including rented hotel rooms and dungeons. In these spaces, visitors were invited to participate and/or watch within fixed but open periods of time, such as twenty-four hours, whether moving in and out of the spaces at will and/or coming in at either unscheduled times or times of specific choosing. By taking into account a range of abilities and nonnormative approaches to sexuality, these less-conventional performance spaces radicalize the intimacies of the artists', audience members', and participants' encounters with each other. In turn, the spaces as part of the performances open up what Mia Mingus has described as "access intimacy [. . .] that elusive, hard to describe feeling when someone else 'gets' your access needs" in permitting unrestricted forms of participation, agency, and consent while allowing for "crip time," or the temporal flexibility associated with countering ableist timing. Hence, the assumed neutrality of space—space that is always already available for the able-bodied and heteronormative subject—is broken down in Rose's body of work. Space's non-neutrality, then, should be thought alongside what Jennifer Tyburczy theorizes in the context of museum space—"how bodies move through space to interact and form relationships with other bodies and objects on display" (6), namely the body-objects of Rose's exhibition and spatial practices. In line with the crip solidarity that Mingus discusses and accounting for what Tyburczy calls "display choreography" (40), Rose's collaborative performances from the 2010s reinscribe spaces, such as the museum, in defiance of how they may be normatively experienced as sites. For instance, her collaborative *Visiting Hours* with Flanagan in the 1990s transformed the museum space into a hospital space and waiting room among the various play spaces that equally reflected the crip intimacies of their BDSM practices in life and art. As Dawn Reynolds explains in relationship to Flanagan's disability, BDSM offers alternative sexual options and "may provide a welcome sexual reprieve from the pain that can accompany some impairments" (42). Likewise, such alternatives must be understood through alternative spaces where they may take place, where attention to accommodation is not only acknowledged but fundamental to the execution of the practices and performances in question. Rose's collaborative performances ask us to consider the possibilities of de-privileging ableist and heteronormative rationales that often define the temporal and spatial arrangement of performative art practices. Significantly, Rose's work reveals a minoritarian bodily aesthetics of space, whether evident in early work such as *Visiting Hours,* where hospital spaces and BDSM spaces were integrated into/as the exhibit, what Petra Kuppers has discussed as "the metamorphosing from [. . .] medical necessity to sexual body play" (94), or in the Sanctuary Studios LAX dungeon space where *Do with Me As You Will* took place over the course of twenty-four hours. These are just some examples that intertwine the sexual politics of disability with extreme performance characterizing Rose's radical art and the destabilization of gender norms that it exhibits across the lines of power and relationality. Rather than represent the minority body's sexual libertinism as restricted, Rose's work expands the possibilities of the body, of performance space, of the body-space, and of the archival space itself.

Collection Overview and the Archival Politics of Editing *Rated RX*

Archives have their own narratives within and outside the contexts of what they are archives of. On the journey to *Rated RX,* I encountered some resistance to this project in its emphasis on Rose instead of Flanagan. Even as some of this book's materials are Flanagan's archive as much as Rose's, the exclusionary, myopic, and sexist logics of thinking about portions of the archive as reducible to Flanagan were disturbingly in place. *Rated RX* is adamant about countering such logics. In 2014 Rose donated her collection of photographs, videos, posters, letters, programs, and other memorabilia to ONE National Gay and Lesbian Archives at the University of Southern California Libraries in Los Angeles. *Rated RX* incorporates selected archival materials from the Sheree Rose and Bob Flanagan Papers at ONE in order to consider the boundaries of time and endurance in the context of Rose's performance art. The book accomplishes this by including rare and previously unavailable material that examines Rose's life-work and the re-performative promises of Rose's recent collaborative performances. Exceeding genre distinctions between photography and performance across a range of visual and subcultural contexts, *Rated RX*

reflects Rose's innovations in incorporating BDSM practices into performance art, which open up critical dialogues about the temporal distinctions between life and death via creative and archival practice. When I
first began digging through the Rose/Flanagan Papers at ONE shortly
after Rose's donation, the labor-intensity of the search was more frustrating than exhilarating because of its almost complete disorganization.
Everything could potentially be relevant, and the sheer range of materials I came across did little to curb or to validate my choices. When ONE's
now-former archivist Cooper T. Moll, whose @lavender_archivist Insta-
gram feed is its own queer archive, took over the cataloging of the collection, it not only facilitated my research by significantly cutting search time
but also allowed for a way to navigate the archive without the normative
imposition of needless linearity or arbitrary categories.

Moreover, researching the Rose/Flanagan Papers was buttressed by
Rose herself as a living archive of experiential-bodily recollection. Rose
often claims that her memory is bad or, like anyone who has been around
a while, that she has trouble recalling the exact year of certain moments
from her past. But during many of my archival junkets at ONE she joined
me and, without missing a beat, recounted the stories associated with and
contexts of the images with impressive detail. Here we might think about
recollection more as "re-collection," that is, what might straddle the spaces
between the performative frameworks of recollection vis-à-vis the archival
collection itself, in line with ephemeral archives of feeling (Cvetkovich,
Archive 1–14), the "archival disorientation" of Ron Athey's work (Johnson, *Pleading* 38), and as "troubling our tendency to think of the archive
as something final or fixed" (Jones, "Performative" 11). This invariably
extends to the destabilizing presence of archival materials recovered outside the domains of official preservation. For instance, along with other
images that Rose used in her University of California, Irvine, MFA thesis show, Rose's friend and collaborator Luka Fisher retrieved the death
portraits Rose took of her mother (image captures by Amanda Majors)
not at ONE but from Rose's home archive. My goal is to let the materials
included in *Rated RX* largely speak for themselves, and I have therefore
approached the arrangement and organization of the materials and essays
in a curatorial rather than didactic manner. The range of scholarly, creative, and personal approaches to Rose's life and work reflects a constellation of deeply relational contexts that Rose has cultivated throughout
her career and friendships.

Rated RX brings together archival photographs and documents with
essays by scholars and artists who were and/or continue to be intimately

involved with the many art and underground worlds that Rose inhabits, whether in terms of scholarship, collaborative practices, or other investments in the larger body politics that her work invites. The "Words" section of the collection offers readers an extensive set of voices in written form: Rose's own writings, scholarly essays, interviews, personal reflections, and creative-performative meditations on Rose's archive. The "Images" section of the book is composed of photography-dominant archival materials largely from the Rose/Flanagan Papers at ONE. Both sections are further divided into clusters of themes, genres of writing, and/or performances. This approach is intended to mirror the archive and the processes of "re-collection" across time vis-à-vis Rose's body of work. Hence this queer historiographic method bespeaks both deferred and reversed time, an always unfinished process of collecting, preserving, and remembering in an attempt to account for the messiness of the performed and lived temporalities in question. As Jacques Derrida reminds us, "The technical structure of the *archiving* archive also determines the structure of the *archivable* content even in its very coming into existence and in its relationship to the future" (17).

Functioning to guide the reader-experiencer of the archive through the materials without being excessively directed, *Rated RX*'s organization of sections into "Words" and "Images" is meant both to reduce and to preserve the chaos that often accompanies the archive and its contents. Its organization takes cues from what Tyburczy calls "queer curatorship as an experimental display tactic that stages alternative spatial configurations" (175). Rather than force the essays and materials into cohesive relationships with one another, *Rated RX* reproduces in its pages innovative ways of seeing or thinking about physical documentation and the ephemera that exists along with it. This is also what Ann Cvetkovich has discussed of archival methods as queer methods; the queerness of these methods pertains to how archives reverse conventional forms of knowledge ("Ordinary Lesbians"). With such queer archival systems in mind, the first section of the book, the "Words" section, is organized into three parts: "In Her Own Words," "Collaborations and Critical Perspectives," and "Performative Writing." The "Words" section includes a range of writing that does not attempt to be exhaustive but that, rather, maintains the queer curatorial qualities of the book. Many essays move away from genre distinctions or classificatory specificity, and, instead of summarizing them here, I invite the reader-experiencer of *Rated RX* to take them in holistically as well as individually and to think beyond the narrow genre descriptions I am using. In addition to essays by Rose—including her "Why Not?" piece, her response-version of Flanagan's "Why," which she recorded with postpunk revival synth artist Terminal A on a release with noise artist Peter Kalisch in 2016—"Words" includes revelatory interviews conducted by Tina Takemoto and me; scholarly essays by art and sexuality studies theorists Amelia Jones and Amber Musser, which offer distinctive, and even somewhat competing, perspectives of Rose's approaches to performance; personally inflected theoretical essays by Tanya Augsburg, Luka Fisher, and Chelsea Coon; performative-experimental writing by Mary Ann Davis and Harold Jaffe; and edifying essays by Rose's collaborators Martin O'Brien and Rhiannon Aarons. Author Jane DeLynn's short story based on Rose, "The Duchess of LA," which originally appeared in *Don Juan in the Village* (1990), is included as a fictionalized take on Rose's involvement in BDSM culture.

The second section of the book, "Images," is divided into two primary parts. "Part 1: 1980s–1990s" features much of Rose's collaborative work with Flanagan and underscores the role that her art played in giving a visual presence to BDSM sexuality, illness/disability, industrial/noise/postpunk music cultures, and the literary underground via radical performance and lived practices. "Part 2: 1999–2018" encompasses when Rose began performing again in 1999–2000 and specifically highlights her more recent performances and achievements from 2013–2018, including winning the Tom of Finland Lifetime Achievement Award in 2018, the photo of which, by Amanda Majors, closes out the collection. The intentionally "misplaced" "Breathing Space" section, placed between parts 1 and 2 of "Images," operates as an emphatic display of death-related materials (Rose's death portraits of her mother and of Flanagan, for instance) and some of the artistic, ritualistic, and documentary practices that transgress a more rigid time-frame grouping. A symbolic gesture that situates some of the themes of re-performance beyond normative time, the breath that this section invites the reader-experiencer to take refers both to the meditative breathing of yoga—Rose is a lifelong practitioner—and to the defiance of breathing restrictions associated with CF. It also experimentally bridges the nonnormative temporalities that characterize Rose's work and its archive.

While placed separately, the "Words" and "Images" sections should be thought of as endlessly referring back to each other. Some of the essays specifically name the associated image clusters in ways that simultaneously push the parts away from and toward each other, to inform each other as modes of survival outside the conventions of existence and performance and leave open the indeterminacies of the always evolving meanings afforded them over time. Rather than subscribe to organizational orthodoxy, the book's organization is thus intended to highlight the role of resurrection/re-performance that Rose's work invites, especially in light of the directions that her recent performances have taken. This organizational logic may even be said to mirror the minority body aesthetics of its contents, what Tobin Siebers theorizes as the "experimentation with aesthetic form [reflecting] a desire to experiment with human form" (10) and "the corporeal variation" (10) that is part and parcel of disability aesthetics. As I update this introduction, Rose's collaborative investments in queer corporeal aesthetics continues: she has already appeared in *This Love Is on Fire,* a video directed by trans performance artist Cassils, which screened as part of the Platinum experimental film showcase at Outfest 2019, and, in September 2019, Rose performed *We Walk with Zombies* with Martin O'Brien and other collaborators in Regina, Saskatchewan, Canada. So, while *Rated RX* may end in 2018, it by no means marks the end of Rose's involvement with performance art.

As would be expected in a book that thinks through the queer temporalities engendered by illness and age, much of this collection showcases Rose's creative output by arranging materials in a manner that does not neatly correspond with what would be expected of an archive in bound pages. Counter to mixing the words and images together, as just discussed, it does not dictate how to experience the archive and is in the service of highlighting Rose's collaborative practices that equally features her work as independent from the male artists with whom she has worked/lived. The reader-experiencer may notice the inconsistent lengths of portions of this book: some clusters of materials contain just one or two pieces of documentation; other sections include much more. Here we should remember that archival research invites unevenness; some areas of the book have more content than others simply because of the availability of materials and the reality of requiring an ending point to what is the never-ending task of doing archival research. I have sought, as much as possible, to have this collection be a book-form of Rose's archive while knowing that much of its historical import pertains not only to the physicality of its contents but also to how it anticipates a visibility of feminist art that did not get the same privileges of circulation and reception that it should have. Much of what *Rated RX* addresses is the question of gaps in the archive, which Rose's collaborative performances such as *Dust to Dust* directly enacted, but, importantly, this book's larger intention is to close some of the gaps in pertinent underground cultural histories and feminist art histories by resisting the problem of Rose's work being collapsed with Flanagan's and the invisibility of her work in collaborating with Flanagan.

Rated RX also includes an appendix of out-of-print materials by Flanagan for and about Rose. *Slave Sonnets* (1986) and *Fuck Journal* (1982) are reprinted in their entirety as a way to reflect how Rose's archive embodies a simultaneity of private/public realms and, significantly, as a sketch of the depth of intimacy that Rose shared with her partner Flanagan through his words. In fact, Rose had Flanagan in bondage while he composed much of the material in these documents. That they are little known and did not get the same circulation as Flanagan's *The Pain Journal* signifies the even greater feminist necessity of their inclusion, since they are almost exclusively about Rose despite being authored by Flanagan. *Fuck Journal* was destroyed by its printer in India, and the transcription here comes from Flanagan's typewritten draft in ONE Archives. These materials will be remarkably useful to readers and researchers since they are out of print and, until now, difficult to locate. *Slave Sonnets* and *Fuck Journal* are transcribed rather than reproductions of the hard copies because plates of the original manuscripts may be difficult to read as images. Included in this collection's "Images" section is Mike Kelley's cover art for *Slave Sonnets*: an illustration of a heart—the organ—pierced with a knife enclosed in an upside-down heart. Besides the obvious BDSM references to love/pain/passion, it symbolically resonates across time in connection with Rose's heart attack in the summer of 2018 and becomes an important way to connect with the broader 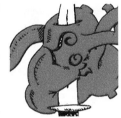 collaborative framework of the collection, especially, for instance, Rose's *p. 240* 2014 *100 Reasons* re-performance associated with Kelley and Kelley's photograph of Rose and Flanagan used in the limited edition compact disc version of Sonic Youth's *Dirty* (1992) album. Rose writes in her epilogue essay in Flanagan's *The Pain Journal,* "Together, we transformed shame and sorrow into a transcendent state that defies logic and reason and death" (178) and, in an interview with Klare Scarborough, speaks of being "fascinated by the question of how [to] immortalize [. . .] something that is corporeal into something that is ephemeral [. . .] yet has an impact on you" (126). It is in this spirit and through these questions that *Rated RX* pursues the possibilities of corporeal-ephemeral transformation in the minority body archive of Rose's work.

Works Cited

Augsburg, Tanya. "Fired Up! From Protest to Projust Feminist Artistic Expression in *F213.*" *F213* exhibition catalog. Northern California Women's Caucus for Art, 2019, pp. 14–21.

Barnes, Elizabeth. *The Minority Body: A Theory of Disability.* Oxford UP, 2016.

Cvetkovich, Ann. *An Archive of Feelings: Trauma, Sexuality, and Lesbian Public Cultures.* Duke UP, 2003.

——. "Ordinary Lesbians and Special Collections: The June L. Mazer Lesbian Archives and Queer Archival Turns." LGBTQ Research Consortium and Department of Women's Studies, San Diego State University, 15 October 2018. Lecture.

Derrida, Jacques. *Archive Fever: A Freudian Impression.* Translated by Eric Prenowitz, U of Chicago P, 1995.

Flanagan, Bob. *The Book of Medicine.* PrimRosePathPress, 2017.

——. *The Pain Journal.* Semiotext(e), 2000.

Gallop, Jane. *Sexuality, Disability, and Aging: Queer Temporalities of the Phallus.* Duke UP, 2019.

Garland-Thomson, Rosemarie. "Seeing the Disabled: Visual Rhetorics of Disability in Popular Photography." *The New Disability History: American Perspectives.* Edited by Paul K. Longmore and Lauri Umansky, New York UP, 2001, pp. 335–74.

Halberstam, J. Jack (published under Halberstam, Judith). *In a Queer Time and Place: Transgender Bodies, Subcultural Lives.* New York UP, 2005.

Hart, Lynda. *Between the Body and the Flesh: Performing Sadomasochism.* Columbia UP, 1998.

Howard, Yetta. Writer Response, *Blue Takes Washington. F213* exhibition catalog. Northern California Women's Caucus for Art, 2019, pp. 96–97.

Johnson, Dominic. *The Art of Living: An Oral History of Performance Art.* Palgrave Macmillan, 2015.

——. "Introduction: Toward a Moral and Just Psychopathology." *Pleading in the Blood: The Art and Performances of Ron Athey.* Edited by Dominic Johnson, Intellect / U of Chicago P, 2013, pp. 10–41.

Jones, Amelia. *Body Art/Performing the Subject.* U of Minnesota P, 1998.

——. "Performative Afterlife: An Interview with Amelia Jones." Interview by Swen Steinhäuser and Neil Macdonald. *Parallax*, vol. 24, no. 1, 2018, 11–18.

Kafer, Alison. *Feminist, Queer, Crip.* Indiana UP, 2013.

Kauffman, Linda S. *Bad Girls and Sick Boys: Fantasies in Contemporary Art and Culture.* U of California P, 1998.

Kuppers, Petra. *The Scar of Visibility: Medical Performances and Contemporary Art.* U of Minnesota P, 2007.

Mark, Brian J. www.brianjmark.com

McRuer, Robert. *Crip Theory: Cultural Signs of Queerness and Disability.* New York UP, 2006.

Mingus, Mia. "Access Intimacy: The Missing Link." *Leaving Evidence,* 5 May 2011, https://leavingevidence.wordpress.com/2011/05/05/access-intimacy-the-missing-link/

Mitchell, David T. with Sharon L. Snyder. *The Biopolitics of Disability: Neoliberalism, Ablenationalism, and Peripheral Embodiment.* U of Michigan P, 2015.

O'Brien, Martin. "The Weight of History Keeps Me Awake at Night (after David Wojnarowicz)." *Survival of the Sickest: The Art of Martin O'Brien.* Edited by Martin O'Brien and David MacDiarmid, Live Art Development Agency, 2018, pp. 56–57.

O'Dell, Kathy. *Contract with the Skin: Masochism, Performance Art, and the 1970s.* U of Minnesota P, 1998.

Reynolds, Dawn. "Disability and BDSM: Bob Flanagan and the Case for Sexual Rights." *Sexuality Research and Social Policy: Journal of NSRC,* vol. 4, no. 1, Mar. 2007, pp. 40–52.

Rose, Sheree. Artist Statement, *Blue Takes Washington. F213* exhibition catalog. Northern California Women's Caucus for Art, 2019, pp. 96–97.

——. "In Semi-Sickness and in So-Called Health, I'm Still in Love with You." *The Pain Journal.* By Bob Flanagan. Semiotext(e), 2000, pp. 174–78.

Saint-Amour, Paul K. "Weak Theory, Weak Modernism." *Modernism/modernity,* vol. 25, no. 3, Sept. 2018, pp. 437–459.

Scarborough, Klare. "Of Coffins and Cameras: A Conversation with Sheree Rose." *Performance Research: A Journal of the Performing Arts,* vol. 15, no. 1, 2010, pp. 123–30.

Siebers, Tobin. *Disability Aesthetics.* U of Michigan P, 2010.

Tyburczy, Jennifer. *Sex Museums: The Politics and Performance of Display.* U of Chicago P, 2016.

Vale, V. and Andrea Juno, editors. *Bob Flanagan: Supermasochist.* RE/Search, People Series, Volume 1. RE/Search Publications, 1993.

——. "Sheree Rose." RE/Search #12: *Modern Primitives: An Investigation of Contemporary Adornment and Ritual.* RE/Search Publications, 1989, pp. 109–13.

SECTION 1

WORDS

PART 1

IN HER OWN WORDS

Home

SHEREE ROSE

I was working at the Housing Authority as a Section 8 advisor, and my office was at Alvarado and 8th, very far from safe Westwood. I grew tired of the long commute, and started looking around for a closer neighborhood. One day, on my lunch hour, I came across a beautiful building on a hill, overlooking Echo Park Lake. There was a "For Rent" sign. I called the number, and the next day I went into an apartment that had the most beautiful view of the lake. I was hooked, and the rent was $700 a month. I went back home, told Bob we were moving, told my ex-husband he could move back into the Thurston house, and that he should sell our smaller Westwood property. My ex, being submissive, agreed, and thus began my budding real estate empire. We refinanced the big house, sold the smaller one, and with the cash, I bought the Echo Park condo for $70,000, and two other houses in Eugene, Oregon, which I never lived in but rented out for many years. I had the real estate bug. Living my entire childhood in one terrible apartment after another, I vowed to own property and never again deal with landlords!

I had a friend who was an architect who had a sister living in San Francisco. It was 1994. I visited them often, and she showed me the plans for a factory conversion in the Mission District that she was designing. I was enchanted. It was glorious. Fifteen-foot-high ceilings, concrete floors, and large windows. It was the loft of my dreams. I bought it with very little down, and planned to rent it out until Bob was well enough to move there. Life got in the way and Bob never got well enough to move. I got an agent, and the place was rented out. I never even got to sleep there one night.

My mother died suddenly on Mother's Day, 1995. I couldn't work anymore. I was living on disability income from my job. Bob died in 1996, my first husband in 1997, and my father in July 1998. I hardly had time to mourn the death of one before another one died. My entire support system was gone. I felt alone. All this time, I had kept control of all six of my properties in three different cities. But I came to the end of my options. My income was low but I couldn't face going back to work. I was done. I had nothing left.

I moved in with my father after Bob died. It was the family home, and I took over caring for him as he approached ninety. I begged my brother to take over managing all my properties. He said no. He didn't want to mix family and business. At that point, I was too devastated to put up an argument, and so, one by one, I sold everything I owned. Looking back, I should have found another agent to take over the management, but my thinking was clouded by grief and despair. I just wanted to be a child again, and to be taken care of. Now, living with my father, I had no responsibilities other than driving him around.

I had the place redecorated and it was pleasant. Unlike my mother, my father was a quiet man, kept to himself, and we never fought. I see now that I was retreating to a sense of family domesticity that I had never experienced as a child. This was home, at last.

I live in a trailer. There, I've said it. For ten years, I've been ashamed. I told no one where I lived. I never invited anyone over for dinner or drinks. I drove myself to parties, art openings, and restaurants. I felt like I was in exile. Leaving the trailer felt like leaving jail. Coming back, alone at night, I felt a sense of profound loneliness. This is the first time I have ever addressed this issue. I have no problem with sharing the most intimate details of my personal life. In fact, I utilize my political and sexual proclivities as fodder for my art with no embarrassment or shame. But I view my living arrangements as a failure, something that is deeply disturbing and troubling. I've hid and avoided this issue as thoroughly as my brother did being gay. And therein lies the root of the problem. My brother hates me and has never forgiven me for outing him to our mother, back in 1978!

In order to sort out my feelings for myself, I will go back into history as best as I can remember. My brother was four years younger than me. My mother never paid much attention to me. I wouldn't say I was neglected or abused, but I don't remember ever being hugged or kissed. I was dark-haired and skinny. My brother was blond and plump. She doted on him endlessly, constantly remarking on his looks and his curly blond hair. I clearly remember her dressing him in frilly clothing, and remarking "wouldn't he be a beautiful girl?"

When he was around six years old, I noticed that he was different from the other boys on the block. He didn't go outside and play in the street, roller skating or playing ball. He stayed indoors, watching television. I told my mother and father that I thought something was wrong with his behavior, but they angrily said "he will grow out of it."

In those days, there was no discussion of homosexuality. I didn't have any idea that such a thing even existed. As the years went by, I noticed that he didn't have many friends, and his looks changed. Blond curls became kinky brunette, and he isolated himself. I became a wild teenager and included him in my dating life. I would have him answer the door when a new date arrived, and he knew when I would sneak out late at night to meet my boyfriend. I was a budding Domme, and he was definitely submissive to me.

At age twenty-one, I married. He was in the wedding party. My husband and I took him under our wing and included him in many of our social activities. We went to dinner, the movies, and house hunting. My family never owned their own home. We moved from apartment to apartment all through my childhood, and I vowed to own my house as soon as I got married. A year after I got married, in 1965, we bought a house that I saved my entire first-year salary for as an elementary school teacher and put a down payment on a house that cost $29,000.

My brother dropped out of college and moved to New York. Shortly after, he was drafted and returned to Los Angeles. My husband had served in the Korean War, stationed in Germany, and we thought that going into the army would be helpful to my brother. We assumed he would never be sent into combat. He was a quiet Jewish boy. Never did the subject of homosexuality come up. My husband and I were very bourgeois, as were our friends. We were clueless. He went into the service, which was a major turning point in his life. A few weeks later, he was given a general discharge, having never made it through boot camp. He never talked about his experience, except to say that he had a sadistic sergeant, who mercilessly tortured him. Meanwhile, I was having babies, moving into bigger and nicer houses, and then going to Europe for a sabbatical, where I drove around in a Volkswagen bus for a year. When we returned in 1973, the world had changed and so did I. I was no longer the naïve wife and mother. I had become aware of the wider world and of my own growing dissatisfaction with my life choices.

My brother was undergoing his own changes. I asked my husband a rhetorical question: "Why don't we have any gay friends?" Soon after, my brother announced that he had joined a Jewish temple. I was surprised because he was never particularly religious. He invited me to attend a Friday night service, where I discovered that my brother was a member of the first gay temple in Los Angeles. My reaction to that was relief. So much of his behavior made sense now! I totally embraced this new information; the sexual and social stirring in my own psyche perfectly matched my brother's proclamation. My brother did not come out to our parents. At that time, homophobia was rampant: Anita Bryant was often on television, railing against the evils of homosexuality.

I separated from my husband and went back to school in 1979 at the University of California, Northridge, where I majored in psychology. In those days, psychology was the Wild West; new theories and experimental treatments were all the rage. Telling your truth, letting it all hang out, becoming liberated were my catechisms. Meanwhile, my brother was living with his lover in a perfect domestic arrangement. My mother often quizzed me: "Do you think Richard is gay?" She was obsessed with the subject, asking questions such as "what do you think gay men do in bed?" I usually brushed off her inquiries, but it bothered me that she never asked my brother himself. Finally, one afternoon we were sitting in a diner and she continued with her constant questioning. I decided to bite the bullet and tell her what I was sure she already knew in her heart. "Do you really want to know?" I said, as firmly as I could. "Yes," she replied, looking me straight in the eye. "Well, yes, he is gay." I wasn't expecting what happened next. She turned pale, stood up from the table, and started screaming at the top of her lungs. She didn't stop screaming. Everyone in the restaurant turned around and stared, wondering, I'm sure, what could have caused this verbal explosion. I felt ambushed by her reaction. I knew she wouldn't be happy with that answer, but I figured she already, unconsciously, knew the truth, and would come to terms with it. After all, he was in his thirties, had been living with a man who baked cakes and brought them to her house when they came for dinner!

Her outburst was just the beginning of a three-year odyssey, during which she declared him dead, sat shiva for him, and would call me up at 3 a.m. to tell me she was cursed and wanted to die. I felt so guilty that I accepted all the shit she heaped upon herself and her son and patiently listened to her crazed ranting. Meanwhile, my brother went along with his life, never having to deal with our mother's insanity. Ironically, after three years, I hosted a Jewish holiday dinner at my house. By then I was divorced, with a new boyfriend, and I invited my brother with his lover and a group of friends along with my mother and father. It was the first time they had seen or spoken to each other. They sat on opposite sides of the long table, but no screaming ensued. I had effectively brought about their reconciliation. They then became good friends with my brother and all his subsequent lovers, frequently going to Friday night dinners at the condo that my husband and I had bought for my parents. I was such a real estate maven that I wanted my parents to have a place of their own. While I was still married, my husband and I put a down payment on a beautiful Culver City condo that cost $32,000 in 1977. My brother and I never talked about the three-year exile and how I never gave up on getting them to reconcile.

Fast forward to 1980 when I met Bob Flanagan. My life took a turn that I really never anticipated. When I got divorced in 1979, my husband and I owned two houses in Westwood. We each lived in one of the houses, and shared custody of our two children. I lived in the big house on Thurston. Bob moved in sometime in 1981, and we set up our domestic arrangement. He was my house slave and we lived a BDSM lifestyle that extended far beyond the bedroom. My children were aware of the relationship, although they never witnessed any overt sexual acts. It's hard to believe now, but I owned two of the most iconic residences in Los Angeles. The first was on Clinton, a crescent-shaped building perched at the end of a cul-de-sac overlooking Echo Park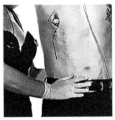

p. 204

Lake. The divorce was final, I was living in the Thurston house, making the long commute from Westwood to 8th and Alvarado, where our gorgeous 1930s offices were located. So I sort of knew the neighborhood. I was entranced when turning a corner at the top of the hill, since the entire lake lay before me with houses and mountains in the distance. It was love at first sight. There were two apartments available. One on the first floor and another one above. They were identical except that the downstairs unit had a wide patio, while the upstairs had a balcony that enhanced the breathtaking view. "How much is the rent?" I casually asked to the agent. "$700 a month." "I'll take it," I blurted out, aghast at the bargain I was getting. I came home to the Thurston residence to tell Bob we were moving next month to Echo Park, so he'd better get packing!

Recently, while being driven downtown on Grand to an art opening at a trendy new gallery, I was shocked to see the proliferation of tents on both sides of the street. I was familiar with the homeless encampments on Skid Row, tucked in the area east of Main where the city does not do street cleaning and police regularly harass the poor citizens. But this was blatantly different. No one could ignore the sight of hundreds of people living on the streets in full view of City Hall, recent monuments, upscale art galleries, and loft apartments. My stomach clenched as I was confronted with the reality and enormity of the chasm between people who had a roof over their heads and the hapless souls who did not.

Where was I on the quality-of-life continuum in Los Angeles? Pretty far down on the list; however, I owned my trailer by virtue of a long, forgotten statute in Culver City that set aside several acres of land for low-income families with the proviso that they could not sell their trailer for more than they paid for it, even if they had made extensive improvements, and even then, only to another low-income family. What a concept: your property value could not go up, but you could live in a secure neighborhood and not worry about being forced out by greedy landlords. So traditional real estate appreciation could be circumvented. Was I living in some sort of communist plot? I realized that there is something intrinsically evil about the rising cost of real estate, in that it means that fewer and fewer people are able to obtain a safe and affordable place to call home. Rather than bemoaning my life as "trailer trash," I should be grateful that I had a place to call my own. Well, maybe. But I couldn't stop thinking about the disparity in people's lives due entirely to what or where they call home.

My brother never gave such a disparity even a microsecond of thought. He and his lover rode the real estate roller coaster to dizzying heights. Several years ago, he bought a million-dollar home in a gated country club in Palm Springs. Then, he bought a condo in West Los Angeles, but he grew dissatisfied with sharing a building with other owners. Recently, he purchased a two-million-dollar house in the Hollywood Hills. Was I jealous of his real estate success? Or was there something fundamentally wrong with two men living like kings in 3,000 square feet of opulence while so many Angelenos live on the sidewalks? It seems to be like something out of the Middle Ages, with rich people living in castles while poor people suffer in hovels. At least they had hovels! Los Angeles looks more and more like Delhi, India, which I recently visited, where street living is indeed a way of life!

As an artist and a depressed woman, I don't expect life to be easy. I have lived almost seventy-five years, been widowed twice, raised two children, suffered financial ruin, been deserted by friends and family, survived a terrible fall and subsequent surgery, but I'm still here, and still raising hell! When I ponder my fate from rags to riches to rags, I consider what part my ego plays in this drama. Do I feel sorry for myself? Do I blame others for my misfortunes? Why do I pity myself? My mental illness? Of course, that is valid criticism if you believe you can control your mind by willpower alone. I took a tumble off a cliff. I was the personification of David Wojnarowicz's bison failing and falling. But I didn't sustain a fatal crash. Bloodied and bruised for sure but, as a semi-Hindu, I realize that karma surrounds us and that all my trials and tribulations were somehow preordained because of my actions in prior lives!

Home is elusive. Where and when did I feel safe and loved? Certainly not during my childhood or teenage years. Until I was ten years old, my family lived in a duplex on Hayworth, one block from Fairfax and Olympic, a predominantly Jewish, middle-class neighborhood in West Los Angeles. I played on the streets, put on plays in the backyard, and played doctor in the garage behind the house. It was a simple time, and I felt as secure as any child would under the circumstances. Abruptly, my family moved from the security and familiarity I had experienced to a series of apartments in questionable sections of Los Angeles. No explanation was given, just a vague statement about a new business venture for my father. Much later, I learned that he had sold the duplex to invest in a boxing arena in Downey, a faraway city east of Los Angeles. We moved to a two-bedroom apartment in the Crenshaw area of Los Angeles, where, for the first time, I shared a bedroom and bathroom with my six-year-old brother. I was yanked from my beloved school in the fifth grade and placed in an unknown environment where I had no friends.

I don't remember much about that year except that I was miserable and lonely. But that was just the first of several other moves over the next ten years. Why we moved so often was never discussed. We just moved. It was always a two-bedroom, one-bathroom unit, forcing me in my adolescence to share intimate space with my brother with little hope of privacy. After some years and several apartments he moved to a cot in the dining room, but we all shared the one bathroom. Later, the apartments got better as we moved to better neighborhoods. But my prominent memory is of moving year after year with no explanation and no input as to how it would affect me or my brother.

I lived at home while I attended UCLA, where the mantra was "you better get married before you graduate." This was something my cousin and my best friend did, so I was feeling the pressure. The pressure was intense not to be an "old maid" at age twenty-two! So, in 1964 I married my training teacher in elementary education, who was the first man I slept with and the first person to show me love and affection. He was eleven years my senior, had been teaching for ten, and still lived at home with his parents. I discovered that he had not saved any money and had no clear idea of his future except going to Las Vegas as often as possible. Well, I sincerely believed that if I didn't marry him, I would end up an old-maid schoolteacher, a fate worse than death in my twenty-one-year-old mind. So, we did the deed, following in the footsteps of many young women in my peer group. One thing was different: I vowed not to live in any more apartments. We did live in a small place for one year after we married. It was a furnished apartment in West Los Angeles, which was $145 a month. My beginning salary at Los Angeles Unified School District was about $5,000 a year, which I diligently put into my own savings account. We spent most of the weekends that year looking at houses for sale. We searched many areas of Los Angeles, but my heart was in West Los Angeles. Finally, we found the house of our dreams, a two-bedroom, one-bath English cottage–style dwelling on the corner of Olympic and Manning for $29,000. I remember taking my mother and brother to see the place. I was so proud of my accomplishment: I had achieved my goal of home ownership at age twenty-three.

Of course, nothing lasts forever, and after several years of living there, I decided to start having babies. My husband, being the simple, submissive man he was, docilely followed my every move and inclination. We needed a bigger place to house our soon-to-be-growing family, and we found the perfect place in the hills of Encino, a new development designed for young families. It had a view of the San Fernando Valley, was two stories, had two- and one-half bathrooms and my own washer and dryer, all for $43,000. Wisely, we decided not to sell the Manning property but to rent it instead, which we did for the next twenty-five years. Life was different in the Valley. Women stayed home with their young children, played bridge in the afternoon, and employed Salvadoran maids for $20 a week with room and board provided. It was a surreal life for me. I was teaching in South Central, a long commute, semi-raising two children a year-and-a-half apart while having a nervous breakdown! I had to leave the Valley or die.

In 1971 one of our teacher friends had just returned from a sabbatical leave in Europe. That became my next mission in life: to travel Europe for a year in a Volkswagen bus with no plans except to follow the sun and find beachfront cities all over Europe and Israel. For a year we were nomads, picking up strangers on the road, staying in obscure places, having the best year of my marriage. Our bus was our home, we shared it with others, and every day was a new adventure. But dreams must end and we came back to Los Angeles in 1973 to live in an apartment on Barrington, until our tenants at Thurston moved out. The Thurston house came closest to being the perfect place for me. It was in Westwood, an upscale neighborhood even then, which we were able to purchase for the cheap price of $50,000 from the profits of selling the Escalon house. I loved being back on the Westside; it felt safe and comfortable. But I was looking forward to living in my own home after such a nomadic life.

Our year in Europe had awakened my interest in archeology since we visited the ancient cave paintings in France and Spain. I soon enrolled in an archeology program at UCLA, which ultimately altered the course of my life. In 1974 my husband was still the only man I had ever had sex with. Times were changing: the pill had come on the market and I was hanging out with a group of archeologists who were the most eccentric people I had ever encountered. Our home became a meeting place for my new friends. We had glorious parties with drinks flowing, guitar music playing, and I had my first affair with a Colombian man named Manuel. My marriage had come to a turning point. I no longer loved my husband. We had no sex life to speak of, and I became aware that there was another life for me outside of traditional marriage. My longing for a home of my own, safe and secure, had kept me in my relationship for fourteen years. It was a leap of faith that propelled me out of it and the knowledge that I owned two houses, one for me and one for my husband, with joint custody of our children.

Depression is a cruel mistress, showing no mercy, enjoying the misery she inflicts. The year before Bob died, I received a phone call at the Housing Authority from my father, informing me that my mother was very sick. I rushed to her home, where she was writhing in pain. She had suffered from arthritis in her knees for years and refused to have surgery. She had been self-medicating with aspirin, and her intestines had finally had enough. I thought an enema would have helped, but she was way beyond that simple solution. My father and I called an ambulance and she was taken to the local hospital. We waited in the emergency room for hours without getting any news of her condition. Finally, a doctor told us she had to undergo emergency surgery. The next morning, the doctor informed us that she had suffered a necrotic intestinal rupture and was not going to recover. I called Bob, my children, and my brother, who drove in from Palm Springs. We gathered at her bedside to say our final goodbyes. It was a ghastly scene. She was in a coma, and we didn't know if she was even aware of our presence. My guilt was acute. Why didn't I insist that she go to a doctor sooner? As an incredibly stubborn woman, she often remarked that she never changed her mind, and she never asked for or listened to advice. She was a difficult person and her death was no different.

By Christmas, Bob went into the hospital for the final time. We had been planning a trip to Las Vegas, but his health had taken a tremendous turn for the worse. I called his parents, who lived in Arizona, and they arrived for what became a ten-day deathwatch. We never left the hospital as we witnessed Bob slowly slip away. We were in the middle of filming the documentary about Bob, and I implored Kirby Dick, the director of *Sick: The Life and Death of Bob Flanagan, Supermasochist*, to be there for Bob's final moments. However, he had taken another paying job, so he was not there when Bob passed. Bob was surrounded by friends and family, and he gave the most amazing monologue just before he died but it was not recorded. The bitterness and betrayal I felt toward Dick has not abated in twenty years.

The day before he died, Bob converted to Judaism and we were married by Rabbi Jane Littman in his hospital room. We did this in order for Bob to be buried in Mount Sinai cemetery, where I had purchased a grave. His Catholic parents were appalled and threatened to disinter the body and move him to Phoenix. I was devastated by their threat; though never enacted, it ended our sixteen-year relationship where they had embraced me as a daughter.

My first husband, Dan, had been suffering from cancer, which had become increasingly aggressive. We had always remained friendly, we had joint custody of our children, and I helped with caretaking. He died on Thanksgiving, in the bedroom of the house we had bought in 1965. Well, I was on a downward spiral, exacerbated by the fact that my husband had not left a will, just a quick-claim deed, and my daughter took the house.

As mentioned earlier, I was living in Silverlake on disability leave, feeling totally alone and desperate. My children were fighting, my brother was living in Palm Springs, and my entire support system was dismantled by death and disloyalty. My future, financial and personal, looked bleak. I felt I had no other choice; my inner resources were depleted, so I sold everything and moved in with my father, to the Culver City condominium I had bought for my parents back in 1975. There I was: no job, few friends, living in Culver City with my ninety-year-old father. The condo was beautiful, a lakeside property that had cost $32,000. It felt like home: my parents had co-parented my children after my divorce, and we spent every Jewish holiday and Friday night there when my mother cooked wonderful dinners. On July 4, 1997, I asked my father if he wanted to go to a party with me. He said no. I asked him if he wanted me to fix dinner for him. He said yes. I asked if he wanted me to heat up the leftover chicken. Before he could answer, his eyes rolled up in his head and he stopped breathing. I called the paramedics and they told me that he had suffered a heart attack and had died immediately. My sense of bereavement was overwhelming. My brother drove in from Palm Springs, having again been spared the agony of witnessing a parent's sudden demise.

The condo no longer felt like a refuge. I had nightmares reliving the deaths of both my parents. I had a friend who lived in Ojai, which had stood in for Shangri-La in the film *Lost Horizon.* Impulsively, I decided to move there, to start a new life ninety miles north of Los Angeles: a fresh start and a new home. I consulted my brother, who had inherited half the condo, and he eagerly advised me to sell it and get out of town. Feeling desperate, I agreed, thinking that I would never live in Los Angeles again. After two years, I realized that I had made a terrible mistake. Ojai might have been paradise, but my nature was not that bucolic. I was a tiger living on a farm. Moving back to Los Angeles was not easy: the real estate market had skyrocketed, and I didn't have enough money to buy a house. My brother had reinvested his money in another house and had washed his hands of me, his difficult, complaining sister. He told me he didn't want to feel guilty about my situation. As the philosopher Martha Nussbaum remarked, "Guilt might not even be quite the right word. It's a kind of sorrow that he has profited at the expense of someone else."

Here I am today: a poor, aging woman living in a trailer, disillusioned about family and loyalty. All is relative—no kidding—and I have a secure place to live, for which I take small comfort, considering how much I have lost, bitterly recalling Judy Garland's mantra "there's no place like home."

Why Not?

SHEREE ROSE

Since I was stuck in my mother's womb since she wouldn't dilate to let me out.

Since she didn't want to be a mother and have to care for a demanding infant.

Since her own mother let her down when she was raped at 15 by a family friend who paid off her father to keep her quiet.

Since she kept her shame and rage deep down inside her only to have it cut open by the doctor's scalpel after 24 hours of agonizing labor, to reluctantly give birth to me, problem child from the start.

Since she finally found an object outside of herself to hate and despise, to air out the rancor that had been festering within her.

Since her venom was so poisonous she was taken to intensive care after my birth.

Since I spent the first two weeks of my life in a crib in the hospital nursery: my hair so black, my face so red from screaming that my grandmother said I looked like a little Indian baby, already on the warpath.

Since I was born a bad girl, the one who ran into the street without looking, the one who ran away from home when I was five because I knew my parents didn't love me.

Since I was a bossy child, the one who took down the pants of little boys in the backyard, the one who masturbated in kindergarten, the one who let a strange man "take care of me" at the Saturday matinee by putting his thumb inside my panties and rubbed my clit, and you want to know the worst part, just like Elizabeth Taylor in *Butterfield 8,* I loved it!

Since my mother's friends were loose women and call girls who went to bars and picked up men.
Since I babysat their children and watched silently as they prepared to go out, dressed in silky underwear, putting on make-up, like actors in a kabuki drama.
Since I feared and envied their beauty, their glamour, their freedom, the reckless abandon with which they carried out their lives.
Since my best friend's mother was a kept woman, a shiksa who lolled around in bed all day, and took us shopping at Bullock's and asked me if she should choose the black or the nude brassiere.

Since I was always the outsider, the outcast, the outlaw.
Since I never was popular.
Since I always said the wrong thing, wore the wrong thing, did the wrong thing.
Since I was gawky, awkward and tall at 13 when the other girls were still little princesses wearing horse-hair slips beneath their flouncy skirts.

Since sticks and stones can break my bones but words will scar me forever.
Since boys don't like girls with bad skin.
Since boys who put their hands inside your bra at the movies don't take you to the prom.
Since Jewish girls who ride on the backs of motorcycles don't get into a social club.
Since girls are made of sugar and spice and everything nice, but I am full of shit and pus and icky stuff that can never be really hidden.
Since gallons of perfume will never completely disguise the stench.
Since buckets of paint can never cover up the ugliness underneath.
Since I am my mother's daughter.
Since what she concealed, I reveal.
Since I can no longer tolerate my mother's rejection.

Since I am compelled to declare that I have survived to transcend my sex and fecundity.

Since I no longer menstruate, but I still bleed when and where I choose.

Since I am no longer in thrall to a timetable determined by nature.

Since this is my true nature.

Since I was sent here for a purpose beyond that of a daughter, a wife, a mother, a widow.

Since I am a warrior.

Since I am my own heroine.

Since I am my own god.

Since I am the resurrection and the light.

Since the light of truth will overcome all darkness.

Since I am a prophet.

Since I foretell a future where gender is what you make or re-make of it, while sex is what you do on Saturday night, as much a sacred ritual as Orthodox Jews who fuck their wives on the Sabbath since their patriarchal god demands it of them.

Since I believe in the Dominant spirit who lives in my heart.

Since I was given the gift of a submissive man.

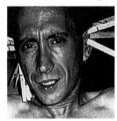

Since Bob Flanagan was my slave of his own free will, he was Saint Bob to my Mistress Rose.

Since he was my best creation.

Since I made him an art star when all he really wanted was to be naked, shaved, and chained under my house, living for the moment I would come downstairs and give him my full attention.

p. 209

Since I tied him to a chair and forced him to write.

Since I made him perform in public the secret rites he practiced alone.

Since I wanted the public to witness the Supermasochist in his pale, frail, sickly body that housed a brave and sturdy soul within.

Since for 15 years I photographed and videotaped his every waking, sleeping, and depraved moments as devoted as Dian Fossey was to her beloved gorillas.

Since I knew Bob was an endangered species.

Since there had to be proof of his existence, so that future audiences could marvel at a man who nailed his own penis to a board to satisfy the object of his desire and to fulfill the desire of his Dominatrix.

Since the Hindu goddess Kali is my guide; since she wields her multi-
armed swords and bloody heads roll.

Since Judith is my ancestor; since she saved her people by entering the
camp of Holofernes and slayed him in his sleep.

Since I cut into the dead body of Bob to send him to his grave with my
mark on his flesh to reaffirm my ownership and to display for eternity
the nature of our collaboration.

Since I honor him today by cutting my own flesh as proof of the depth of
my commitment.

And this be my blessing:
Lead us from unreal to real.
Lead us from fear of death to knowledge of immortality.
May the entire universe be filled with peace and joy, love and light.
Victory to the light!

Long live this revelation.
Long live the Mistress.
Long live the memory of Bob.

Amen. Blessed be. Namaste. Shalom.
Om om, hari hari om.
Hari, hari om.
Hari om, hari om
Hari, hari om.

She-ma Yis-ro-el, adonoi elahaynu, adonoi e-chad

"Love Is Still Possible in This Junky World"

A Conversation with Sheree Rose about
Her Life with Bob Flanagan

TINA TAKEMOTO

See Commitments, Consent, Contracts; Public/Private Exhibition(ist)s; and Music, Literary, and Sexual Subcultures image galleries.

In this interview with Tina Takemoto, Rose discusses her life, work, and sadomasochistic relationship with Flanagan. Rose also offers a candid and moving account of her experience of love, sex, loss, and grief inspired by their sixteen-year relationship.[1]

TINA TAKEMOTO: Can you begin by talking about your interest in art and feminism?

SHEREE ROSE: I'm interested in what gets in the canon and what gets left out. In 1966, I went to the Los Angeles County Museum of Art for the first exhibition of Edward Kienholz's *Back Seat.*[2] At the time, there was a big controversy over whether the museum should keep the back seat of the

---

1. This interview originally appeared in *Women and Performance: A Journal of Feminist Theory*, vol. 19, no. 1, 2009, pp. 95–111. Copyright © Women & Performance Project Inc. Reprinted by permission of Taylor & Francis Ltd, http://www.tandfonline.com, on behalf of Women & Performance Project Inc. The phrase "Love Is Still Possible in This Junky World" is taken from the title of a poem by Bob Flanagan. See Flanagan, *The Kid*, 8–9.

2. Edward Kienholz, *Back Seat Dodge '38*, artwork, 1964, presented at the Los Angeles County Museum of Art in 1966.

car open because of the sexual content of the piece.[3] Of course, Kienholz was still alive as was his wife Nancy Reddin Kienholz. What I remember about that show is that her name was not mentioned or credited. In the 1960s, the women artists who were the collaborators and wives of the male artists were not given credit, even though these women were equally involved in making the work.

TT: Now we are seeing a number of feminist art shows such as *Wack! Art and the Feminist Revolution* and *Global Feminisms*.[4] What do you think about this phenomenon?

SR: I think that anything involving feminism and education is good. When I got divorced, before I was an artist, one of my goals in life was to empower women to be economically independent. I was a counselor and worked with single mothers. I said to them, "Stop having more babies and stop being so dependent on men. Get yourself an education and find a way to support yourself." These women were young and eager to be good parents, but they were often trapped in bad relationships. Education and economic independence were crucial for change. If you have these two things then you don't have to tolerate an abusive relationship. I taught this message long before I got into the art world. I wouldn't have necessarily called myself a feminist then, but I think I was a proto-feminist.

TT: It sounds like you were already involved with feminist issues.

SR: I was a middle-class recently divorced housewife, and my assignment while getting my master's degree at Cal State Northridge was to work at the Women's Center.[5] There, I joined the Feminist Socialist Network. We met once a week and read about women's rights and the history of feminism. This was around the time of women's consciousness-raising

---

3. See *Edward Kienholz* 15, 44–45; "Los Angeles Art Uproar"; A.V.F., "For Adults Only."

4. *Wack! Art and the Feminist Revolution*, MOCA: Museum of Contemporary Art, Los Angeles, 2007 and *Global Feminisms / The Dinner Party*, Brooklyn Museum, Brooklyn, 2007. See also: *Agents of Change: Women, Art & Intellect*, Ceres Gallery, NYC, 2007; *Take 2: Women Revisiting Art History*, Mills College, Oakland, 2007; *What F Word?*, Cynthia Broan Gallery, NYC, 2007; *Women's Work: An Homage to Feminist Art*, TABLA RASA Gallery, Brooklyn, 2007, *Kiss Kiss Bang Bang: 45 Years of Art & Feminism*, Bilboko Arte Eder Museoa, Bilboa, 2007.

5. Currently known as the Women's Research and Resource Center, Cal State University at Northridge.

groups. I had a boyfriend at the time, and he wasn't very nice to me. One woman in a consciousness-raising group said to me, "Don't you know you are sleeping with the enemy?" She said this without irony because this was 1979. [Laughs.] But this comment did get me thinking about my own relationships with men. I thought, "Well, she's right because men can be pigs. But not every woman can become a lesbian. There has to be other options." I have always been very supportive of gay and lesbian sex, but I was also trying to figure out other options within heterosexuality.

TT: You have always presented yourself as very sex-positive and supportive of alternative lifestyles and sexualities.

SR: Generally, I believe that sex should involve consent. If it is consensual it is okay. I draw the line at sex with children and animals because children and animals cannot consent. There is no other reason that it is unacceptable. It's not disgusting or anything else. If there are two consenting adults then any form of sexual relationship is fine. Even if nobody else understands the relationship, it doesn't matter. Sex is not about what anyone else thinks. That is my sexual philosophy.

TT: So you were exploring feminism as a new mode of thinking and a way of making sense of your life.

SR: Feminism taught me about independence, about cultures where women are deities, and about the systematic oppression of women through patriarchy. I liked these ideas because they gave me a context for understanding why I was always considered "bossy." That was the description that people used for me. What they meant was I didn't follow directions very well and wanted to do things my own way. Rather than getting a positive response, I was told I was bossy. I accepted this because it was better than being a dishrag. After my divorce when I started dating, I decided that I was going to be the aggressive one. This was a complete role-reversal and totally different than the way I was brought up to behave. I was doing it as an experiment because I really didn't have much experience sexually. In fact, I was a virgin until I got married. So I would go to a bar, find the guy I thought was cute, and pick him up. I found it was very easy. Men are very indiscriminate when it comes to sex. During those three years, I slept with a lot of men but, overall, it was very dissatisfying. Numerous one-night stands become tiring and uninteresting. After a while, it was just blah.

TT: Tell me about meeting Bob Flanagan.

SR: I met Bob through my interest in poetry. The flowering of the Los Angeles poetry movement started in the 1980s in poetry workshops, and one of the best places for poetry at the time was Beyond Baroque in Venice, California.[6] I was their primary photographer, and I have thousands of pictures of everyone who went through there over the years, people like Exene and John Doe of the band X, Dennis Cooper, Amy Gerstler, Benjamin Weissman, and David Trinidad. Bob was also very involved with that scene. We actually met 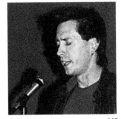 at a Halloween party organized by poetry friends. I was dressed as the late Jayne Mansfield, completely made-up with a blonde wig and big boobs. He was dressed as one of the characters from *Dawn of the Dead* covered in blood and gore. Both of us were dead characters, and it was love at first sight. We fell for each other right away.

p. 237

TT: Was Bob the first person to support your assertiveness and sense of adventure when it came to sex and sexuality?

SR: Absolutely. Bob was ten years younger than me. I was 37 and he was 27. For me it was a little unusual because I generally dated older men. My ex-husband was ten years older than me. I was just beginning to explore my sexuality, and like many women in their late thirties, I was hitting my sexual prime. A man like Bob in his twenties is a perfect match. And Bob was perfect! Our sexuality interests and energies were totally in sync. I had never been with someone with whom I felt so sexually compatible. Also, his interest in sadomasochism (SM) opened up something for me that I had never experienced. When he told me he was a masochist and that he wanted to be somebody's slave, these were very new concepts to me. The women's groups didn't say to me, "You should go out and find yourself a slave." They didn't say *that* to me. Plus, he was smart, creative, and obviously a very nice young man. He wasn't just someone I had picked up at a bar. He was someone I could sexualize as a decent and respectable person.

TT: How did you find out about Bob's health condition?

---

6. Beyond Baroque Literary/Arts Center began in 1968 in Venice, California, to offer public readings, workshops, a bookstore, publications, and a small press archive.

SR: On our second date he told me that he had cystic fibrosis (CF). I come from a family of extremely healthy people. I have no family history of terminal illnesses or cancer or heart attacks. No one in my family had even spent a night in the hospital. So my knowledge about chronic illness was very limited. I asked him what having CF meant. Bob said, "It means that I have to take a lot of pills because I don't have this right enzyme. It means that I have this thick mucus, so I have to cough all the time." But Bob was walking around and dancing, and he seemed fine to me. Plus, he looked adorable. He was thin, like a punk rocker, but I liked that look. I thought, "Okay, he has a health condition." Initially, I didn't take it more seriously because I had never heard of cystic fibrosis before.

TT: You didn't know about the short life expectancy or the health problems associated with cystic fibrosis?

SR: No, not at all. I did find out more about cystic fibrosis a few weeks later. I learned that most people with CF die by the time they are thirty years old. Bob's own sister had died at the age of 21, a year before I had met him. Bob said to me, "Maybe I will live for two more years. All I am looking for is a good two-year relationship." I thought to myself, "What's wrong with having a sickly Irish poet for two years? He's adorable and I am crazy about him. I can do this." That was my mindset. Plus, he was so funny. He brought me down to Cal State Long Beach to see a musical that he had written and starred in. It was called *Juice* and he played a character called Mr. Natural. It was hysterical. From the very beginning Bob made me laugh, and that was his greatest gift to me. At that time, I wasn't thinking about a long-term relationship. I figured, "Okay, I will take him on for two years. He wants to be a slave to a woman. He could be my slave." That's really how our relationship started.

TT: Was this the beginning of your written sadomasochistic contracts with Bob?

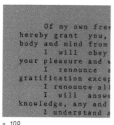

p. 198

SR: Yes, we always had SM contracts. That was something we thought was a good idea. Instead of going through the "I love you forever, until death do us part" marriage vows, I thought we should have a contract for a set period of time. At the end of each contract term, we would go over it and see what worked, what didn't work, if either of us wanted out, or if we needed to make some changes. These were written contracts.[7] First, we had three-month contracts followed by three-year contracts, until much later when it was clear we were going to be together until he died. The SM contracts were the start of our idea that everything had to be consensual, and we had to agree on everything. So even though I was ostensibly his Mistress and he was my submissive, everything we did together was totally consensual.

TT: Can you describe one of your early collaborative performances with Bob?

SR: We did a performance at LACE for a pro-choice benefit exhibition in 1992.[8] In this performance, Bob portrays a conservative, religious, anti-choice character based on Randall Terry, who was the founder of Operation Rescue.[9] Bob begins a ranting monologue saying things like, "women are meant to have babies" and "God wants you to have babies" and the typical Randall Terry rhetoric. While Bob is speaking to the audience, I enter with a basket filled with plastic babies that look remarkably real. After a while I begin attaching babies to his flesh using fishhooks and wire, so that babies are dangling from the front and back of his body. He winces each time the fishhook goes in, but he continues with his Terry rant. At the same time, the audience begins to hear an audiotape of babies crying. The babies' cries get louder and louder until they completely drown out Bob's speaking. I attach the last baby to the head of Bob's penis and he starts swinging it between his legs singing, "Rock-a-bye baby . . ."

TT: This performance is so physically and politically provocative. How did you develop it together? Can you describe your collaborative working process?

---

7. In a 1993 interview with Andrea Juno and V. Vale, Flanagan recalls, "The contracts were just copies of Sacher-Masoch's: I would be Sheree's slave and do anything she said. I would be in charge of cleaning the house, and I couldn't masturbate or have any kind of sex unless she said so. My body belonged to her completely, to do with whatever she wanted. I wasn't allowed to be with anybody else, but *she* could be with whoever she wanted to be with. There was no penalty of death, of course—this was a totally non-binding, non-legal agreement specifying in concrete terms what our boundaries would be" (Juno and Vale 38).

8. Bob Flanagan and Sheree Rose, *Matter of Choice*, performance for *Issue of Choice*, a pro-choice benefit and exhibition, LACE: Los Angeles Contemporary Exhibitions, Los Angeles, 1992.

9. Randall Terry founded the conservative and religious anti-choice organization Operation Rescue in 1987.

SR: We wanted to demonstrate our point in a visceral manner without having to give a political lecture. That was one of our goals in working together. Each piece had to have humor, and it had to feature Bob as the star. The spotlight was never on me. I was just there to make things happen. Bob was the ham. He loved to be on stage, and he really loved to perform nude. Because he was so thin and frail, his nudity was acceptable to the audience. You never felt that what you were seeing was too sexy or aggressive because he never used his body or his penis in a sexual or threatening way. He engendered more sympathy rather than horror or terror. The response was, "Oh that poor guy, he is so skinny." In this way, our performances took the fear out of looking at a naked male body.

TT: And how often do we see a male body with babies? We usually see women and babies.

SR: That's right. For me, the pain of attaching the baby with a fishhook was really important. A fishhook hurts going in and even more coming out. It is not so easy to get a fishhook out. You're hooked. That's what happens to women when they have babies—they're hooked. Men think, "Oh, babies are so great and wonderful." But they aren't hooked forever the way women are. I thought that using fishhooks was a good way of communicating this idea.

TT: This performance also conveys such a strong feminist message. I often wondered if you were the driving force behind a lot of the conceptual aspects of your pieces with Bob.

SR: It's true. This topic doesn't get discussed much. No one remembers my name. It's always Bob's name that people remember. But part of that has to do with who I am. It has to do with me—being a Mistress, a mother, being the one behind the scenes, and pushing Bob to stardom. That is still part of my role. In truth, I was more like a Svengali. I had these ideas and Bob was the one who fleshed them out. The thing that people don't understand is that Bob was *my invention.* He was my means to get my message across. And that was part of his role as my submissive. He was the compliant man who would willingly do anything for his Mistress.

TT: I understand that *Fuck Journal* was your idea. As Bob's Mistress, you commanded him to write about every time you had sex together. Is it true that if you caught him being lazy or cheating with the writing, you would withhold sex or force him to do things like write from the top corner of the page to the bottom corner of the page?

SR: Yes. I gave him a lot of instructions for his writing. I had to push him and I never stopped pushing him. It made his writing better. As my submissive, he knew the main rule: "Make me happy." Bob wrote a poem once saying he could do this and that but he could never make me happy. But he did. The truth is, he did make me happy. I just had a difficult way of showing it partly because I had to be the Mistress too. I couldn't just be the wife or the collaborator in the conventional sense.

TT: I once heard you described as a muse who is more like an irritant—or the speck of sand that helps create a pearl.

SR: That's true. I was an irritant. Bob wanted it that way. If you read Bob's poem "Why" he talks about wanting "a mommy, a mean mommy, especially a mean mommy." He wasn't kidding. He didn't want a cream puff. I had to irritate him. People would say to me, "Oh, you were so awful. How could you be so mean to him?" They didn't understand the relationship. It wasn't like that at all. The truth is, oftentimes, I didn't do enough. I did as much as I could comfortably do, and sometimes uncomfortably do, as his Dominatrix. But, he always wanted more.

TT: Looking back, how would you describe the trajectory of your life and work with Bob?

SR: I would say that there were three main phases in our relationship. The first phase was our personal life—just him and me and all the crazy, wild, fun things we did together during the first couple years. Even though I photographed everything, this documentation was just for us. The next five years, the second phase, were spent organizing the sadomasochistic community, which had not been done before. SM was a really important aspect of our lives. We believed in it enough to pour all of our energy into making SM a national movement and creating public and community spaces for it.[10] We became spokespeople for sadomasochism, giving lectures and demonstrations and raising awareness about the SM com-

10. As founding members of the Los Angeles Janus Society (now called Threshold), Bob Flanagan and Sheree Rose were instrumental in forming this non-profit organization dedicated to the education and support of safe, consensual, non-exploitive adult sadomasochism and power exchange. See Weymouth and Society of Janus 20.

munity.[11] Nowadays, it's gone much further than we ever expected. But at that time, the SM movement was just beginning. And, because we got such good responses within the SM community, we flirted with the idea of bringing SM out into the mainstream. That was the beginning of the third phase, the art phase.

TT: How did this "art phase" begin?

SR: It started with the RE/Search book *Modern Primitives* (Vale). We had a friend Stuart Swezey, co-founder and co-publisher of Amok Books, and he knew that I had done photographs of pierced and tattooed people. He introduced us to V. Vale and Andrea Juno, who noticed a subculture of pierced and tattooed people developing in San Francisco. At that time Bob and I were working at the Gauntlet. It was one of the few places to get body piercing. We did a performance in honor of the *Modern Primitives* book at Olio in Los Angeles, 1989.[12] This was a watershed performance. To my knowledge, it was the first time that art, SM, music, dance, literature, and performance were presented together to a "straight," meaning non-SM audience. This was our biggest contribution to bringing sadomasochism into the mainstream. Until then we had only given SM performances for SM audiences and poetry readings for poetry audiences. This was the first time both worlds were brought together. Club FUCK! was started

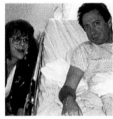

after the performance at Olio. Michael Tolkin, who wrote and directed *The New Age,* was there. It inspired him and many others, also because the event was covered on the news. From that time on, Bob and I were invited to participate in numerous shows and exhibitions.[13] Bob was not interested in making money or being famous. Those were things that just happened along the way.

p. 219

TT: In 1997, the documentary *Sick: The Life and Death of Bob Flanagan, Super-masochist,* directed by Kirby Dick, was released. Can you speak about your experience working on this film?

---

11. See, for example, Flanagan and Rose.

12. Bob Flanagan and Sheree Rose, *Nailed!* performance, Olio, produced by Amok Bookstore, Los Angeles, 1989.

13. Bob Flanagan and Sheree Rose, *Visiting Hours,* exhibition, Santa Monica Museum of Art, Santa Monica, 1992; New Museum of Contemporary Art, NYC, 1994; and the School of the Museum of Fine Arts, Boston, 1995.

SR: Kirby and I had a very strange relationship. He came into the project during the last two years of Bob's life. I had been photographing and filming Bob from the beginning of our relationship. During the last two years when we knew that Bob was going to die, I realized that I didn't want to be the one holding the camera at his death. I didn't want that responsibility. I felt it would be too much emotionally, and I just wanted to be able to be there with him. After talking it over with Bob, we approached Kirby about making a documentary. We picked Kirby because socially we had been good friends for over ten years and we had seen his other movies.[14] It was supposed to be a collaboration among the three of us.

TT: How did this collaboration work out given the fact that you had always been the primary person who documented your life and work with Bob?

SR: It was very hard. But, I felt that the completed film was going to be more important than anybody's individual ego. I was willing to rise above potential conflict, and I trusted Kirby, which turned out to be a big mistake. Toward the end, when Bob went into the hospital for the last time, I begged Kirby to come to the hospital. He said, "I'm sorry. I am directing and I have to go to this paying job." I said, "Kirby, this is very important. This is going to be the most significant part of the film. I really want you to be there." He said, "No."

TT: Did Kirby understand that it would be Bob's last day?

SR: He knew, but he picked his job instead. So there I was in the hospital room. I had a video camera that wasn't working very well. I set it up on an angle and I turned it on when I could remember to do it. I shot all the footage that exists of Bob's last days in the hospital. Some of the best moments I do not have on tape. Bob gave a fifteen-minute farewell speech that I don't have on tape because I could not bear to leave his side to turn on the camera. No one else even knew where the camera was. If Kirby had been there, or if Kirby would have sent somebody to the hospital, it would have all been recorded. It was devastating. Bob was dying, and I had to photograph his death, which was just what I did not want to do. I did it because I felt that if I didn't then no one else would. It took a lot out of me, and Kirby never apologized. Afterwards, I was so upset that I gave Kirby all the footage and I said, "You do the editing. I don't want to have anything to do with it." That's how I felt.

---

14. See Dick, *Private Practices* and *I Am Not A Freak*.

TT: Yet, the documentary has been very successful. Do you feel that the film has been important?

SR: Oh yes. It is getting the word out about Bob. But it's not completely accurate. There were scenes that I begged Kirby to put in. For instance, there is a scene of my mother going to the museum to see Bob in *Visiting Hours* and the conversation they had together. Kirby left that out. The footage that he did include of my mother is very harsh and wasn't even intended for this film. I shot that footage for another project about my family. Also, Kirby has never given me any financial compensation. In our contract, I am supposed to get one third of the net profit. I didn't know the difference between net and gross profit at the time. He got me to sign the contract the night before I was leaving for Tibet. I was going on a pilgrimage for Bob one year after his death. Kirby got me to sign the papers without a lawyer. I didn't know what I was signing because I was still crazy with grief. It was a very vulnerable time, and Kirby took advantage of me. But, on the other hand, the movie is out and people know about it. I probably wouldn't have been able to complete the film on my own. I do resent that fact that he didn't even want my name on it. We had a big fight about getting my name on the film at all. But, I guess that's what Hollywood does to you.

TT: In the commentary section, the editor Dody Dorn says that one of her primary intentions in editing the film was to demonstrate how it was a love story and how much of Bob's life revolved around you.

SR: It's true. Bob had two main goals. First, he wanted to express himself. Second, he wanted a life with me. That was his choice and my choice too. With our contractual agreements, our relationship was totally consensual, and it became much more than each of us could ever imagine. What started off as a personal relationship ended up having a significant impact on the art world and the SM community. At the same time, we were very real people, with real desires and problems. I know that I wasn't perfect and I often disappointed him. But, we did the best we could. You can't expect perfection. That's what life is.

TT: In my own research, I have been thinking about what it means to collaborate with a loved one who is sick. How has Bob's illness affected your understanding of intimacy and grief?

SR: It changes you. After I was with Bob for a very short while, I met a woman on an airplane who said to me, "You know, you should never get involved with anybody who has an illness like cystic fibrosis because you won't be able to get out of it. You should get away while you can." She was a nurse and a stranger. I was so shocked by what she said, because it never had occurred to me. It was such a new idea, the thought that Bob was going to die and that I would be involved in it. I felt a shock all the way down to my toes. When I came back home, Bob was in the house, sitting on the couch and playing guitar. Bob had this quality. He was like a little boy. I felt this love that was beyond sex or intimacy. I thought, "He's here now, but he is not going to be here forever." I had the first inkling of the mortality of someone I loved. Of course, I had thought about the mortality of my parents but they were still alive. This was very different. This was the first time I had the feeling that Bob was going to die. It was only three months into our relationship. It felt like love and grief mixed together. But at that point I made the decision that I wasn't going to back out of it. I knew our relationship was something very profound.

TT: Did this awareness of Bob's mortality intensify your desire to document him and your life together? Was there a sense of urgency about it?

SR: It felt urgent, absolutely. Also, I thought Bob was such a genius. He was not just a little funny, or a little weird, he was amazing. What happened to him was fate—his brothers didn't have cystic fibrosis. But what Bob did with his condition, that's what made him unique. It was the illness that drove him, that made him, that gave him that extra spark. I thought he just couldn't go unnoticed.

TT: Did making work about illness produce the feeling of agency, as if you are slowing down time or somehow combating illness by transforming it into something else?

SR: Yes. I think it did. It transformed illness from something horrible and tragic into something else. In the beginning, I got into it because I had this romantic idea of being with a sickly dying Irish poet. It made everything we did seem more poignant. It was like the story of Camille reversed. Instead of the dying young woman with the cough it was the story of the dying young man with the cough. He would write songs that said, "If it wasn't for SM, I'd be dead. If it wasn't for Sheree, I'd be dead. She gave me all these extra years." And it's true. He couldn't have died on me. I wouldn't have let him. As his Mistress I would say, "You are not going to die. How dare you?" That's exactly how I was with him. I knew he was sick. I felt it, but I decided I wasn't going to let it affect how I treated him. I never treated him with pity—never once, even as sick as he was. Of course, there were times when I thought, "I need to get away from this. This is too much. This is too heavy and intense for me." But, with a child or with anyone you love, there is no way you can just leave.

TT: How did your role as Bob's Mistress change as he got sicker? Was it difficult for you as the sadomasochistic dynamic of your relationship began to shift?

SR: Bob found it harder and harder to submit to me as he got sicker. When he got very sick, the illness was overwhelming and nothing else really mattered. The truth is, he really couldn't submit to me one hundred percent because he had to submit to his illness. It was difficult for me to come to terms with this. But I learned early on that I wasn't his true Mistress. Nevertheless, I did the best I could to maintain my role. Being his Mistress wasn't just about sex. In fact, it often had very little to do with sex. But, as his condition worsened, I think the grieving started then too. It became part of what I knew.

TT: Grief becomes such an intense aspect of being with a loved one who is sick. How did you deal with this feeling especially during the last couple years of his life? With all your performances and exhibitions, your relationship had a very public dimension, which must have impacted your private relationship. This aspect of grieving is one that people don't really want to talk or think about.

SR: Definitely. But, again, even amidst all the sex and the craziness I still saw him as a little boy. I was also a mother, and I think that part of it was feeling, "What would I do if he was my child? How would I treat a child who was dying? Would I abandon my child?" He was not only my lover, my collaborator, but he was also my child. The only way I could deal with it was not to admit that there was a higher authority than me. At the same time, we weren't delusional. We talked about death all the time. But we were never going to give in to it. He lived with death. Death was always there. He didn't have to think about it, he knew it.

TT: And by choice, you also lived with a sense of mortality. I think for some people it may seem morbid or counterintuitive to choose to live this way. Not everyone would make that choice, because that is the harder thing to do.

SR: It may be morbid. But when I fell in love with him, it wasn't because he was dying. It was because he was very attractive. He was very good in bed. He cleaned my house, washed my dishes, and took care of my junk. He was funny. He kept me laughing, and he could play the guitar beautifully. I didn't fall in love with him for any of the wrong reasons. His illness was a very minor issue in the beginning. Remember, we were together for sixteen years. It wasn't until the 1990s that his health started getting really bad. We had many years together that weren't recorded, years that weren't in the public eye. Also Bob was someone who taunted death and made fun of death. He is famous for singing, "It's fun to be dead." I even had that line written on his tombstone.

TT: Do you think that Bob's humorous approach helped you talk about issues that you may not have been able to do otherwise?

SR: Absolutely. His humor was always something that I admired. Toward the end, as the work got very macabre, we were discussing what we were going to do when he died and laughing about it and making fun of it. Humor was another way we dealt with the grief. Even on his deathbed, he made fifty people laugh. He reminded me of this enlightened being Satchidananda, who passed away a few years ago. Why was he so wonderful? He had the greatest sense of humor. He made everybody laugh. It wasn't that he was a funny man. But he saw life in this very large way, so he could see the humor in it. He was very similar to Bob. Whenever Bob couldn't do something, he would say, "Well, I can't do that anymore, so I will do this instead." There was no self-pity. He didn't want pity. And yet, I think he was as afraid of dying as anybody else and as angry about it as anybody would be. We weren't sad and depressed all the time. Yet, death was always on our minds, and we were always dealing with it in one way or another. At the very end, when he was actually dying in the hospital, he said, "What's happening to me? Am I dying? I don't understand. This is stupid."[15]

---

15. See final scenes of *Sick.*

TT: Maybe in his own mind he couldn't comprehend it, because he had been defying death for so long. Or, I suppose, there is no way to understand death when it happens.

SR: Yes, his words, which I have rewatched on videotape, really affected me afterwards. I will always regret that his deathbed soliloquy is not on tape. It was as good as Hamlet, only funny. Believe me, people were laughing. I don't remember a word of it, except for the very end. Bob's last words were, "Sheree, I love you. It was the best collaboration ever in the whole world." Those were his last words. I am teary . . . So I don't think he was too upset with me. It wasn't a quiet deathbed scene. There were fifty people in the room, family and friends. We didn't say "no" to anyone who wanted to be there. We had made that decision together. We felt that with his death, people wanted to be there because they cared about him deeply. People still remember him because he was so open even until the very end.

TT: Dying is an experience that most people aren't willing to think about or to share with others. There is still so much fear and shame around dying that people feel that it needs to be private.

SR: That's true. Yet, we lived our most intimate moments on stage. Death is such a strange thing. To see it happen in front of you—not in the dark of night and not when the person is asleep or in a coma—is unbelievable. Bob was alive and thinking up until the very moment he took his last breath. People are very curious about death. Especially in this world where there are so many young people who have life-threatening illnesses. They are going to die very young and they know it. I am not talking about getting shot or getting hit by a car. I put that kind of death in a different category because you don't have time to say goodbye or to put your life in order. I am talking about someone who has time to think about it—who has knowledge of his own death. In the old days, when people had terminal illness, they would take a long time to die. They would be in their own home and people would come to say their good-byes and to have that moment with them. Today, there are so many deaths that aren't natural. There are so many deaths by accidents and murder and war that people don't have time to process it. Then there's Bob who had all the time in the world to think about it. Bob was able to spend so much of his creative and intellectual time thinking about his own death. It was a rare opportunity and most people don't get a chance to do that. I have gotten so many letters over the years from people who tell me intimate things about their experience of illness and the loss of loved ones. Beyond the artistic aspects and on a very personal level, our work has really affected a lot of people.

TT: Did being with Bob change the way you think about mortality?

SR: Oh yes. I am much more conscious of it. In yoga, they talk about the breath of life, and the idea that you are only allowed so many breaths. When you take your last breath, you don't know when that is going to be. Yoga is so much about breathing and deep breathing. I think about Bob a lot during yoga because he could never deep breathe. He never had a comfortable breath. Yet he was a singer. He was a person who transcended so much adversity. Also, living with someone with a chronic illness like Bob, was living with this sense of not knowing. You wonder, "When is it going to happen—today, tonight, or tomorrow?" You want to leave because you can't take it anymore, but your love is stronger. Grief and love get very mixed together. You are like rubber. You change.

TT: What is your experience as the survivor of this relationship?

SR: That's a hard question. It's been ten years since Bob died. I still don't think I have gotten over his death. I sort of had this delusion that Bob wasn't really going to die. Intellectually, I knew he was going to die, and I thought I was strong enough and somehow more prepared to deal with it. After his death, I engaged in many activities that were very symbolic and ritualistic of grief. In the Jewish tradition, you sit shiva for seven days. You don't leave the house, you tear your clothes, and you don't wash. Everyone comes over to your house and they talk about your loved one and people take care of you. Then I made that twenty-foot inflatable statue of Bob, the *Bobballoon*.[16] It was an homage to him that was shown in Japan. I went to Tibet and Nepal to throw his ashes into the river. The first time I saw Bob in the hospital I said, "Oh dear, now I will never be able to go to the Himalayas." It was always one of my fantasies to go there, but I knew he could never go because of the altitude. So I went on the year anniversary of his death and I spread some of his ashes there. I tried to come to terms

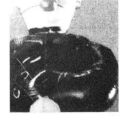

p. 224

16. Sheree Rose, *Bobballoon* (a twenty-foot-tall inflatable Flanagan with pierced penis, ball gag, and straightjacket), Japan, 1996.

with Bob's death with my psychologist, with my friends, and in so many other ways. Yet, as time went on, I didn't feel better. I felt worse. When it actually happened, when it actually hit me that I would not see his face or hear his jokes, it really paralyzed me. I went into deep freeze mode. I was living and doing things but I felt like a part of me had been ripped out, like my leg or my intestines had been removed. I felt like a big part of me wasn't there. And it has taken me ten years to get over that feeling. In fact, I haven't really loved anybody since Bob. I haven't been able to open my heart because the devastation of his death was so horrible for me. It took away some of my interest in art as far as making art.

TT: Now that Bob is gone, do you have a more private and protective relationship with his images and the work you did together?

SR: While he was alive I had no problem sharing him with the world. But now that Bob's dead, I feel that whatever I do with his images would be difficult for me. I have so many photographs of Bob, and my friends have urged me to show and publish them. But Bob has become very personal to me now. And it's strange. I didn't think this would happen, but it has. At this point, I have become somewhat morbid. I think that the world might have to wait until I'm dead for people to really understand what we did together, and for the work that I haven't shown to be shown. I still give lectures and respond to people who are seriously interested in our work. I would like the legacy of our work to continue, and I think about the future of our vast archive of materials. But I am loath to put down my own words and feelings. I mean, how can you express how you feel when your lover or your child dies? It is still that personal and painful to me. I think about Bob's mother, who loved Bob and her daughter dearly, and she knew they had death sentences over their heads. She had to deal with her love for them. I know about this because I loved her son. So now I do yoga every day because I know that Bob could never do it. I do yoga to honor him. That's how I deal with his loss now. I honor Bob's pain and his creativity and his courage, and I try to stay connected to his very deep love.

Works Cited

A.V.F. "For Adults Only: The Revolting L.A. Art . . . ?" *San Francisco Chronicle,* 24 Mar. 1966.

Dick, Kirby, director. *I Am Not a Freak,* 1987.

———. *Private Practices: The Story of a Sex Surrogate,* 1986.

———. Prod. Sheree Rose. *Sick: The Life and Death of Bob Flanagan, Supermasochist,* 1997.

Edward Kienholz. Los Angeles County Museum of Art, 1966.

Flanagan, Bob. *Fuck Journal.* Hanuman, 1987.

———. *The Kid Is the Man.* Bombshelter Press, 1978.

———. "Why." *Art Journal,* vol. 56, no. 4, 1997, pp. 58–59.

Flanagan, Bob, and Sheree Rose. Lecture for Symposium on Bondage and Discipline, Society for the Scientific Study of Sex, San Diego, 1985.

"Los Angeles Art Uproar: Supervisors Ban Museum Showing." *Los Angeles Times,* preview edition, 23 Mar. 1966.

Tolkin, Michael, director. *The New Age,* 1993.

Vale, V. *Modern Primitives* (2nd ed.). Re/Search Publications, 1989.

Vale, V. and Andrea Juno, editors. *Bob Flanagan: Supermasochist.* RE/Search, People Series, Volume 1. RE/Search Publications, 1993.

Weymouth, T. and Society of Janus. *Society of Janus: 25 Years.* SOJ, 1999.

Why Kirby Dick Is a "Sick" Prick

SHEREE ROSE

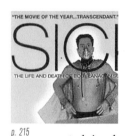

p. 215

In 1997 Kirby Dick's *Sick: The Life and Death of Bob Flanagan, Supermasochist,* won an award at the Sundance Film Festival, which effectively began his distinguished directorial career. I was co-producer on the film as well as the co-star: Bob Flanagan was my consensual "slave" for sixteen years, until his death, from cystic fibrosis, in 1996.

For the first fourteen years of our relationship, I documented, in photographs and video, many aspects of our unique collaboration, which involved S/M activities, writing assignments, art practices, hospitalizations, and political activism. Mr. Dick was a personal friend, and we attended parties and other social situations together. We knew he was a filmmaker, and we attended the premiere of his first documentary, *Private Practices,* about a sexual surrogate, produced by his wife's ex-husband.

As Bob's health worsened, we decided to bring someone else into our lives to document the last years of his life, since I wanted to be by his side and not have to worry about always having a camera handy. We chose Mr. Dick because we felt he knew us and had directed a film that dealt with unusual sexual practices.

We invited him into our private lives, with the understanding that he would take my place and document Bob's final days. We never had a contract; we never formally said we were making a film for distribution.

Three days before Bob died, Mr. Dick abandoned the project because he was offered a paying job as a director on a feature film, *Guy*, starring Vincent D'Onofrio. So, Mr. Dick was not present for the last days of Bob's life, and I was left on my own to photograph and videotape his last moments—the very thing I did not want to do. Mr. Dick was fired from this job, and subsequently came back to our project, and did videotape the funeral. I gave him all the footage and photos I had taken at Bob's death, settled into a prolonged grieving process, and let Mr. Dick handle the editing process.

After a year, I planned a trip to Nepal, to spend the first anniversary of Bob's death in the Himalayas. On the eve of my departure, Mr. Dick came over to my home late at night and proceeded to get me drunk and stoned. He then produced a document, which he said he should have in case I died while trekking in the mountains. He told me not to worry about anything, that he would take care of me, and I shouldn't be concerned with the legal aspects. He said he would give me 33 1/3 percent of the profits. I was very woozy and thinking, yeah, I might fall off the mountains and die—so I signed the document in good faith.

Unfortunately, Mr. Dick had no good faith. He not only swindled me out of my fair share of the money, he also didn't want to put my name on the film and acknowledge the fourteen years I had spent documenting Bob, long before he was involved.

I sued Mr. Dick and forced him to add me as co-producer, but he wouldn't budge on the 33 1/3 of the net profits. I was forced into bankruptcy, from which I have never recovered. But worst of all, Mr. Dick has never paid me one penny of the money he has made from *Sick*. He has never provided me an accounting of his costs or the many deals he made with various movie studios. To this day, I am completely in the dark about the financial status of the film. I take responsibility for many foolish decisions, but Mr. Dick took total advantage of my impaired mental condition and totally exploited the film to his own advantage. He built his career on the back of *Sick* and has never acknowledged the debt—both moral and financial—that he owes me.

Shame on you, Mr. Dick—your name says it all.

PART 2

COLLABORATIONS AND CRITICAL PERSPECTIVES

Performing Again (after Bob)

TANYA AUGSBURG

See *Nailed, Again!* image gallery.

Los Angeles, 1999

Sheree Rose was coaxed back into performance art in August 1999 during a private art event in downtown Los Angeles. More than three years had passed since the death of Bob Flanagan—her husband, art collaborator, and submissive—from cystic fibrosis in January 1996. I had driven from Phoenix to attend the party, which was hosted by two artist friends at their apartment. I brought along as my date, an aspiring actor who happened to be nine years younger than me.

We made an unlikely pair. His movie-star looks and self-assured confidence clashed with my mousy appearance and jumpy demeanor. We had been only casually hanging out for about a month, but we were already used to receiving side-eyes and double takes whenever we were seen together. We enjoyed the attention. He liked surprising people, while I appreciated getting noticed for a change.

We didn't know any of the guests at the party. I recognized the names of one couple, as their reputations preceded them: Columbia professor Sylvère Lotringer and his then-wife Chris Kraus, an experimental film-maker and writer. Together they ran Semiotext(e) press. While all the guests were cordial to us, we still were subjected to various curious looks.

At one point during the party, the aspiring actor, a lover of literature, came across a copy of Bob Flanagan's *Fuck Journal* and showed it to me. A woman named Sheree stared as I explained who Bob Flanagan was, since my companion was unfamiliar with contemporary art. I didn't realize that Sheree, whom we had met briefly a few minutes earlier, was *Mistress Sheree,* Flanagan's widow. As I was telling the art initiate how important Flanagan's work was to the art world, Rose interrupted me, saying, "Bob Flanagan was my husband." My immediate reaction was not so much surprise as it was relief—thank goodness I had discussed Flanagan's BDSM practices and art in positive ways that were both scholarly and theoretical!

Later that evening Rose told both Chris Kraus and me that she had not performed since Flanagan's death. But Rose was adamant when she asserted that she was not suffering from a lack of new artistic ideas. Rose let us know that she was still making art, most notably the huge balloon installation called *Bobballoon,* which had been exhibited in Tokyo in August 1996. She was done with performing, however. Rose disclosed that she just didn't feel right performing any more without Flanagan since she believed that he had been the performer of the two.

Rose's declarations about the end of her performance career seemed to me a bit premature. Rose's performances as Flanagan's dominatrix were performances in their own right, even if they were intended to be relational to Flanagan and supportive of his performance work. After all, as Flanagan often admitted, he would not have had been known as a performance artist if it hadn't been for Rose.

I pulled Rose aside at the first opportunity. I encouraged her to submit a proposal to perform a commemorative piece about Flanagan for a performance studies conference in Phoenix the following March since I was a member of the local conference planning committee. She laughed. Little did I know that only a few minutes earlier Kraus had done the same thing, inviting Rose to perform at an earlier academic conference that she was helping to organize in New York. I thanked Rose and told her that I would follow up with her, which I did.

A Common Feminist Plight: The Struggle for Recognition

Thanks to Kraus, Rose performed *Nailed, Again!* for the first time during the Simone Weil Conference in November 1999 at the Galapagos Art Space in Brooklyn. In retrospect, it makes perfect sense that Rose would agree to Kraus's invitation. At the time Kraus and Rose were discussing the possibility of Semiotext(e) publishing the journal Flanagan kept at the end of his life. *The Pain Journal* was published by Semiotext(e) the following year with a foreword written by Kraus. Like Rose, Kraus at the time was struggling to be recognized for her own work apart from her collaborations with Lotringer, a predicament that she chronicled in her early novels *I Love Dick* (1997) and *Aliens and Anorexia* (2000).

Thanks to my own initiatives and efforts, Rose performed *Nailed, Again!* for the second time during the Sixth Annual Performance Studies international conference (PSi) in a decommissioned chapel at Arizona State University (ASU) in March 2000. It makes less sense that Rose would have said yes to me so soon after meeting me. All that she knew of me initially was what she observed: she saw a thirty-something woman talking about Bob Flanagan to a twenty-something man who seemed quite attentive to her.

Reflecting back on that night almost twenty years later, I'm fairly certain that my interactions with the younger man at the party reminded Rose of her own dynamics with Flanagan during the early days of their relationship, since he had been about ten years younger than her. If Rose initially thought that she and I shared a similar erotic makeup, she would eventually find out that she was mistaken. But what we did ultimately bond over was the mutual struggle to be taken seriously for our own original contributions. Much to her chagrin Rose's solo art practices, as well as her unique contributions to her collaborations with Flanagan, had been overlooked by fellow artists, curators, collectors, and critics while Flanagan was alive, and his death did little to change prevailing perceptions for a number of years afterward. The challenges I faced organizing Rose's performance at ASU exposed some very ugly truths about how my own work was viewed by some of my colleagues there.

Performance Proposal

As a state university, ASU back in the period 1999–2000 was and still is (albeit to a much smaller degree) dependent on state financial support. At the time I was a lecturer teaching for the second year on a three-year contract in a relatively new interdisciplinary studies program that had a questionable campus-wide reputation. It was my third year teaching at ASU, as I had taught as a visiting lecturer during the 1997–1998 academic year in what was then the Communication Department. The local organizer of the Performance Studies international (PSi) conference invited me to join the local conference organizing committee because I had been on the local planning committee of a previous PSi conference in Atlanta before I had arrived at ASU. Nevertheless, it quickly became apparent during the planning process, and subsequently during the conference, that not everyone thought I should have been on the local steering committee at ASU given my contingent position at the university. My participation throughout the conference planning process and even afterward was persistently downplayed—to the extent that I was only credited as having given "assistance" to the steering committee in the official conference program.

Since I very much wanted to be a conference planning committee member, I had no choice but to ignore the superabundance of noncollegial behaviors directed toward me right from the start. After consulting with Rose, I wrote a performance proposal for *Nailed, Again!* on her behalf. I submitted the proposal not knowing whether it would be accepted or not. The performance proposal indicated that Rose not only would perform in a transparent outfit but would also symbolically cut herself. When the committee met to review all the submitted conference proposals, I was there and able to observe directly how an artistic work could become a litmus test for institutional tolerance of artists considered "extreme."

The other conference organizers were sharply divided among themselves about whether to accept Rose's performance proposal. Some strongly saw the value and importance of having Rose perform in memory of Bob Flanagan, while others could only see nightmarish visions of the Arizona state legislation cutting funds after finding out that the public university had allowed a performance that possibly involved nudity and bloodletting on its campus. I proceeded to make my case for Rose's proposal with my eyes wide open, understanding all too well the professional risks I was undertaking at the time. I could only hope for the best while fearing the worst: the end of my academic career.

"Safety Precautions"

To be fair, the conference planning committee members who initially wanted to reject Rose's proposal quickly acquiesced and accepted it— although they insisted that Rose perform only under certain conditions and with strict safety precautions. The committee agreed that Rose would perform in Danforth Chapel, a decommissioned chapel located in the center of campus. However, while it would be listed in the conference program, there would be no advance publicity. In strict compliance with fire safety regulations, only fifty people would be allowed into Danforth Chapel. Not surprisingly, a number of conference participants were unable to figure out where the performance was taking place. Several who made their way to Danforth Chapel didn't make it inside. The support for Rose's performance turned out to be quite tenuous insofar as it was highly managed, taking place under surveillance, control, and secrecy.

Were all the "safety precautions" surrounding *Nailed, Again!* really necessary? Or were they really serving as a ruse to marginalize Rose's performance from the rest of the conference? Could they also have been maneuvers to keep a lowly lecturer's efforts in the shadows? The following account, which I wrote approximately four months after Rose's March 2000 performance, will allow readers to answer these questions for themselves.

Sensing historical importance, I prefaced that account as I have done with this text—that is, with a detailed recollection of how I met Rose. Additionally, I saved several key performance artifacts, such as the performance proposal, a portion of the original performance script (the sermon poem Rose wrote for the performance), and a copy of the performance program. I also took some photos during the rehearsal, the performance, and dinner afterward. Aside from revisions made for clarity and accuracy, the following description of *Nailed Again!* during PSi 6 at ASU remains faithful to the original unpublished 2000 text.

Nailed, Again! at Arizona State University, March 10, 2000

Entering Danforth Chapel

Before entering the small chapel, each aspiring audience member is individually told the following warning, "The performance contains explicit and sensitive material." Once each person acknowledges the warning, thereby accepting responsibility for what they are about to see, they are allowed inside.

The Performance Program

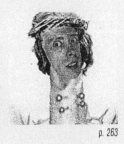

Upon entrance each audience member is given a performance program. Printed on pink paper, the program has on its cover a photograph of a man's genitals poking out of dark underwear. A crown of thorns is tattooed above

p. 263

the genital area. The man's scrotum is bound. Superimposed on the head of the erect penis is a photo of Flanagan's head with a crown of thorns. The words "He is risen" in Gothic letters are clearly visible below the image. The words invoke both religious and sexual connotations and play upon the tension between the two. Is it blatant sacrilege? Or is it merely bawdy humor?

The inside of the program doesn't provide any answers. The top of the second page contains Hebrew letters. Below it is one of Flanagan's poems from his *Slave Sonnets* (1986) that describes how Rose and Flanagan met in 1980 on Halloween:

> I was the walking dead, blood-splattered shirt
> and a knife in the back the night we met.
> You were dead, too, but beautiful, alive
> again, Jayne Mansfield, and with a good head
> on your shoulders, which turned surprisingly
> toward me: your humble and obedient
> zombie ever since. "It's fun to be dead,"
> someone once said, and we're the living proof.
> I'm the sick skeleton in your closet:
> you're my reason for living: it's real life
> and it scares us to death. Some big bruiser
> we know just dies, no reason. How 'bout me?
> Let's make it Halloween. Get out your knife,
> carve me like a pumpkin, and then let's fuck.
>
> Bob Flanagan

The third page of the program provides an outline of the performance in six parts: Processional, Invocation, Transfiguration, Sacrifice, Redemption, and Recessional. The outline indicates that the performance is organized anthropologically in terms of ritual yet framed overall as a religious service. Religious iconography included on the last page of the program emphasizes spirituality. On the top half of the last page is an image of a circle. Inside the circle are symbols of Christian, Jewish, Islamic, Buddhist, and Native American religions. On the bottom of the last page, a Jewish prayer and its translation:

> *She-ma Yis-rael, a-do-nai e-lo-he-nu, a-do-nai e-chad*
> Listen, the source of all our being, that source is one

The invocation of a pan-religious, global spirituality sets a commemorative mood of oneness with oneself and in relation to the world for the performance to follow.

Mise-en-scène and Pre-Performance Opening Remarks

Once seated, the audience waits with anticipation in the small chapel. Two video cameras are set up: one in the back and one to the right side of the altar. A video projector is set up midway up the aisle; a video screen is behind the altar.

Some audience members are expecting quite a show, familiar with Flanagan and Rose's previous work. Others work for the university and have been invited by colleagues to come. Collectively they all wait.

A frazzled and visibly nervous woman (the author of this essay) walks up to the front of the chapel and greets everyone. She introduces herself as a lecturer at ASU. Her nervousness is not an act. Instead, it is a clear sign to everyone that what they are about to see will be controversial, especially for a public university funded by a conservative state legislature. The tenseness in the air is almost palpable.

Nailed, Again!: The Performance

I. PROCESSIONAL

Nailed, Again! begins with an audio recording of Flanagan reading his prose poem "Why." It is followed by a taped rendition of Richard Wagner's "Bridal Chorus" ("Here Comes the Bride"). Rose's friend Fluffy Swenson walks down the aisle like a flower girl at a wedding while carefully avoiding the video camera and video projector. Instead of rose petals, the flower girl throws kosher salt. LR Smithline, who is both Rose's friend and Swenson's partner, ushers Rose down the aisle. The bride wears a loosely fitted white gown. Her hair is platinum and obviously a wig.

The trio walks together toward the chapel altar. In front of the altar stands a three-foot-tall erect phallus. Made of white satin, the soft sculpture was fabricated by Rose. On the altar table are various symbolic tokens of Flanagan and Rose's life together including a toy Superman, a toy Elvira, candles, and a phallic-shaped Japanese *sake* bottle. The usher walks toward the video camera on the right side of the chapel altar and sits behind it. The flower girl sits on a chair to the left of the altar.

II. INVOCATION

The bride walks around the altar table, lighting first the candles, and then incense. She next strikes a bowl to signify the beginning of the performance ritual. She bows.

III. TRANSFIGURATION

Rose stands before the altar table. With the help of the flower girl, the bride removes her white gown to reveal a white vinyl nurse's outfit and thigh-high white platform boots. The flower girl, after a bit of a struggle, affixes a large nurse's cap on Rose's head. Rose acts out the metamorphosis of her primary roles during her marriage to Flanagan—specifically her transitions from his lover and bride to his nurse and caretaker.

Danzig's "It's Coming Down" blares in the background. The nurse takes off her dress. Underneath, Rose wears a bustier and white pantyhose along with white platform boots. Is Rose now revealing her "true," naked self? Or is she celebrating her Dominatrix identity?

Rose next prepares for the ritual. She swabs iodine on her chest. She removes the bustier. She takes hold of a scalpel and holds it above her head as if in offering. She pauses dramatically. She then proceeds to cut.

IV. SACRIFICE

Slowly and methodically Rose cuts a large S into her chest. Behind her, video footage of a live performance of Rose cutting Flanagan is projected onto the screen. As Rose cuts herself live before the audience, the audience sees simultaneously in the video Rose cutting an S onto Flanagan's chest. Some of the audience members cringe while watching the double acts of cutting that took place more than a decade apart. Others grimace and look away.

For Flanagan the choice of letter was ambiguous: S stood for Sheree as well as submissive (and alternatively, slave). Sheree cut Flanagan during his life, and she cut an S onto his body after he died. As she admits at a later point in the performance, the act of cutting Flanagan's dead body was more than branding—it was an act of possession.

By cutting herself, Rose arguably is reclaiming ownership of what she gave Flanagan. Rose's act of self-mutilation can also be regarded as an act of self-assertion and self-validation. The choice of the letter *S* remains a bit ambiguous for Rose as well. Evidently the letter *S* stands for Sheree. But *S* also suggests that Rose is a slave to Flanagan's memory, and by cutting herself Rose is willingly submitting herself to it.

Rose beats the wound with a small whip. Blood slowly drips down her chest, stopping at her nipple.

Finished with cutting, Rose walks over to the podium at the side of the stage in front of where the flower girl is sitting. The flower girl assists Rose in putting on a tallit, which is a Jewish prayer shawl. Once it is on, Rose kisses its ends in accordance with religious custom. She begins to pray, invoking Jewish and Buddhist prayers. She then delivers her "sermon": the prose sermon poem called "Why Not?," her poetic response to Flanagan's prose poem "Why" that the audience heard a recording of him reciting at the start of the performance. Flanagan's poem began each line with "Because." Each line of Rose's poem line begins with "Since."

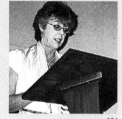

p. 264

The sermon poem "Why Not?" is an affirmation of Rose's life and all from which she has managed to break free. Rose identifies some of her life's major obstacles—beginning with her mother's nondilating womb. Rose recalls childhood stigmas, from being an unwanted child to being a bad girl who saw plenty of loose women after whom she could model. She admits to being a sexual child who masturbated in kindergarten and who pulled down a boy's pants. She discloses that a man fingered her in a movie theater. But instead of describing the molestation as traumatic, she confesses to having "loved it."

During adolescence Rose was branded as an outsider, unpopular, gawky, and awkward with bad skin. Rose asserts that all of these early instances of rejection, stigmatization, and sexualization have strengthened her resolve and determination to affirm herself as a powerful, mature post-menopausal woman, warrior hero, and god as the following lines indicate:

Since I am my mother's daughter.
Since what she concealed, I reveal.
Since I can no longer tolerate my mother's rejection.

*Since I am compelled to declare that I have survived to transcend my sex
  and fecundity.*
Since I no longer menstruate, But I still bleed when and where I choose.
Since I'm no longer in thrall to a timetable determined by nature.
Since this is my true nature.
*Since I was sent here for a purpose beyond that of a daughter, a wife, a
  mother, a widow.*
Since I am a warrior.
Since I am my own heroine.
Since I am my own god.
Since I am the resurrection and the light.

After declaring herself a prophet who foresees "a future where gender is what you make or re-make of it, while sex is what you do / on a
Saturday night, as much a sacred ritual as Orthodox Jews who fuck their
wives on the Sabbath / Since their patriarch[al] god demands it of them,"
Rose gives testimony of her life with Flanagan: "the dominant spirit who
lives in my heart . . . my best creation." In so doing Rose sets the record
straight about Flanagan's performance art: it was a collaboration between
him and Rose because Rose as his Mistress demanded it of Flanagan, her
submissive:

*Since I made him an art star when all he really wanted was to be naked,
  shaved and chained*
*Under my house, living for the moment I would come downstairs and
  give him my full attention.*
Since I tied him to a chair and forced him to write.
Since I made him perform in public the secret rites he practiced alone.
*Since I wanted the public to witness the Supermasochist in his pale, frail
  sickly body that housed*
A brave and sturdy soul within.

She then recounts her contribution to the collaboration:

*Since for 15 years I photographed and videotaped his every waking, sleep-
  ing, and depraved*
Movements as devoted as Dian Fossey was to her beloved gorillas.
Since I knew Bob was an endangered species.
*Since there had to be proof of his existence, so that future audience could
  marvel at a man who*

Nailed his own penis to a board to satisfy the object of his desire and to
    fulfill the desire of his Dominatrix.

She ends the sermon as a woman warrior, defiant and vengeful but with
purpose to a higher cause:

Since the Hindu goddess Kali is my guide; since she wields her multi-
    armed swords and bloody
Heads roll.
Since Judith is my ancestor; since she saved her people by entering the
    camp of Holofernes and slayed him in his sleep.
Since I cut into the dead body of Bob to send him to his grave with my
    mark on his flesh to
Reaffirm my ownership and to display for eternity the depth of our com-
    mitment to each other.
Long live this revelation.
Long live the Mistress.
Long live the memory of Bob.

Amen. Blessed be. Namaste. Shalom.
Om om, hari om.
Hari, hari om.
Hari om, hari om
Hari, Hari om.

She-ma Yis-ro-el, adonoi elahaynu, adonoi e-chad

V. REDEMPTION

After the sermon ends, Rose grabs the soft white satin sculpture, a phallus piñata, at the front of the altar. She lays it down, straddles it, and proceeds to nail it with a huge hammer. While audience members watch Rose
perform live, they also see above and behind her on the video screen an
excerpt of Flanagan and Rose's co-directed 1989 video *Nailed!* that documented a private performance by Flanagan. In other words, as the audience watches the video documentation of Flanagan nailing his penis, they
simultaneously witness Rose's symbolic albeit live re-enactment. Cis male
members in the audience noticeably cringe. For these audience members,
the background-mediated imagery of a past performance prompts more

immediate and visceral responses than Rose's live performance taking place right in front of them.

Once Rose finishes nailing the satin phallus, she looks inside the "wound" and pulls out red candy. Meanwhile in the video Flanagan pulls out the nail, causing blood to spurt everywhere, including [on] the camera lens. Rose performatively transforms Flanagan's bloody, gory, masochistic act into a sweet offering.

VI. RECESSIONAL

Rose marches down the aisle to the recorded sound of Felix Mendelssohn's "Wedding March." The flower girl and the usher walk out together behind her, arm in arm.

Finis

Postscript, 2018

Rose expressed disappointment after the performance over how few people were in the audience, but she was a good sport about it. Afterward, I took Rose, Fluffy, and LR to a local restaurant, where I took photographs of Rose proudly showing off her *S*.

As Rose seems to suggest in *Nailed, Again!*, self-affirmation is important. I have invoked the personal throughout this essay in order to recover Sheree Rose's pivotal performance *Nailed, Again!* from the dustbins of history. By finally feeling empowered to reveal publicly my documentation of *Nailed, Again!* along with some of the circumstances revolving around its inception and production, I have, with Rose's encouragement, reclaimed my own contributions and achievements.

The account that I wrote back in 2000 focused on three aspects: Rose's feminism, American cultural politics, and institutional university politics. The latter two did not have much to do with the performance itself, but rather addressed its context and (lack of) reception. In 2000 I was interested in how Rose explored and ultimately rejected traditional female roles and stereotypes. Re-reading my account in 2018, I realize that I did not adequately address in 2000 how Rose explored gender performativity and transgressions of socially prescribed gender roles. In her sermon poem "Why Not?" Rose explicitly rejected the negativity imposed on her previous adherences to femininity before assuming powerful, traditionally masculine roles such as warrior and god. While she appreciated cis female acquaintances such as Chris Kraus and me who encouraged her return to performance, she leaned on the support of her friend Fluffy, a trans woman, to help her perform on her own. In feminist solidarity Rose bonded with women in their common struggles to be fully acknowledged and recognized. In transfeminist solidarity, Rose transgressed heteropatriarchal gender roles dictated by society, family, and religion.

Nailed Again! literally and figuratively marked Rose's return to performance. Rose demonstrated with her first performance after Flanagan's passing how revisiting and reclaiming one's past can be necessary steps in moving forward. Arguably, Rose framed her work as re-performance with her choice of title. She invoked Flanagan's memory from the start by beginning with a recording of Flanagan reading his poem "Why" before reading her sermon poem, "Why Not?" *Nailed, Again!* was also a re-performance of her own previous performances of cutting Flanagan as well as a symbolic re-enactment of Flanagan's 1989 performance *Nailed!*, which she had documented in the similarly titled video that was co-directed by Flanagan and Rose. As a rather complicated performance that featured multiple types of re-performance, *Nailed, Again!* anticipated many recent debates regarding performance, its documentation, and its re-enactment that were prompted by later re-performances such as Marina Abramović's 2005 performance series *Seven Easy Pieces*. Ultimately, *Nailed, Again!* memorialized Rose's personal and artistic partnerships with Flanagan through re-enactment while reasserting Rose's own personal self-identity as a visionary feminist performance artist.

Recorded Leftovers

Digesting Sheree Rose's Video Archive

LUKA FISHER

See Public/Private Exhibition(ist)s; Music, Literary, and Sexual
Subcultures; and Breathing Space image galleries.

Sheree Rose's video archive currently contains around 360 videos. Between 1982 and 2009 Sheree and her associates filmed an eclectic range of scenarios: performance documentation, lectures, poetry readings, family dinners, protest marches, documentaries, art films, music videos, video diaries from both Bob Flanagan and Sheree, and other miscellany, including her largely forgotten documentary projects with Tim Keenan, and videos related to her University of California, Irvine, MFA thesis show, *Leftovers,* which explored Sheree's relationship to her family and her thoughts on motherhood. The sheer volume of material is daunting, and it is notable that much of it, including and especially *Leftovers,* has rarely, if ever, been considered by those who have explored Sheree's legacy.

The archive is arranged by audiovisual format type, and then chronologically. The videos are usually titled by Sheree in a descriptive manner: *Anniversary Tape, Chest on Cross, 1991,* and so forth. This arrangement, with its rough chronology and its appearance of thoroughness, reveals a great deal about Sheree's artistic obsessions and political commitments. It also obscures other relations among the videos, such as what motivated her to create them, and how they fit into her overall practices as an artist/ documentarian. There is no structuring narrative that could explain them fully. As a result, it is hard to understand the contents of this archive, because Sheree has not left a lot of written statements about her video practice and its intentions. There is no comprehensive catalog of what she produced. She did not always keep copies, nor does the archive even include all the footage that Sheree would want included.

Sheree donated these materials and her archive when she lost the house in which she was storing them and she began to fear that they might be destroyed by her daughter if she were to die unexpectedly, and so the archive was established in a state of crisis. Now that these materials are not so endangered, it may finally be time to think about what the "complete" archive might consist of if it were to be organized and if "lost" materials were to be introduced.

It is difficult to draw boundaries when considering her practice and to then determine what ought to be included in a "complete" video archive, because her work so thoroughly collapses both formal and artistic boundaries as well as those between art and life as she turned her life into a series of performances, art objects, and documents. Should it include only videos that she shot or directed? Should it include videos of her performances? If so, from what periods? Does the presence of her or Bob in a video merit its consideration for inclusion in the archive? What about videos from her other collaborators? Is any video in the archive art by virtue of its inclusion in the archive, or only when presented as part of an edited film, or only when Sheree shot it? Or was the archive fixed the day Sheree signed its contents over? I think that these are important questions to consider because they determine both the scope of Sheree's practice and how much of it will be remembered.

Although the films are varied, many of them could be described as having the aesthetics of home movies, which is not surprising given that Sheree used consumer-grade camera equipment and tended to just turn on the camera and let it roll. However, unlike other home movies which are meant to be private affairs shared among loved ones, Sheree was consumed with documenting as much of Bob's life as possible so that he might be remembered by future generations as well as documenting the political and social scenes that she inhabited as a participant-observer so that they might one day be unearthed and put to use. By placing these videos in an archive open to the world, she has made these works, at least poetically, available to the entire world to sort through and construct meaning out of. This can make Sheree's work a bit difficult to digest, as it can be hard to pin down what exactly we are being asked to consider.

Instead of being directed to watch one or two videos with clearly defined titles, we are presented with hundreds of videos with different subjects, often with little or no editing, and we are provided few recorded details outside of their titles. This is partly the result of her method, which favors improvisation.

While I was working with Sheree on various performances, she often stressed the importance of improvisation backed by a fear that too much planning will make the piece boring or dilute its truthfulness. She is committed to presenting her version of reality without much reflection, or editing, about what that reality means or says. At times this can be frustrating, but there is also a refreshing generosity to her approach in that Sheree asks you to consider the work for yourself rather than telling you what it means or how to feel about her. She had the courage to publish *The Pain Journal* and other materials which are, arguably, deeply unflattering to her out of a loyalty to Bob and a commitment to truth.

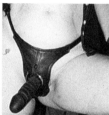

p. 208

Why am I interested in Sheree and her archive? It is a combination of two things: random chance, and an appreciation of her desire to destigmatize sex and upend traditional gender roles by staging public performances of private lives.

I first met Sheree when she took my seat at a small poetry reading in the back of a coffee shop on a hot day. I was irritated and felt like an asshole for being irritated. She was, after all, older and clearly needed the seat more than I did. Eventually she took the stage and started reading "Why Not?," an autobiographical poetic account of her life before Bob. I was transfixed. I approached her about contributing to a poetry zine that I was putting together. In other words, I met Sheree the way she met most of the people she documented before and after Bob: first as an admirer and then as a collaborator.

As we became friends, I wanted to better understand both her work and where she was coming from, and to present the Sheree that I knew to an (art) world that I felt had largely ignored her contributions in favor of the default cherishing of the "tortured male" artist. This is why I started to think about her video archive, what it might tell us about her process, and how it might be presented to a wider public. I wanted to explore the lesser known, underexplored sides of Sheree, so I largely stayed away from tapes that were Bob-centric or that focused on the lives of others, such as Dennis Cooper's wedding to Chris Lemmerhirt or Ron Athey getting his face tattooed. Instead, I favored videos exploring aspects of her life that have been less considered, such as her work as a documentary filmmaker, or her time as an MFA student at University of California, Irvine. It is a lot of material, and after each viewing I would spend time with Sheree trying to unpack what I had just watched and how, if at all, the archive fit together.

One of the first videos that I had sought out was *Needles and Pins.* I was interested in it both because it is one of the only documentaries that Sheree has completed, as both the director and editor, and because it was created in 1987, a decade before *Sick: The Life and Death of Bob Flanagan, Supermasochist,* a documentary by Kirby Dick that was co-produced by Sheree. *Needles and Pins* is a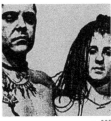

p. 235

lo-fi documentary about Jim Ward's piercing studio. The film begins with strangely erotic, historical paintings of pierced martyrs accompanied by uncredited music from Joyce Lightbody, and then transitions into a production that is part television newscast, part after-school special, and part softcore porn through its intense eroticization of piercing. The video starts with Sheree acting like a television reporter in Jim Ward's studio, in which she asks him pointed questions about piercing culture and then cuts to various people getting pierced, usually in their genitals, both at the studio and at private leather parties. The film premiered at the Erotic Art Festival at CalArts, which was organized by Mike Kelley, and then screened at several film festivals. While the film, with its focus on piercing culture, may not seem so shocking to today's audiences, it was quite radical for its time, in terms of both its subject matter and its frank depictions of genital piercings. In it, the film's talking heads—Jim Ward, Bob, Sheree, and others—assert the primacy of pleasure. For me, a key to understanding Sheree's motivations for making this film occurs when Jim describes his first encounters with piercing culture, and Sheree says that it must have been a "good feeling" when Jim realized that he was not alone.

This suggests to me that much of Sheree's work can be understood as a form of activism in which she is trying to make taboo topics like sickness, LGBTQ rights, body modification mainstream, first by saying that they are activities worthy of documentation, and second by using tools like photography and video which hold the promise of reaching a mass audience. As someone who grew up queer and confused, I thrived on the few glimmers of a culture that existed outside of the mainstream: gems that were usually buried in the discount bin at a local comic store, misfiled at the bookstore, or just hiding in plain sight at the bookstore. Indeed, as a teenager, I had unknowingly encountered Sheree and Bob's work through Danzig's X-rated video "It's Coming Down" and would routinely show it to my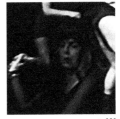

p. 232

friends as a kind of litmus test of their sensibilities and aspirations. I guess that, even then, some part of me wanted to watch people drive nails through their cocks. But today, I am a lot less enthralled by blood, and I am beginning to think that perhaps it is more transgressive to have empathy, particularly for difficult people.

While talking with Sheree about *Needles and Pins,* I discovered that this film was but one of a series of films that she was working on with Tim Keenan, and from what she can remember, they worked on the following films: *Eyeful,* which was a mishmash of happenings and "weird things" that they documented in Los Angeles; *Tattooed Women,* which documented women in tattoo culture; a film about the Wobblies; and a film about the 1984 Nihilist Olympics. With the exception of *Needles and Pins,* most of this footage has been lost.

This discovery also tipped me off to the possibility that much of the archive might not be as random as it appears, and that much of the films are just raw footage that Sheree had generated over the years for a series of finished and unfinished documentaries / art works. Sheree confirmed this theory and identified two such projects within the archive in addition to *Needles and Pins* and *Sick: Fortitude and Forbearance* and *Leftovers.*

Fortitude and Forbearance was a documentary film/book project that Sheree started working on in 1999. The project focused on Dragon, a 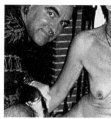 pagan that operated a BDSM service in Santa Barbara and organized an annual BDSM parade float for the family-oriented May Day Parade. The Santa Barbara government was unhappy with his activities and went out of their way to throw him in jail for two years on pimping charges. Sheree documented this process through interviews, trial footage, and correspondence

p. 253 while he was in prison. While incarcerated, Dragon created a number of drawings, which Sheree had intended to publish.

The archive also houses a series of family films that form the basis of an unrealized documentary project investigating her parent's fraught marriage, her relationship to her mother, and questions about legacy. This research culminated in her University of California, Irvine, MFA thesis show, *Leftovers.* Because I had never read anything about her thesis show in any of the interviews and critiques of her work, I was intrigued and began focusing most of my efforts on that portion of the archive and what came immediately after it. Beginning with *Murray and Rose Birthday Dinner; Silent Vigil St. Vibiana's, 1991–1992,* Sheree begins to document her parents' birthdays, holiday dinners, and her mother's weekly Friday dinners. Once the family gets past the constant presence of a camera, these videos become recordings that capture the private performances of family life. Many of these conversations are tedious and full of small talk that does not seem to shed much light on Sheree's thought processes or interests, interrupted by startling moments that provide genuine insight into Sheree's life. For instance, in *Friday Night at Mom's, 1993*, we learn that after discovering that Richard, Sheree's brother, was gay, their dad, Murray, at age eighty, left his Orthodox temple and began going with his son to Beth Chayim Chadashim, a gay synagogue in Los Angeles. Watching Sheree's family discuss the hot-button issues related to HIV, the struggle for equality, gay adoption, and other topics can at times be quite interesting. But, really, what emerges from these videos is Sheree's attempt to understand and make peace with her mother, Rose.

Sheree had planned her thesis show around her mother as a kind of grand gesture of love and reconciliation after years of fighting and defining herself in opposition to her. Rose was upset that her son was gay, and angry with Sheree for her divorce and subsequent life choices. At the same time, it is understandable why she was so bitter. Like many women of her generation, she had been ignored and her wishes had been repeatedly thwarted. *Murray and Evelyn, 1994*, reveals that Rose wanted to separate from Murray, but he refused, believing that they had to "stick it out." Having spent the majority of her life as a housewife and mother, Rose came to define herself almost exclusively by her cooking. As a result, Sheree wanted to document her mother's passion for cooking through video, photographs, and a staged dinner performance of her mother's Friday night dinners as her MFA thesis show. Unfortunately, Rose was hospitalized before Sheree could stage her show, and of course Sheree was there to document it.

In a video titled *Mom in Hospital; Mom's Funeral; Bob's Electrocardiogram, 1994*, the tape begins with Sheree asking her brother, Richard, to go and talk to their mother. Richard is not pleased by the camera's presence.

RICHARD: I don't want this to be a circus.

SHEREE: It's not a circus—this is for my documentary, I can't stop now.

RICHARD: Yes you can.

SHEREE: I don't want to stop it. I want to remember her every way.

RICHARD: Wait Sheree. I don't agree with this. I don't. I really truly don't.

RICHARD: Crazy Daughter.

SHEREE: I love you and I want to document you. I want to document
how I feel about you.

RICHARD: [inaudible] let her live her life.

SHEREE: No it's not true.

Off-camera it sounds like Richard says "I don't agree with this Dad,"
but it's hard to tell.

Bob enters and tells everyone that he got a letter from the Make-A-
Wish Foundation, requesting that he meet with Sarah, a seventeen-year-
old who is also suffering from CF. Sheree expresses how amazing it must
be to have someone want to meet him as their last wish, which feels a
little strange given that Sheree's mom, at that very moment, is dying and
perhaps thinking about what her final wish might be. Then Sheree begins
to address her mother and their relationship:

SHEREE: I want you to know that I think you did a really good job as
a mother. I think you did the best you knew how to do. And you
always were your own person. You never made any attempts to
change. And that was hard for me to maybe accept when I was
younger but I do understand and I do accept you now and I have
for a long time. And maybe we saw the world a little differently,
but you are my mother and I respect that. I took your name: so
Sheree Rose. I took that knowing it was your name. And all my
work that I've been doing at school is all about you and me and
our relationship. So I want you to know that. So if I get to be a
famous artist on my own someday it will be because of you. So—

RICHARD: Great art comes from aggravation.

SHEREE: [laughs] Right. Make a person aggravated enough and they
become an artist. Right it's like a pearl. . . . It's true I think that's
how a pearl is made with a little bit of irritation and out of that
irritation comes the pearl. It's a precious thing. And there's millions and millions of oysters but there's not millions and millions
of pearls. And Jenny [Sheree's daughter] for all her faults which
are many, many has your strength and your determination. It's
in her. And she has my brains.

RICHARD: Combination. [laughs]

SHEREE: So she's sort of a dynamite kid, you know. So she has your
blood flowing in her too. So that's important things to think about
and to remember. So there's nothing that I hold any grudges

about. There's nothing that I hold any resentment about. You're my mother and I respect and honor and love you. And I never changed the person I was, either. I taught . . . I learned that from you.

Richard brings up that Sheree used to find "reasons" to get mad at their mother, and that one of those reasons was for purchasing too many pies.

SHEREE: Well I don't think I realized then, that how she was able to show love, was through food . . .
RICHARD: Well she can't express it in too many ways.
SHEREE: But she did through there and that was her way of expressing it.
RICHARD: Still does. All those Friday night dinners.
SHEREE: Still does. Right. And so the art will have to have a different kind of ending to it . . . but it's still going to be—I just want you to be there for the art opening—to make chicken soup for the art opening.

The camera turns off when Lilian,[1] a longtime family friend, enters, and when the camera turns back on, we can tell that some time has passed because Richard refers to how awful Rose was the night before when she did not have enough medication to keep the pain at bay. Sheree keeps zooming in on Rose's face. Richard thinks that she is dead and mentions that Rose had had this fear of being taken away before she died. Sheree too wants to capture her death, explaining to Richard, "She's still breathing, I want to catch the last breath." Sheree tries to get Murray to come over to her side. Although it is hard to hear exactly what is said, it sounds like Richard gets mad at Sheree for directing reality.[2]

After Rose dies, the camera stops. We are now in a funeral home where we watch Murray, Richard, and Sheree go coffin shopping. Sheree overrides her mom's wishes for a cheap coffin in a favor of more aesthetic one, and notes that she purchased a brand-new outfit for Rose.

---

1. When asked about Lilian, Sheree told me that she was an old Jewish lady who was friends with her and her mother. "She was kind of glamourous. Every time a husband died, she found a new one. They would always die and she would never be alone. It wasn't very nice of me but I once told her that I had wished she had been my mom."

2. Sheree was too emotionally upset to shoot Bob's death, and Kirby did not provide a camera person to capture it, as he had promised, when they started making *Sick*. Thus, there is no recorded record of Bob's last words. Sheree is still haunted by this.

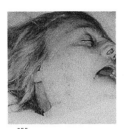

p. 255

Although it is never stated, it would seem in retrospect that Sheree is beginning to art-direct her mother's final portrait.[3]

I felt extremely emotionally conflicted about Sheree's choice to document her mother's death and somehow complicit in it through my choice to circulate that incident through this essay. And yet we all process things differently. Sheree's mom expressed herself through food, and it would seem that Sheree expressed love largely through who she turned the camera lens on. Perhaps it is not unrelated, then, that Sheree began her work as a documentarian when she started photographing her children in Europe.

A few weeks after Rose's death, an old flame from Murray's life sees the news in the *Jewish Journal* and reaches out. Sheree captures their first meeting in *Murray and Evelyn, 1994*. Evelyn had briefly known Rose, and the two women begin to discuss Rose and her acrimonious marriage to Murray, and what it meant to be a woman in that period. Evelyn notes that her daughter also got a divorce and congratulates Sheree on her decision to leave her marriage when she realized it was not working. Because Sheree's divorce had deeply upset Murray and divided her family. Sheree's response is worth quoting:

> SHEREE: But it's been hard. It's been hard on me . . . like your daughter too . . . we're that transitional [generation]. It's like we're still part of that older generation that wanted to be traditional wives . . . take care of the kids, sacrifice your life for the kids . . . but I had other feelings inside . . .

About a year later, Sheree holds her thesis show, *Leftovers*, which is captured on a tape called *Leftovers Opening Night Dinner Performance; UCI Art Gallery, 1995*. The video is one solitary shot of a long dining table that eventually becomes the site of a dinner. We can see a pedestal with Rose's chicken soup. I am told that, off-camera, there is a picture of Rose in her casket. All uneaten food was left to rot for the duration of the exhibition.

Sheree's gesture of placing her mother's life's work, chicken soup, on a pedestal in the white cube seems to elevate the physical and affective labor that her mother had invested in her craft as a housewife into *art*,

---

3. Sheree told me that Bob's family were extremely upset with her coffin choice for Bob's funeral, which they felt was too modest.

and in so doing, draws attention to how our patriarchal society has too often ignored, and too often denigrated, such contributions in favor of the tortured "male genius."

Around this time, Sheree records her first video diary, *Video Diary, c. 1983–2000.* The video is shot almost entirely upside down, until Bob comes in and tries desperately to explain how the camera functions. At first, the video is a bit random and a little creepy as she zooms in on teeth and makes vaguely threatening remarks ("closeness is dangerous"), but after a few minutes, the video really finds its center when Sheree starts talking about her mom. It is moving, and in a way it captures how I felt trying to dig through Sheree's leftover footage.

> SHEREE: I like to document whenever it feels like a change is happening. The first one being my mother's death, which is almost going to be a year ago now . . . and I do still want to try and get to something about her. And I don't even know what it is I am trying to get. I'm not trying to say she was a monster: "let's hate her," [or] she was a sick person: "let's pity her." She was courageous but crazy: "let's praise her." You know I don't know what to do. And it's important that I work it out, because every mother imparts a legacy to her children, and it's part of how history gets handed down. And I don't want her to be remembered in only one way, and it's like a mystery to me to try and unravel who she was. And I have so many questions and so few answers.

It is worth remembering that a little over a year after Rose died, Bob would die, and then her father would die, and then her first husband, with whom she briefly reunited, would die. This must have been a tremendous blow to someone accustomed to collaboration and community.

And among all this death, not a lot of people were there to support her art and help her make sense of all this pain. So, the archive, with its vast gaps and unfinished projects, is a kind of symbolic love letter to the people that mattered in her life, and a symbolic open wound to a past that still haunts her.

And while Sheree's urge to document has died down considerably, you can still see her, some nights, with her iPhone, documenting the world around her today. Will these materials ever find their way into the archive, or is it strictly limited to what was shot between roughly 1982 and 2009? The fragments from her life that we can examine are both fascinating and at times extremely difficult to sit through. I think part of that is because, as viewers, we are conditioned to expect simple, easy-to-digest narratives with simple takeaways. Rarely are we given such access to the inner life of someone who we are not related to. Sheree's archive, like her life with its records ad nauseam, is anything but simple and resists easy categorization.

Though I must confess that it has been a strange experience to go through these materials as I write about her MFA thesis show with its explorations of family and its meanings, while my father is slowly dying from leukemia and I avoid contemplating my own MFA thesis show, *Binary Terrorism: Artist as Producer,* in order to write about her life and her art. It feels absurd to pass judgment on the banality of her family dinners or to be put off by her choice to document her mother's death when I had to bail on a vacation with my father in order to focus on someone else's life. We all become artists for different reasons. I guess I create art and produce work with others as an act of love and as an act of avoiding all the things that have hurt me; perhaps others shoot video or make soup as a means of connecting with others.

There are still hundreds of hours to go through and I am not sure if I will ever get through it all. And I am not even sure if that is the point. I think Sheree left us with an amazingly rich sampling from her life, and I think it is up to those interested in her life's work to consume these leftovers in a manner that fits their taste and interests. For me, this archive is both an objective and a symbolic reminder that Sheree has always been so much more than an Encino housewife, so much more than a Dominatrix, a mother, a documentarian, or whatever other titles we care to throw at her. Sometimes, I watch so much that I feel a bit dizzy and a bit sick, and yet I keep coming back for more. Right now, I am looking for a tape in which Sheree and Rose walk through *Visiting Hours* together. I cannot imagine how Sheree's mom would have processed such an exhibition of psychosexual materials, but I want to know, and so I keep looking, hoping that this tape still exists.

Sheree, Bob, and Me

Performing Painful Histories

MARTIN O'BRIEN

See *Dust to Dust*, *The Viewing*, and *The Ascension* image galleries.

The Scar: A Beginning

On my left breast there is a fading scar. If you look closely enough you can see it is an *S* shape. The letter constructed with three straight lines, resembling an inverted *Z*. The cut which led to this scar was made in 2012 by Sheree Rose during a twelve-hour performance, *Regimes of Hardship #3*, in London. It was the first of many times I have been cut by Sheree. Her famous mark, which she inscribed into the flesh of Bob Flanagan as well as all of her other slaves. *S* for Sheree: a mark of ownership, *S* for slave: a mark of lifestyle, and perhaps most significantly *S* for sick: a mark of identity. As someone suffering from CF the *S* also stands for surviving: a mark of what I'm doing, or survivor: a mark of what I am. This text is a plotting of history and a telling of a story. It's the story of that *S* and the significance of that mark on my p. 251 body. This is less an essay and more a polemic, a recounting and a theorizing of what Sheree and I have been doing together since 2011. The *S* scar on my body opens up a way of thinking about the politics of our work. This writing is structured around a series of short segments that describe moments of performance and think about the wider implications of these actions in relation to illness, mortality, and history.

S Is for Sheree

The story of Sheree and I starts well before this mark appeared on my body. It begins well before we ever met. An anecdote I've published elsewhere explains the beginnings:

> I distinctly remember, before I was making performance work, acci-
> dently stumbling upon an image, in a book, of a male groin that had
> been sewn up. The skin of the scrotum was wrapped around the
> penis and sutured. Two nails were pierced through the front edge
> of the scrotum attaching it to a piece of wood. I was around eigh-
> teen years old and attempting to understand my identity as a queer
> man and as someone with a life-shortening chronic illness. I was still
> unaware of the potentials of performance as a space in which these
> politics could be explored, but this image changed my life. At first,
> it was the affective power of the photograph that struck me. I let out
> a quiet squeal trying to contemplate what it must feel like. My eyes
> glanced around the page of the book, which was *The Artist's Body*
> by Tracey Warr and Amelia Jones, and noticed the name Bob Flana-
> gan, an artist of whom I had never heard, along with another image
> of the artist lying in a hospital bed with Sheree Rose sitting next to
> him. My heart stopped. I couldn't believe it. Here was an artist mak-
> ing performance about my disease. I wasn't alone. There are others.
> (O'Brien 56–57)

Learning of others, people with CF and artists with CF in this instance, like you is significant. CF is a peculiar disease in that we are not supposed to be in the same room as other people with the illness due to potential cross-infection, meaning it is a lonely disease. So, some years later when Sheree and I met in person, it was a connection with CF (through her relationship with Bob) that I hadn't experienced since childhood. I arrived at Paddington station in London to meet Sheree and her son Matthew in March of 2011. Sheree and I had been in conversation online for some time. We had never met face to face. The following day, Sheree and I performed *Thank You Ma'am, Please May I Have Another?* The performance was based on her collaboration with Bob Flanagan and Mike Kelley, *100 Rea-
sons*. The piece was short and consisted of me over Sheree's lap, spanked one hundred times. After each thwack, I said "Thank you ma'am, please may I have another?" For me, this action was a direct homage to the inspi-
rational work Sheree and Bob had done during the 1980s and '90s, but it

turned out to be much more. This simple performance began a collaborative relationship which, seven years later, is still going, growing, and is becoming ever more complex and developed.

S Is for Slave

After this piece, all of our other performances together have begun with the signing of a contract as an explicit demonstration of the consensual nature of the work and our positions within it. I become the slave, Sheree the Mistress. For example, the contract for our 2012 piece *Regimes of Hardship #3* stated, "On June 7th, 2012 at 12 noon at] performance s p a c e [in London, England, I, Martin O'Brien being of sound mind of my own free will give over my body to Sheree Rose for the next 12 hours to do with as she pleases." The contract within this context is important. It signals a form of commitment to the carrying out of the performance, acts as a reminder of this commitment, and signals the consensual nature of the work.

This contract recalls a short video, which was included in the documentary *Sick,* called *The Contract* (1982), in which Bob is naked in the same position as I was. The film is in black-and-white and is in a domestic space. Rose walks over to him and cuts her signature *S* on his right breast. The camera zooms onto the wound and it ends. Throughout the entire short film there is a musical soundtrack and a voice-over of Flanagan reading the following contract:

> Of my own free will I, Bob Flanagan, grant you, Sheree Rose, full ownership and use of my mind and body. I will obey you at all times and will whole heartedly seek your pleasure and well-being above all other considerations. I renounce all rights to my own pleasure, comfort, or gratification, except insofar as you desire or permit them. I renounce all rights to privacy or concealment from you. I will answer truthfully and completely to the best of my knowledge any and all questions you may ask. I understand and agree that any failure by me to comply fully with your desires shall be regarded as sufficient cause for severe punishment. I otherwise unconditionally accept, as your prerogative, anything you may choose to do to me either as punishment, for your amusement, or for whatever purpose, no matter how painful or humiliating to myself. (Flanagan and Rose in *Sick*)

My own contract with Sheree could serve to remind spectators (if they are aware of this earlier work) of my body, at a similar age to Flanagan when this contract was made, as one moving toward the same fate. My contract with Sheree is, of course, different. It is predicated upon the conventions of performance and the appropriation of the aesthetics of BDSM. It exists only for a twelve-hour period. The contract for Bob and Sheree, however, was a lifestyle choice. Through her obsessive documentation of their lives together, this lifestyle gained a conduit to public exposure. Their actions became political, and, although performed with and for each other, they always held within them the possibility of wider spectatorship. Life and art were one and the same thing. The radical politics of Flanagan/ Rose's life-as-art project relies upon the fact that this is a decision to live in this way and make this private activity public. In doing so they resist normative conventions of existence within patriarchal society and they do this within the public eye. They ask us to reflect upon our own bodies as impeded and disciplined subjects, and through their project we are able to imagine an existence predicated upon our own terms.

Regimes of Hardship #3 asked spectators to bear witness to our commitment of the contract by being in the same space as us for up to twelve hours. It functioned as a micro version of Sheree's previous and more excessive conception of life as an artistic endeavor. In my signing of the contract to give my body to Sheree there is the implication that I own it in the first place. The act of having Sheree's signature cut onto my chest is a gifting of my body to her which can only be done if it is mine to give. This act of cutting draws attention to the contract as being contingent upon my own political agency. In presenting my body as hers to sign with a scar, I am also claiming my body as my own. Sheree's invested power within this contractual structure exists only insofar as I hold agency over my own body.

S Is for Substitute

In 2015 I was artist-in-residence at ONE National Gay and Lesbian Archives, Los Angeles. I was the first person to dig through Sheree and Bob's archive. The idea was that Sheree and I would create a piece of work in response to it. What became apparent were two missing pieces. Bob and Sheree had conceived of a Death Trilogy. The first part, *Video Coffin*, had been made, but the second two were unrealized before Bob's death. The two of us decided that we had to make them happen. We realized a version of the second piece, *Dust to Dust,* at the end of the residency, and just over a year later, we were commissioned to make *The Viewing* at DaDaFest, Liverpool, United Kingdom. In these pieces, I was a substitute for Bob. My sick living body standing in for his dead body. In these works and in other pieces where together we re-enact her history, I am also rehearsing for the inevitable.

Our version of *The Viewing* was twenty-four hours long. I spent the entire time lying in an open-top coffin. Spectators were in a different space, only able to see via four CCTV cameras framing my body from different perspectives. Every hour, Sheree would enter with Rhiannon Aarons and perform various actions on my body: whipping, stapling, piercing, dressing me up as a drag-

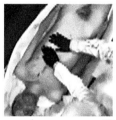

p. 292

zombie, dripping hot wax on my body, mummifying me, breath restriction. I remained "dead" with actions being done to me. In the final action, I sat, reaching out and biting Sheree. My jaws clamped around her flesh. A public moment of intimacy and a playful imitation of zombie movies, the infecting of another. In reality, she had infected me all those years ago when I saw Bob's sewn-up groin, and she continues to infect me every time we collaborate.

We are continuing a practice across generations. These works are about an enduring legacy. They are about ensuring that the torch is passed on and that we make what-should-have-happened happen. I am not Bob, Sheree and I are not lovers. But we are family, not by blood but by something else. As an artist I feel a responsibility toward history, and now more than that. The work Sheree and I are doing is not historical re-enactment. It is continuing a practice; to use a zombie metaphor: it is spreading the infection.

S Is for Sick

In 2017, Sheree and I performed *The Ascension.* As part of this piece, I gave a sermon on sickness. I wanted to include this in full as a section in this writing. It demonstrates our views on sickness: as something not to fear or pity but to embrace. The performance itself took the form of a religious ceremony and ended with me suspended by hooks through my flesh. This text was spoken just before the suspension.

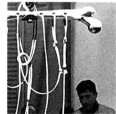

p. 305

A Sermon on Sickness According to Martin

In the name of the Mistress and of the Slave and of the Ghost of Bob.

The prophet rode into a small town with their twelve disciples of sickness. It was warm and this was a town known for its healthy people. Everyone had a tan, everyone loved to swim and play football. No one ever coughed in this town and anyone that sneezed was put into quarantine. Anyone that was sick, soon fled the town as they were no longer welcome. The dying moved to neighboring towns where they could receive treatment. Everything in this town was clinical and clean. The town was full of health food shops and people seemed to live off salad. In the restaurants everything was described as foraged, handpicked, or locally harvested. No one ever showed any real emotion in this town, fake smiles were the look of the day. The sex was boring in this town. There were never any orgies, and no one liked BDSM. Sex was done once a week with the lights off, missionary style, mainly by younger people in order to have children once they were in stable relationships. Most people were heterosexual and the few who weren't were gay rather than queer. The people here were neither happy nor sad because they didn't have the emotional capacity to truly feel. Everyone had an expensive car and a big house, everyone had plenty to eat. No one particularly liked or disliked each other in this town and it was usually warm weather. There was a beautiful coast nearby and people with perfect bodies loved to bathe here. Nothing exciting ever happened in this town. People tried to outdo each other: bigger houses, faster cars. There was little need for hospital in this town, its main use was as place where the citizens could get plastic surgery: bigger dicks, bigger breasts, chiseled faces, and luscious lips. Many of the people looked the same as each other. This was a town of younger people. The elderly people moved away when they realized there was nowhere to get treatment they actually needed and when they saw that they were no longer respected. As they left, they remembered the ways they used to treat the elderly when they were young and wished they had done it differently. This was the perfect town if you were healthy, pretty, and rich.

The prophet and the twelve disciples of sickness came to the town because they had heard about this place and its lack of sickness and of the values they cherished so dearly. The prophet was disgusted at the health and wealth of the town. As the prophet entered the town, the sound of the disciples' coughs rang out through the streets. People heard the sound and bolted themselves inside for fear of becoming sick. The streets were empty, the sun was setting and the prophet took to the bandstand in the main square to preach but no one came. The disciples knocked on the doors but people looked out of their windows and saw the sickly looking visitor so didn't answer. "Only the sick will survive" preached the prophet. "We are here to spread the good word: fight sickness with sickness." After a few minutes of preaching, a healthy woman came to the prophet and said "prophet, I have lived in this town all of my life. I do not know what it is to suffer. But I also do not know what it is to feel love or to feel happiness. Will you show me how to feel oh prophet?" The prophet looked at the healthy woman and said, "sickalluja. You will be cured of this curse of health. I bestow upon you the gift of sickness." With that, the prophet lay their hands on the woman and she immediately began to cough. She returned home and left her boring, misogynistic husband. People witnessed this through their windows and began to come out to watch. Soon a large crowd gathered in the square and another person said, "please prophet, show me the ways of the sick." The prophet placed their hands on the person and they too began to cough.

With the cough came a new take on life, a new understanding of existence. Soon people were queued up in front of the prophet. The prophet gave out the gift of sickness through the night and the sound of fast cars zooming around was replaced by the sound of coughing. The hospital, which once was a place for rich people to get plastic surgery, soon became a place of care. The town hall was transformed into a disco for the infected. The beach became a place for people of all ages and body types to meet and philosophize about what it means to be alive. Everyone started experimenting sexually. The prophet and the twelve disciples of sickness watched as the town collapsed and a new society started to form. Outsiders from around the country started to gather in this town and it became a haven for anyone that didn't fit in elsewhere.

Those who wanted to remain healthy fled for a new town. Those who wanted things to return to the old way left but couldn't sell the big houses because no rich people wanted to move here. Instead these houses became accommodation for many people. The doors were always open. There was no crime or homelessness. Eventually the prophet and the disciples left. They could not stay here although they longed to do so; they needed to go and spread the gift of sickness elsewhere. So, one night they rode out of town, leaving behind a chorus of coughing.

The only way to survive is to join the unwell. Sickness is a desired state of being. It is the only way to survive. Only the sick can survive in this world. Being sick becomes a lifeline, a way to live in a hostile environment. It becomes the only way to be. Sickness becomes life-affirming. Paradoxically it becomes a way of surviving, of enduring, of living. There is no other way, there is no option but to join the unwell. Those who learn to embrace sickness thrive, the rest become prey. The rest are just meat. The rest cannot evade death. Only the sick will survive. Only the sick will survive. Only the sick will survive.

In the name of the Mistress and of the Slave and of the Ghost of Bob.

S Is for Survival

Sheree and I have a mantra: keep breathing. It is a statement of dedication to survival. The scar on my chest reminds me of the same thing. Art can be a survival strategy. In 2016 we collaborated on *Sanctuary Ring* for Spill Festival of Performance in Ipswich, United Kingdom. It was a three-hour performance in a church. We moved slowly up the center aisle toward the altar, performing various actions en route: Sheree shaving all my hair off, 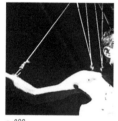 piercing me, whipping me, sewing up my scrotum, bathing me, and then fucking me up the arse with a strap-on in a bath of water. It climaxed in a suspension. I was lifted using ankle cuffs. I rose, naked, above the altar. On the wall, a video of the same action happening to Bob in a synagogue in the music video for Godflesh's "Crush My Soul" (1995). The ghost of Bob was present that

p. 306

night. This action felt like a collaboration between Sheree, me, and him. As Sheree and I keep surviving, so does his legacy.

The final action of the performance was a cut. Like the one I described at the beginning of this writing. This time, however, Sheree cut her *S* onto my chest and I did the same to her. Although I submit to Sheree in our work, here we were equal, tender, and performing a ritual to Bob but also to sickness, survival, and deviants everywhere. Before each action, we spoke a text. I want to end with that text. Before the cut we said:

> SHEREE: In the name of Bob, I cut you
> MARTIN: In the name of Bob, I Obey
> In the name of Bob, I submit
> In the name of Bob, I fight sickness with sickness
> AUDIENCE: Keep Breathing

Works Cited

Dick, Kirby, director. Prod. Sheree Rose. *Sick: The Life and Death of Bob Flanagan, Super-masochist*, 1997.

O'Brien, Martin. "The Weight of History Keeps Me Awake at Night (after David Wojnarowicz)." *Survival of the Sickest: The Art of Martin O'Brien.* Edited by Martin O'Brien and David MacDiarmid, Live Art Development Agency, 2018, pp. 56–57.

Rose/Flanagan/O'Brien

The Aesthetics of Resurrection

AMELIA JONES

> See Breathing Space, *Do with Me as You Will, Dust to Dust,*
> *The Viewing,* and *The Ascension* image galleries.

Why? Because it feels good, because it gives me an erection . . . because
I'm sick, because I was humiliated by nuns, . . . because I felt like I was
going to die, . . . because I'm a Catholic and I still love my penis, because
my parents said do what you want to do and this is what I want to do.
. . . Because of the inquisition, . . . because of motherhood, because of
Amazons, . . . because it's nasty, because it's fun, because it flies in the
face of everything that's normal, whatever that is. . . . Because I had to
take my clothes off and lie in a plastic bag so the doctors could collect
my sweat. . . . Because I learned to take my medicine . . . like a man, . . .
because no pain no gain, because spare the rod and spoil the child,
because you always hurt the one you love.

> –Bob Flanagan, reading of "Why," from *Sick: The Life and Death of Bob*
> *Flanagan, Supermasochist*

We were very interested in the reciprocal interchange between the artist
and the viewer–the blur, the relationship between subject and object, and
the use of sadomasochism as deliberate perversity. Our personal saint
was Saint Sebastian, who was always depicted with scores of arrows
piercing his flesh. . . . Bob gave me his body, it wasn't much of a body,
but I made the most of it.

> –Sheree Rose, comments made during Amelia Jones's public discus-
> sion with Rose and O'Brien, February 7, 2015

Endurance can be powerful, and there is a sense of it being celebratory for me—I can still do it, but certainly I don't see it as a triumph against adversity, I'm not enduring despite CF, I'm enduring with CF.

    —Martin O'Brien, c. 2015[1]

The original title of this essay—"Family Romance, or, the Melancholia of Mourning: Sheree Rose and Martin O'Brien's *Goodbye Bob*"—referred directly to Sheree Rose and Martin O'Brien's 2015 performance, *Goodbye Bob,* and deliberately referenced the work of Sigmund Freud, not once but twice ("Family Romances"; "Mourning and Melancholia").[2] This new version of the essay is written in the glorious shadow of another, more recent performance by Rose and O'Brien, *The Ascension,* which took place at Jason Vass Gallery in Los Angeles on December 30, 2017. Family romance and the visceral suffering it can incur reach an apotheosis in this latter performance, wherein O'Brien is almost literally crucified.

Freud's storytelling—his obsessive fascination with the ways in which individuals channel personal experiences but also larger psychic and social structures of power and meaning in interacting with others—provides a framework through which to understand some of the more theatrical elements of these two Rose/O'Brien performances, both of which are homages to the earlier art and performance projects of Rose and her life, art, and BDSM love partner Bob Flanagan (1952–1996). At the same time, I am aware that this framework both encourages a resistant approach, given Freud's heteronormative method, and biases the interpretation in the direction of psychodrama—I do this willingly to position Rose and O'Brien's work as producing nonnormative relations and to address the strong emotional charge of *Goodbye Bob* and *The Ascension.*

In Freud's essay "Family Romances," not surprisingly, he begins from the assumption that there is a desirable healthy or normal family romance driven by inevitable and necessary generational conflict.[3] In this scenario,

---

1. O'Brien continues: "I use queer imagery as a way of disrupting any triumphant/powerful/macho politics, then the illness adds something else, I 'crip' up the queer images. This allows me to think about the convergence between being queer and being sick, the illness stops me from becoming a pretty gay boy and the queerness stops me from becoming a macho man or a sick man in need of sympathy."

2. Original essay written July 2016. Revised and expanded 2018.

3. In the essay Freud notes, "The liberation of the individual, as he grows up, from the authority of his parents is one of the most necessary though one of the most painful results brought about by the course of his development. It is quite essential that liberation should occur. . . . Indeed, the whole progress of society rests upon the opposition between successive generations" (237).

before puberty the child (presumptively male in the essay) discovers that his parents are flawed and not superhuman and thus seeks to replace particularly the parent of his own sex (i.e., the father in this case) with an ideal parent—usually one of higher social status. Once he learns about procreation, the child becomes aware that "paternity is always uncertain, maternity is most certain" (239) and thus imagines himself to be born of another father (symbolically "killing" his own). Through this "depravity of the childish heart" (240), in Freud's terms, we could say that the son thus phantasmagorically enacts the oedipal drama, establishing himself as the new generation of patriarchal authority coming to replace the father.

Freud's model of the family romance reiterates the very heteronormative structure with which he begins by assuming it to be true—the normal boy necessarily must identify with (rather than desiring) yet also want to eliminate the same-sex (male) parent in order to secure patriarchal values for a new generation. At the same time, he calls attention to the "depravity of the childish heart," a term that seems to apply quite well (and with positive, queer valence) to Martin O'Brien, in relation to Rose, who is both his collaborator and (with Flanagan) predecessor.

*

Goodbye Bob

Goodbye Bob was staged at the ONE Gay & Lesbian Archives at University of Southern California in February 2015 as a collaborative memorial gesture to the epic poet and performer Bob Flanagan, Rose's partner, who died of cystic fibrosis in 1996 at the age of forty-three. Martin O'Brien—who never met Flanagan—is a London-based artist, also with CF, and has gotten to know Rose through his interest in Flanagan and their collaborative works of the 1980s and 1990s. O'Brien and Rose have produced several joint performances over the past five years—including *Mucus Factory,* for the Access All Areas performance festival in London, 2011 (where Rose

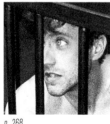 repeatedly spanked O'Brien as he hung over her knees, indirectly loosening the mucus in his lungs), and *Do with Me as You Will / Make Martin Suffer for Art* in 2013, a twenty-four-hour performance in a BDSM dungeon in Los Angeles, with actions (Rose to O'Brien, or vice versa) determined by the suggestions on the part of audience members. In *Do with Me as You Will*, Rose also cut a line

p. 268

in O'Brien's arm every hour, and together they recorded entries in a video diary (O'Brien).

The collaborative works both restage elements of Rose/Flanagan's earlier life relationship and performances (the spanking and cutting in the new work echoes their mutual passion for BDSM actions, with Rose in the role of dominatrix) and bring these elements to an entirely new place, not the least through the replacement of the now deceased Flanagan with the young (but equally CF suffering) body of a British gay man who is not Rose's lover. To the contrary, Rose has been explicit about viewing O'Brien as a collaborator, their relationship being *not* "like mother and son" and certainly not like BDSM partners with her dominating ("I don't dominate him. My dominatrix days are over"; Rose and O'Brien). It has to be said, however, that, as Rose made these comments after the performance during the public discussion at the ONE with myself and O'Brien, the latter made a humorous face and then, in response to Rose noting that "Martin is a sweet, kind person . . . he doesn't browbeat me," he stated with affection, "I [just] give in, basically" (Rose and O'Brien).[4]

In honoring Flanagan and in their collaborative work in general, Rose and O'Brien enact an *alternative* "family romance," one that epitomizes the kind of queer affiliations that challenge rote and rigidly mainstream conceptions of kinship and family. At the same time, dedicated to Flanagan, *Goodbye Bob* serves as both a cross-generational paean to radically alternative modes of attachment and filiation and an act of mourning on Rose's part in particular, but also for O'Brien as well as for audience members who might have known Flanagan (as I did) or at least know his work.

As O'Brien is well aware, the performance work of Rose and Flanagan—a presumptively heterosexual but in practice radically queer couple—deliberately perverted conventional gender roles and trashed these assumptions and patterns subtending heteronormative family relations. A key element of Flanagan's masochistic relationship with Rose involved being her slave: cleaning her house, cooking for her and her two children (from her first marriage), and performing all other tasks demanded of her, Flanagan took on the feminine role around the house. In his words, nothing less than "gender demolition!" would do. Adding to this, he was explicit about his queer sexual preferences: "being penetrated is great. . . . I think I like being penetrated more than Sheree does, so it's a good switch" (Vale and Juno 63; see also Jones 229–35). Flanagan's life and work was

---

4. O'Brien also noted affectionately: "I've learned a lot from Sheree. . . . The whole process in collaborating . . . compromise . . . Involves things you wouldn't normally do, particularly with Sheree."

about navigating his perverted relationship to norms—including that of a healthy body: in his epic 1985 poem "Why" Flanagan plaintively notes in answer to the poem's question, which implies "why sadomasochism?": "because it's nasty, because it's fun, because it flies in the face of everything that's normal, whatever that is."

Honoring the gender-bending ethos of Rose and Flanagan's BDSM relationship and performance work, Rose and O'Brien's *Goodbye Bob* completely refuses the grounding assumptions of Freud's normative family romance narrative. Rose is (as noted) neither the mother nor the romantic or erotic love object of O'Brien. O'Brien is neither a son wanting to kill a father nor an aspiring lover. The "family" that Rose and O'Brien create is one of collaboration and mutual understanding, forged against the grain of the conventional and oppositional structures of identification and desire which underpin Freud's heteronormative family narrative.

Only one element of Freud's story might apply here: O'Brien could be imagined to be taking Flanagan as his "ideal" father substitute, in turn hoping to replace him through identification.[5] But going down this path assumes that our interest is in psychoanalyzing O'Brien, which it is not (determining his identifications would not get us very far); and it is at any rate too pat an explanation to be of any use here. Flanagan is not only *not* a conventional "father"; he explicitly refused the castration-anxious, armored conventions of heteronormative masculinity altogether (see Jones 229–35). And he is no longer with us, although he haunts our imaginaries—largely through his writings and the documentation taken by Rose during their collaborative period. O'Brien's access to Flanagan is thus almost entirely *through* Rose, an interesting permutation through which to understand this particular family romance. The "father" is gone—and in this case, never existed as such (viz. Flanagan's cheery refusals of normative masculinity, both verbally and in his lived and performed relationship with Rose, begging the question: is Rose, the dominatrix, more of a "father" than Flanagan ever was?). Flanagan's refusal of the authority generally assigned to adult (white) men encourages us to ask: did the "father" Freud imagined ever, in fact, exist? If nothing else, Rose-Flanagan-O'Brien's project exposes the "father" as a fantasy and a construction, dangerous in its role in anchoring heteronormative patriarchy.

---

5. Freud is clear on this point—the ideal father is a projection relating to the "actual" father, and for healthy adult development both are dealt with through identification such that the male subject comes to take his proper place as an adult man / potential father (Freud, "Family Romances" [240–41]).

In the case of Rose-Flanagan-O'Brien, gendered and generational roles are thus confused from the get-go. Generational and gender issues here are complex and rich, rather than reductive and binary (as in Freud). O'Brien is both "son" (spanked by the dominatrix/mother Sheree Rose) and the extender as well as the caretaker of Rose's and Flanagan's legacy, an echoing of Flanagan in his CF-compromised corporeality. He is, of course, an entirely different person from Flanagan, and yet reminds those of us audience members who knew Bob or who know his work of our lost object. Most importantly, in *Goodbye Bob*, performance is used as ritual, to produce an elegiac experience of two people finding their way with each other and after a profound loss (personal for Rose, historical for O'Brien).

It is in this sense that *Goodbye Bob* resonates with Freud's other text noted in the title—"Mourning and Melancholia." The piece functions as a partial acknowledgment, a working through, of the loss of Flanagan— for Sheree Rose, obviously, but also for his audience (for me, he was a friend and a hugely admired poet and artist). Sparked by time O'Brien was spending with Rose organizing the Rose/Flanagan collection for the ONE archive, *Goodbye Bob* is also about activating photographic documentation from the past to create a new narrative in the present: it is about the role of the archive in remembering and writing into history (a person, a practice). If the archive is the site of the memorializing of family (imagine the family photo album), then Rose's relentless documentation of Flanagan's living and working becomes a counterarchive, never cohering into a conventional family romance such as that imagined by Freud.

In *Goodbye Bob* the archive structures the entire performance. Images (by Rose) of Flanagan from the archive are projected onto a screen during the first part of the performance. The second and third parts of the piece take off from a historic work planned by Flanagan and Rose but never executed. In this way, O'Brien's appearance in the performance can be seen as a channeling of Flanagan's CF-compromised body as Rose's collaborator. The work narrates the open and alternative family romance I have suggested that Rose and Flanagan initiated in their work of the 1980s and 1990s, while also commenting on the process of mourning attached to this homage to Flanagan.

In the beginning of the performance, Rose and O'Brien are treated as effigies—their bodies lie under sheets (in front of the screen showing Flanagan in Rose's photographs, at home and in performance works). They are uncovered by assistants and then painted white by a black-clad, bird-masked plague doctor figure. Dirgelike music plays during this prolonged process. Once painted, the two move to an adjoining room (announced by one of the assistants as "the crypt"), where a "coffin" lies filled with a life-sized effigy of Flanagan, topped by a photograph of his head. The artists pick up "confetti" from the ground and place it in the coffin—as audience members are invited to do the same, we realize the confetti is actually tiny photographs from Rose's archive of images of Flanagan performing. The representational replacement of Flanagan is ratcheted up—almost relent-less in its insistence and volume. We cannot escape his image, nor the energy oriented towards recalling his importance to Rose and the Los Angeles performance scene.

The referencing to the past was also explicit: this part of the perfor-mance in the "crypt" enacted a version of *Dust to Dust,* the second part of a trilogy proposed by Rose and Flanagan to the Solomon R. Guggenheim Foundation before his death. *Video Coffin,* the first part, was achieved in

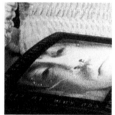

1994 at the Otis Art Gallery in a show called *Narcissistic Disturbance* (Cohen 28–29, 31; and see Jones 229–35). The head of a casket (decorated with icons of death such as bullets and body parts) was laid open to show a text ("I was promised an early death, but here I am, some forty years later, still waiting") and to expose a video monitor with a loop of Flanagan's face. Approaching the flower-

p. 256

bedecked casket, the visitor was compelled to move closer and closer to view the "dead" Flanagan, only to find her/his face replacing Flanagan's on the monitor.

As articulated in Flanagan and Rose's application for the Guggenheim award in 1995 (for which I was an evaluator), the second part of the tril-ogy, *Dust to Dust,* would involve a simple pine box (like the one he was

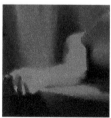

actually buried in) with the entire lid open to show a mound of confetti. On closer look, the visitor would real-ize that the "confetti" is actually thousands of minuscule photographs of Flanagan (again, taken primarily by Rose) from various stages of his life (in Flanagan's words, "viewers [could] . . . scoop up hand fulls [*sic*] of the tiny squares so that they are literally holding another

p. 283

person's life history in the palm of their hands"; Flanagan and Rose). Here, Flanagan's ability to ride the sharp line between living and dying, between the boisterous and pleasure-seeking body in performance and the dead corpse of representation (the performative body frozen in its documents), is fully dramatized. Rose and O'Brien found a way to work this dynamic into their live memorial project.

Finally, *The Viewing*, the final part of the trilogy, is almost impossible to fathom in its original formulation, developed before Flanagan's death. He died before it could be completed, so, although the Guggenheim application was successful, neither of the second two parts was produced (until Rose and O'Brien reworked the second part, *Dust to Dust*, in *Goodbye Bob*). As originally conceived, *The Viewing* was to document the decomposition of Flanagan's body through the placement of a video camera in his coffin underground. The camera would be connected to a monitor placed in a gallery or other public place, to be accessed at will by visitors apprised of its contents (that is, it would be up to the viewer whether to turn the monitor on or not—whether to engage or not with this decaying body, bereft of a "self"). Watching this body return to the earth, we would be compelled to acknowledge our dependence on the flesh to sustain our existence (the fact that the self cannot survive the body is proof not of the self's transcendence but of its incontrovertible contingency in relation to the body). At the same time, we might also become acutely aware through this "viewing" that Flanagan does still "exist" in and through the others who have engaged him (in particular, Rose), marking the contingency and embeddedness of the self on/in the other: it is this interrelatedness of the live and the dead that Rose and O'Brien's piece taps into. Flanagan becomes "alive" in their memorializing (and in Rose's living body, where traces of Flanagan shape her psyche).[6] The originally conceived trilogy addressed death both as imagined by a man predicted to die young (Flanagan survived to the age of forty-three, highly unusual at the time for CF sufferers) and as an event the aftereffects of which were to be theatrically represented. The structure of each of the pieces was to highlight the relation between self and other, a relation that death challenges: Flanagan and Rose literally replace Flanagan with the viewer in *Video Coffin* and activate the viewer as mourner in *Dust to Dust*. In *The Viewing* the bond between those who view/know/desire Flanagan is literalized even after death—we become activated as potential voyeurs of his corpse's disintegration.

As noted, in *Goodbye Bob*, Rose and O'Brien stage *Dust to Dust* in revised form as the second part of their tribute to Flanagan. The coffin was cardboard, the confetti pictures mounded on the floor to be sprinkled inside the coffin—with its effigy of Flanagan—by Rose, O'Brien, and

---

6. Rose introduced a further element to the unfinished trilogy, staging a huge, twenty-foot-long balloon "sculpture" of Flanagan in bondage and with an erection—the *Bobballoon* (this was exhibited in the exhibition *On Camp / Off Base*, organized by Kenjiro Okazaki, at the Tokyo International Exhibition Center in Japan in August of 1996).

audience members. Flanagan's likeness is multiple and yet of course does little to bring him back to life; his vitality is, rather, in the remembered bodily/psychic aspects of who he was for Rose (and those of us who knew him). And of course Rose and I will also die, along with everyone who ever knew him. Whither Flanagan's living memory then? Just as Rose and O'Brien hope to sustain Flanagan's creative force in *Goodbye Bob* (while also, through the gesture of saying goodbye, putting him "to rest"), so in writing this piece I hope to sustain my memories of Flanagan, but also to confirm my creative relationship to Rose and to O'Brien, as a writer interpreting their homage.

Eventually Rose and O'Brien stand, each cuts a rough angular S or zigzag into the other's whitened chest. This signifier, etched into flesh, stands for "Supermasochist," but also "Sheree" and "slave," and exactly replicates the shape that Rose had cut into Flanagan's chest just before he died, and which is visible *on the chest of his corpse* in a harrowing moment at the very end of the film about Flanagan's life and work, *Sick: The Life and Death of Bob Flanagan, Supermasochist* (1997, directed by Kirby Dick and co-produced by Rose). We see these cut lines on Flanagan's chest (which are livid and nonbleeding, because the body is "gone") after we have effectively watched him die in Rose's arms. The sign in the flesh becomes a signature, a mark of Flanagan's body (he called himself "Supermasochist" in performance and in the book *Bob Flanagan: Supermasochist*) through which his otherwise alien corpse can be identified (Vale and Juno). But it is also a sign of Rose's loving creative agency in relation to his body/self, as he paradoxically commanded her to dominate him, here through the act of cutting.[7]

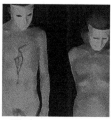

Each of the two performers (Rose, O'Brien) then presses blotting paper into the other's wound, making bloody signs; these are then stuck to sticks like flags, and they file out carrying them, as if leading a medieval funerary procession. They are followed by the audience and pallbearers carrying the casket, now filled with confetti pictures of Flanagan. Audience members are given

p. 285

7. Flanagan himself was acutely aware of the paradox of masochism. While nominally the "slave" in his relationship to Rose (and the "object" of the audience's gazes in the artistic performance), it was he who directed every action and even motivated the S/M orientation of their relationship in the first place: "I am ultimately (this is what every masochist hates to hear, or admit) in full control" (Vale and Juno 32). The masochist *commands* the very action by which he suffers. And yet, Flanagan also stressed the consensual aspect of BDSM practice: for Rose and Flanagan, the BDSM confusion of passive and active positions becomes a confusion of gender polarities as well.

lit candles, increasing the mood of elegy and remembrance. All gather around a hole dug in the garden of the ONE, and the casket is lowered and then lit on fire—Rose and O'Brien throw their banners into the flames, and audience members are asked to throw their candles in. The fire roars and Rose and O'Brien quietly process out of the garden.

Ashes to ashes and dust to dust. . . . The performance is over, Flanagan's ghost both raised and put to rest. I miss him more afterward than before, but I am also reminded of his humor, his lightness, and the fact that he is no longer suffering. Perhaps this confirms that the séance was successful.

*

The Ascension

On the cusp of New Year's Eve, marking the transition from one difficult year in American history to another (2017 to 2018), *The Ascension* took place in conjunction with an exhibition of Rose/Flanagan works at Jason Vass Gallery in east downtown Los Angeles. The display of Rose's photographs and BDSM paraphernalia became the setting for a queer procession of naked and almost-naked performers in BDSM garb leading or

following O'Brien, walking on all fours. A man with a loincloth and a basket throws more of the Rose photographs of Flanagan as confetti; two dominatrixes dressed as nuns flog O'Brien periodically; a woman in a mask and kimono follows. They process into a darkened back space behind the gallery, where Rose awaits in front of a shrine covered with skulls and memorial images of Fla-

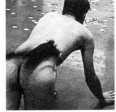

p. 303

nagan (her skirt is made of bloody plastic arms, like gruesome life-sized *milagros*). She performs a ritual, which culminates with O'Brien in a bathtub being "bathed" in liquid and covered in glitter and blood-colored rose petals, finally cutting the signature *S* in his chest (the bathtub ritual is

completed by performance artist Ron Athey, garbed in a caftan and moving like a sage or shaman). The apotheosis of the performance consists of O'Brien being hoisted up via hooks slicing through his shoulders and wrists into a crucifix formation. He hangs silently, turning slowly. Rose then approaches and a gasp goes up as she embraces O'Brien around the waist and hangs off his

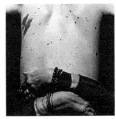

p. 307

already tortured body, straining the holes where the hooks slice through his body almost to the breaking point.

Tapping into the extreme imagery of medieval crucifixes and paintings of saints during the Catholic reformation, *The Ascension* ramped up the symbology and excessive bodily suffering of Rose's works with Flanagan to reopen wounds for those who lost Flanagan as a friend—freeing the viewer (who is also a participant) to cry and re-experience the loss, as well as to mourn pre-emptively for O'Brien (who is now also a friend for many who followed the work of Rose and Flanagan). O'Brien's dangling body opens up a state of emotional release that is almost ecstatic in its catharsis.

As Freud points out in "Mourning and Melancholia," the grieving subject experiences mourning as an appropriate response to the death of a loved one. After a suitable amount of time, in this prolonged process of mourning the psyche repeatedly activates "reality-testing" in relation to encounters and memories that remind the sufferer of her loss. Eventually, through the results of this testing (which shows "that the loved object no longer exists"), the sufferer accepts the loss of the beloved, working to substitute another for him. While the sufferer may cling to the impossible (a wish that the lost one is still alive), at some point "normally, respect for reality gains the day," and she emerges with a new substitute object (Freud, "Mourning and Melancholia" 244). The case of Rose, channeling Flanagan and working with O'Brien, would hardly fall into the model of a "normal" psychic development such as this pattern outlined by Freud. Melancholia, Freud argues, is an unhealthy condition where the grieving subject cannot accept the loss of the beloved object, turning inward in "self-reproaches and self-revilings," culminating in "a delusional expectation of punishment" (244). Melancholia, which we would today call depression, is essentially narcissistic, whereas mourning allows the subject to turn outward again, in a supposedly healthy move to become reinscribed in normative social relations.

Rose and O'Brien's genius, in mourning Flanagan, has been to refuse either the forgetting necessary to "healthy" recovering through mourning *or* the twisted narcissism of Freud's other alternative—melancholia. Rose of course still *lives* Flanagan, having internalized him through incorporations so profound we cannot know them or see how they work. O'Brien brings him to life again, but with a difference—a younger-generation CF sufferer and performance artist echoing and expanding upon Flanagan's insights, as understood not through a lived connection but through documentation and a relationship with Rose.

Ultimately, *Goodbye Bob* and *The Ascension* both highlighted the failure of representation to stand in for the lost or dead object of love and desire, and the failure of the live body itself to secure immortality (O'Brien's coughing throughout our public dialogue was another reminder of this tragic state of affairs, true for all of us but far more pressingly evident for someone with CF). Neither the body of Flanagan nor his archive can/ could secure his living presence in the world forever. However, all is not lost. Rose continues to inhabit and perform his psychic imprint on the world, furthering our memories and thus his "voice." And O'Brien, his beautiful, young body wracked by CF coughs, interprets Flanagan for new generations. This is all Flanagan could have hoped for, given the impossible yet inevitable annihilation of death. Rest in peace, Bob.

Works Cited

Cohen, Michael, editor. *Narcissistic Disturbance.* Otis Gallery, Otis College of Art and Design, 1995.

Dick, Kirby, director. Prod. Sheree Rose. *Sick: The Life and Death of Bob Flanagan, Supermasochist,* 1997.

Flanagan, Bob. Reading of "Why," from *Sick: The Life and Death of Bob Flanagan, Supermasochist.* 1985. http://www.youtube.com/watch?v=nWtgdnuNiKQ. Accessed 28 Mar. 2018.

Flanagan, Bob and Sheree Rose. "Project Description" for grant application to Guggenheim; Flanagan, revised by Rose, 1995/1996.

Freud, Sigmund. "Family Romances." 1908–9. *The Standard Edition of the Complete Psychological Works of Sigmund Freud,* vol. 9, translated by James Strachey, in collaboration with Anna Freud, Alix Strachey, and Alan Tyson, Hogarth Press and the Institute of Psycho-Analysis, 1959, pp. 235–41.

———. "Mourning and Melancholia." 1917. *The Standard Edition of the Complete Psychological Works of Sigmund Freud,* vol. 14, translated by James Strachey, in collaboration with Anna Freud, Alix Strachey, and Alan Tyson, Hogarth Press and the Institute of Psycho-Analysis, 1953, pp. 243–58.

Jones, Amelia. *Body Art/Performing the Subject.* U of Minnesota P, 1998.

O'Brien, Martin. http://martinobrienperformance.weebly.com/performance.html. Accessed 29 July 2016.

Rose, Sheree and Martin O'Brien. Comments made during the public discussion I led at the ONE with Rose and O'Brien after the performance on 7 Feb. 2015.

Rose, Sheree and Martin O'Brien dialogue (n.d.), originally available at O'Brien's website: http://martinobrienperformance.com/dialogues-sheree-rose.html. Accessed 10 Nov. 2017.

Vale, V. and Andrea Juno, editors. *Bob Flanagan: Supermasochist.* Re/Search Publications, 1993.

Obliquely Chronophilic

A Dialogue with Sheree Rose and Martin O'Brien on
Do with Me as You Will–A 24-Hour Performance

YETTA HOWARD

See *Do with Me as You Will* image gallery.

On June 23, 2013, at noon through June 24, 2013, at noon, Rose and O'Brien collaborated in a performance called Do with Me as You Will, *which explored the contours of temporality and submission. Rose permitted audience members literally to do whatever they wished to Martin O'Brien's body over the course of a 24-hour period. The performance took place at Sanctuary Studios LAX, a dungeon near the Los Angeles International Airport, an exceptional and fitting space for the performance piece. We might think of the performance as a way to modify the concept of chronophilia, which loosely has been designated as "unnatural" attractions to persons of a particular age group, a kind of "uneven" age dynamic, if thought of in normative terms. But if we expand the notion of chronophilia to mean a fetish for time, then perhaps we can begin to arrive at an understanding of how to approach Rose and O'Brien's 24-hour performance. The stakes of experiencing time were made explicit, not just through the differences in their ages or how the work calls up O'Brien's illness and Rose's artistic practice with Flanagan but in the way the performance radicalizes the framing of a quotidian temporality. Even with such a revision of chronophilia, time is the vehicle through which a range of other philias took their forms on and through O'Brien's body as orchestrated by Rose. The chronophilia in this performance is therefore oblique and disrupts as it reimagines how we characterize "late" versus "early" while breaking down the distinction between day-time activity and night-time activity through an erotic framework defined by relinquishing control. The following discussion took place about three months after the performance, in October 2013.*[1]

---

1. This interview originally appeared in *Fiction International* 47, 2014, pp. 73–84. Special issue, "Phobia/Philia."

YETTA HOWARD: Talk about how you came up with the idea for the performance.

MARTIN O'BRIEN: Maybe a year before, we worked on a 12-hour performance together: we were interested in ideas of endurance and time and Sheree really wanted to do this work over a 24-hour period, thinking about doing something over the entire period of a day and what it means to be engaged in an art practice together for an entire one-day period.

SHEREE ROSE: Martin's work is all about endurance and duration and he did these three amazing *Regimes of Hardship,* three separate 12-hour pieces. The first two, he did everything to himself, but then I got involved. We would set up 12 or so different events every hour and he gave up his control to me and we did it very formally with a contract. That was in the last 12 hours and it was quite active: we did things I'd done with Bob [Flanagan] and things that Martin I came up with. We had a great time finding all the materials and it went really fast. One of the fun things was my dressing him up as this little go-go dancer with beautiful four-inch heels—and he's not a cross-dresser—with a beautiful wig. We got a gorgeous wig. He looked adorable and he went around the room dancing to "Love to Love You Baby" by Donna Summer, who just died, so it was sort of an homage to Donna Summer, and then he went up to different people and said, "Wanna fuck me?" or whatever. What was it I had you say?

MO: "I'm a dirty slut. Would you like to fuck me?"

SR: That was sort of improvisational and what I really like to do in all my performances is to get the audience involved. I don't like it to be just a spectacle where they're watching people do weird things. And we had talked a lot about doing a 24-hour piece because I love Marina Abramović and what she was doing. My first idea was Martin and I would be in this room and there'd be all this equipment around and people would call us up or tell us what we should do with the equipment. But then I thought that maybe that was too much Marina Abramović.

MO: There's sort of two things going on with this piece in developing it from the other, which was, first, about developing the time aspect and spending a longer period of time together working through particular ideas and in a different context. The second thing was the control idea, which was the first time I had ever given over control to an audience.

I had given over control to Sheree before. I had never in a performance allowed audiences to come and do things to me. That was the other aspect for us, wasn't it?

SR: Right, it was. I was very nervous about the whole thing.

YH: What were you nervous about?

SR: Well, I was giving up control to a certain extent. I had flyers made up, *Make Martin Suffer for Art*, and what was the other name of the piece?

MO: *Do with Me as You Will.*

SR: *Do with Me as You Will.* Right. Those were the twin ideas that were going on so I asked a lot of my friends and we put it on Facebook, but what I liked about it was that it was totally up to the whim of what was going to be happening. I had no idea who was going to show up. I had no set ideas about what was going to happen *when*. I had friends coming. My friend Pony Lee Estrange came and shaved all of Martin's hair. Later on, Pony and I put needles around Martin's penis and scrotum.

YH: What point was that? Early the next morning?

SR: No, it wasn't that late. 24 hours is a lot of time. But we did do a video diary. Every hour, we marked the hour with me cutting Martin on his arm: making just a very simple little cut to mark the hours and then we would talk for a few minutes together.

YH: So a lot of this performance is obviously about inviting these unexpected moments. Were there any moments within that 24-hour period that were truly surprising or unexpected?

MO: One of the things about the performance that elicited particular responses was that it was in a dungeon so it was already set up with a contract which had to do with submission. So I think that people came with an idea of doing something that came out of that context, if they were interested in it themselves. Some of the things that happened to me I was completely unprepared for: one of the most intense experiences was when Durk Dehner from the Tom of Finland Foundation rolled up at about 11 o'clock at night. The room was really full and at that time I had done a few things that were a little difficult but nothing too major and I was a little bit tired but was quite enjoying it. I just remember the doors swung open and these two leathermen came walking in and then I just remembered Sheree telling me the day before, "These two guys from the Tom of Finland Foundation are going to come and they play heavy." He spent about 45 minutes, 50 minutes—one of the things he did was psychological play. He really scared me. For a long time he didn't really do anything but he made me lay out all of his equipment on the table: these huge elbow-length fisting gloves and huge dildos that would never fit in my ass, and I was completely terrified and he was speaking very calmly to me. But in the end, he beat me a little bit and whipped me with a single-tail whip quite a lot on my chest and back—the marks stayed on me for a couple of days after that. That was really one of the most intense experiences. One thing to note here is Sheree's position in all this as a sort of orchestrator, as someone in charge. One of the things I found interesting was how she positioned herself in relation to different people. She had known him for a long time and she just kind of sat away, laughing and enjoying it, whereas with other people, I felt her really close to me, just a few yards away. For instance, the girl who we didn't really know, who put ginger in my ass. Sheree was quite close at that time, just making sure . . . But nothing went wrong. I felt Sheree was present in those moments.

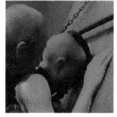

p. 270

SR: Well you never know. One of the things you have to do in a performance like this, part of it, for me, was having to give up a certain amount of control and trust that the things that were going to be happening would be all for the good. No one was going to do anything untoward or really harmful. But I didn't really know and I didn't know everybody who was doing things with him. But I found that a lot of the people were very shy about it. One woman, very early on, led him around on a dog leash and had him eat some baby food in a dog dish and that was her first time that she had ever done anything like that, so you got that range of experience: people who had never been in a dungeon before, number one, or seen a naked man in a cage—I mean, just the visual of that alone set up the mood. Toward the very end, in the middle of the night, some of the women who were professional Dominatrixes and my friends came in and they gave him some pretty good workings over with whippings and fire. I love the serendipity, synchronicity, coincidence of who came when and there were never too many people or people waiting or not enough people. It all just sort of flowed in a very natural way. For me, there was only one thing that happened that I still worry about a little bit or think it wasn't exactly what my plan was, but I gave up because I wanted it to be spontaneous. A friend of mine, who had just come out of the hospital, and had hip surgery, comes into the room . . . okay, Martin, you can tell the story from there.

MO: I could see him speaking with Sheree, but I didn't really know what was going on. What he wanted was to be stripped naked, tied up, whipped by someone else, and then sponge-bathed and dressed again by me.

SR: His concept was that he had just come out of the hospital, and he's disabled, so part of it had to do with Martin's CF and taking care of people, the idea of being taken care of. It wasn't my agenda, it was his agenda, and I had to make a decision to say no, but I'm of the belief that when you're doing something you don't want to say no. That sort of stops the flow of things. So I agreed to it and I also ended up cutting his hair. But it was a little bit uncomfortable because this was supposed to be make *Martin* suffer for art, not you be his surrogate and suffer. He was somebody I've known for many years, a dear friend who left the hospital to come to this so I didn't feel that I wanted to stop the action at that point.

YH: That gets to this question of where to draw the boundaries. Did you have boundaries going into it or was it just this situation that made you think about boundaries in a different way?

SR: Well, I was aware of it. Most of the activity either I was involved in or I could see was about scenarios like spanking, or it was about things that weren't going to be dangerous. A woman that came in was a beautiful young Dominatrix, dressed all in latex, and she had called me earlier and said, "Can I have him drink my urine?" and I thought to myself, well, I don't know if she has any diseases and I didn't want to do anything that would jeopardize Martin. That was my number one concern. I wanted nothing that would jeopardize Martin. So I told her no, but she did a wonderful scene with him. Actually it was one of the best scenes where she had him eat all these cookies from a platter and then she carved a little ginger and put the ginger up his ass. You can explain how that felt, Martin.

MO: Just the pure sensation . . . that was the worst, the least enjoyable part of the performance. It was this intense burning: a small piece of ginger up my ass just to sustain the intensity of the burning. I did not like it at all. It was very intense and it kept slipping out as well, because it was quite small. Every time it slipped out, she would bend me over, laugh, and shove it back in. And each time it went in, she didn't lube it or anything. It was just dry and burning and I could just feel it dragging across the edges of my asshole. It was a really horrible thing but a really good scene.

SR: Well, it was distressing, but it wasn't dangerous. So that was my concern. I wanted him to be distressed. I wanted *that* danger, that unknown quality of what was going to be happening. I wanted that. I was excited about it, too. That kept our energy up, I think: the unknown quality of it and not knowing.

YH: It almost seems like drinking the urine would have been more preferable in that situation.

[laughter]

MO: It was interesting the way the 24 hours went. There were real peaks and the energies changed all the time so that there were moments when there was absolute silence in the room or when it was crowded when Durk Dehner was there, for example. Around that time, it was absolutely silent and it felt very intense and there were other times when it was quite playful, like when you were there at the beginning. People were talking and drinking wine later in the evening and things. But it just sort of moved naturally.

SR: At about five or six in the morning, there was nobody there and Martin and I were alone for a couple of hours and I was blabbering to him as I usually do. We thought it was over. We thought, okay, it's over, no one's going to come and, then, around nine in the morning, about three or four young men came in and a couple of them were really smart, and I wish I would have recorded some of the things they said about the performance—do you remember . . . ?

MO: I don't remember anything from that moment. At that time in the morning my capacity to speak was . . . [laughter]

SR: But we did it the whole 24. At first I was really nervous that nobody would do anything. That we would just be sitting there but we decided, well, that's okay, too. If that's what's going to happen, we'll just sit there and be bored and that will be alright. I think part of it, for me, was I felt like I had to do something. I had to make it happen. If it was boring or dull . . . To that extent, I had all kinds of different things: I had pens. I was going to write on his body. We had games. We were going to play bingo. We were going to play chess.

YH: There was a whole stage full of sex toys . . .

SR: A whole stage full of things that I had set up in case there was a lull in the action, thinking, what if nobody shows up? What am I going to do— this is 24 hours.

YH: Do you think you could have gone on longer if you didn't set that 24-hour period of time or was that enough of an exercise in endurance? Something like 36 hours?

MO: I could've, but when I do my work I usually set a particular time limit and I sort of work toward that and there's a feeling that it's building, it's building, it's building toward the end and I've got an endpoint. So by setting 24 hours, that was the natural end for the performance, for me, at least. And it also makes sense, as well, to have 24 hours, so it's kind of like, how do we fill a day, a day in the life of Sheree and Martin. How do they fill a day in the dungeon.

SR: I was very interested in that whole aspect of time, because for Martin and me, for different reasons, time is extremely precious. Because I'm older and because he has CF, we're very aware that time is limited and we only have so much of it, and how we decide to fill that time . . . and that's everybody's existential dilemma. It's not just Martin and me but we're bringing it to the forefront, especially in this piece and in all of Martin's work, time is definitely of the essence. So, we were really playing with that concept of the 24 hours. Also, we were in a dungeon, so we had no idea what time it was in terms of day or night. We didn't have any cues, like the sun or nighttime or anything like that. But your body does have rhythms and we definitely played to those rhythms and, at five in the morning I was awake and thinking about it and thinking about this whole piece and it was very spiritual in the sense that this time—it's never going to happen again and we're *doing* this particular time and it made me feel very happy. I was pleased with how well it had gone. Trusting the universe.

YH: You felt that time was cooperating with you—it didn't feel like it was moving too fast or too slow.

SR: Not at all. It really cooperated.

MO: It's quite interesting: a lot of the work that I do is much more where I'm sort of actively doing particular tasks that are usually quite repetitive, some of the things over and over again . . . After a few hours, I start to really feel the endurance of it and that word is really important in my work: *endurance.* That I'm going through this thing and I really feel it and I'm thinking what time is it? How long do I have left? But it was quite different I think in this piece for me. There was something about lying back and taking it and letting time wash over me and I didn't really feel as though I was enduring it so much. Overall, there were certain periods of endurance within it, when I had ginger up my ass or when I was really feeling that I wanted it to finish. But I just felt as though, in this performance, my experience of time was rather distinct from how it usually is in my other performances. In this one I felt as though my relationship with time was a little bit different. It could have been going on for three days, two months, or ten minutes. I really lost a sense of time in this performance. I lost a sense of how long things were lasting. I really didn't know how long each person's session lasted at the time. The endurance element of it, even though the length was so prolonged, was less than it sometimes is in other pieces when I've been more active on my own. There was something about the kind of community that was built there which helped. People who chose to spend some of that time with us came and this bizarre ad-hoc community inside this dungeon formed. Some people brought me chocolate, some people beat me up, some shoved things up my ass or stuck pins in me, but whatever they came to do they came to do it to spend part of this 24 hours with us and act in this community somehow.

SR: One of the major elements was making sure that people would come. Whenever you give a performance, the idea of an audience is very important. At one point we thought about maybe stopping it at midnight and then having people come in and then we thought, no, no, whoever wants to come in, even if it's 3 in the morning, let them come because this was our parameter: 24 hours. I think it worked out far better than I even imagined. We had so many different people from all different walks of life, too: people who had never been in a dungeon to people who were professional Dominatrixes and professional Masters. It was a great mix of people. There were a lot of academic people there. I thought that was really interesting because Martin is an academic as well and so I think people got the idea of it. And I thought 24 hours, wow, but then there's the Chinese artist Tehching Hsieh who did several performances that lasted a *year*, as did Eleanor Antin and Linda Montano. So when I thought about that in contrast to our thing, I thought we can do 24 hours, that's a piece of cake. That's going to be easy compared to doing something for a year.

YH: Would you do another version of this and, if so, do you think you would do it in some place other than a dungeon?

SR: Oh yeah, it would be something different. . . . When we first met, it was an amazing experience where I spanked him 100 times in front of an audience and that was one of the best experiences and I've done that piece many times . . .

YH: That's a version of *100 Reasons* [Sheree Rose/Bob Flanagan performance].

SR: After that, I felt this connection with Martin. It was such a beautiful spontaneous connection that we had. I didn't want to leave. I didn't want to just say, oh, I don't want to see you again forever, so we devised a 30-day performance.

MO: Sheree was in LA and I was in London, actually I was living in Oxford at the time, so we were trying to figure out a way of continuing the collaboration across continents. We came up with a project for 30 days, a period of one month's time. Each morning, Sheree would send through a task or a starting point and then I would have the day to either complete the task or to make something from the starting point and then send back the documentation to Sheree that evening. The starting points ranged from responding to the work of different artists and performances to dressing up as a princess on the day of the Royal Wedding and walking around in Oxford and then going for high afternoon tea.

SR: I had so much fun with that because Martin just did whatever I said. I went to the library and got a bunch of books on performance art and on Allan Kaprow and the Happenings. The difference between the 30-day piece and the 24-hour piece was that the month-long piece was just between Martin and me and we didn't have an audience. I like an audience. I feel, if it's going to be a performance, you need an audience because that brings it to another level of understanding and complexity. But I don't know . . . Do we have to do something longer now because we did something 24 hours? Does it have to be months? . . . I've been at this for a long time. Let's just say that. Although I don't think I've really slowed down necessarily. I'm having a show of *100 Reasons* coming up in a couple of months here in Los Angeles. It will be the first time I'll have photographs of 100 different asses bruised in some way all with captions by Mike Kelley, so, an homage to Mike Kelley, who unfortunately passed away last year . . . and that piece was done in the '80s. It was done over a period of 5 or 10 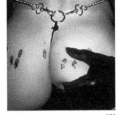 years in the '80s and now finally, in 2014, it's going to be shown. So it's p. 273 slow, but it's happening.

YH: Along those lines, you mentioned Mike Kelley, you talked about your past collaborations with Bob [Flanagan], and you discussed Marina Abramović earlier. Do you both see *Do with Me as You Will* as working in a particular kind of lineage or—I hate to use the word *tradition*—of radical performance art, or do you really see it departing from those other kinds of endurance-based performances?

MO: For me, I think the fact of me and Sheree working together puts it within a particular lineage or at least calls a particular history to it: that Sheree was making all this work in the '80s and '90s with Bob [Flanagan] and then I come along 20 years later with cystic fibrosis and that our first collaboration, really, was about a kind of homage to the work that she was making with Bob. For me, it was about thinking through their influence on my work and addressing those ideas. How can I address this within a performance—how can I do this without being overshadowed, but also acknowledging the influence of the work that they were doing? The way to do it was to actually work with Sheree. I think the work fits into a particular lineage especially since we were doing it in an SM space, a dungeon in LA. That was important for me.

SR: When Bob and I started doing our work, we performed for SM audiences only. We did not perform for an art audience. In 1989 when the book *Modern Primitives* came out, Bob did a performance called *Nailed!* at

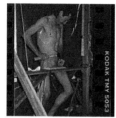

a very small venue in Los Angeles, and there were about 200 people that came in and that was the first time we actually combined my slides and SM activities . . . Bob nailed his scrotum to a board. I had a woman bound up and I cut her breasts and there was blood dripping on the floor. Plus, we had go-go dancers and all kinds of other things happening. That was the very first time, for

p. 262

us anyway, that we mixed in the SM and the art scene together and that, I think, started a whole new sort of lineage because after that many of the other artists expanded their audiences, including Ron [Athey], who had been doing work before, but, again, those were more limited audiences . . . Our work really started blending SM into the art world saying, SM is not something horrible and nasty that you can't talk about but actually can be an art form if done artfully. Now, I don't know. I think that legacy is there and we acknowledge it and we're proud of it. I'm very proud of it. I think I've spawned all these younger artists who are willing to do all kinds of things now, much more radical than anything Bob and I ever did. But we started it. We were the founders and I think it's blossomed in a way that's really beautiful. What I'm going to do now with Martin, I don't know. Obviously the issues are still there, for me, the issues of aging . . . Death seems to be hovering. Several of my best friends now are dealing with cancer and are terminal. And my daughter had cancer last year. She had breast cancer and had to have a double mastectomy. So issues for me of mortality and illness and my own mortality . . . my own body that is not what it used to be . . .

YH: I think what you're also talking about is fascinating in that this performance, even though it's about time, is working with time in these theoretically innovative ways that exceed the temporal characteristics of the performance—not just in terms of age-play, but how illness and age have affected your approach to the performances. I know you were about 10 years older than Bob and that Martin is significantly younger, but he has cystic fibrosis, so it really revises time in relationship to age.

SR: Yes, it does. Also, I like playfulness. Martin and I are not grim or morbid around each other. We're very playful with each other, as Bob and I were. Even though he was dying, he still had the most amazing sense of humor and we laughed to the very end. There was no grimness even in his death. It was poignant and heartbreaking, but, at the same time, we approached it with humor and with the acknowledgment that this is life. We don't shy away from those realities. Bob never did and I hope I never do and certainly Martin doesn't.

MO: Well, I suppose now it's quite a few months after [the performance], so one thing to note is how to think back to a performance that was about time. All this time has passed since I was there in LA. I was contemplating that time and trying to remember what took place. Earlier today, I was reflecting on some of the things that happened in the performance and the way in which, over time, things decay or you lose things . . . trying to remember these things that slipped away that I had forgotten about that came back into my head . . . A performance about time over time: some bits are forgotten, some bits are remembered so strongly and it's just remarkable what time does to memory.

YH: Memory is so inaccurate, too. It's not a precise form and it definitely changes what the performance might even mean in terms of how you experienced it.

SR: If I do a new performance, it might have to be about memory, which I find difficult. I don't remember things. If I'm reminded of them, then of course I remember them perfectly. But it's bringing them back to mind. Things fade, but it's like photographs. I used to photograph everything I did with Bob. I photographed him every day for 16 years, but those photographs are faded. So what's left? I think what's left for me are the emotions that I felt doing it, how my body was excited and engaged for 24 hours, which usually doesn't happen. The days go by and you sleep for maybe some of those hours and you don't really recall everything that happened. But I really want to try to record and keep alive the memories.

Sheree Rose, the Maternal, and the Erotics of Care

AMBER MUSSER

See *Do with Me as You Will* image gallery.

Do with Me as You Will, a collaboration between Sheree Rose and Martin O'Brien, offers insight into the erotics and vulnerability of mothering. The twenty-four-hour performance, which was staged from noon on June 23,

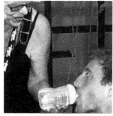

2013, until noon on June 24, 2013, in a dungeon in Los Angeles, required participants to ask Rose for permission to act on O'Brien, who, as the title of the piece suggests, invites those in attendance to do with him what they will. Through this enactment of radical dependence, O'Brien relinquishes control over his own body to Rose and others, and in this way makes visible the pleasures

p. 269 and perils of the work of mothering, especially when considered through the lens of caretaking.

Though the mother might act as the catalyst for the oedipal, she is not usually given a role beyond that of first object of love. Generally speaking, the mother functions as a theoretical conundrum—a cipher often reduced to the body and disavowed for her corporeality. In 1970's *The Dialectic of Sex,* Shulamith Firestone argues fiercely against motherhood: "The heart of woman's oppression is her child-bearing and child-rearing role" (65). According to Firestone, gender inequality could only be addressed through the "seizure of control of *reproduction*: not only the full restoration to women of ownership of their own bodies, but also their (temporary) seizure of control of human fertility—the new population biology as well as all the social institutions of child-bearing and child-rearing" (11). A feminist revolution would sever the link between reproduction and women and break "the tyranny of the biological family" (11). Though dramatic, Firestone's understanding of the problem of motherhood is one that hovers around feminist theory. Here, I briefly cite Simone de Beauvoir's discussion of the multiple, deep ways that maternity prevents women from being fully realized subjects. The mother becomes the symbol of the impossibility of subjectivity, agency, and desire. Lynne Huffer writes, "As the ground of meaning, the mother can only ever be the empty foundation of meaning; she is never meaning itself, but only that which allows meaning to come to be. The political and ideological implications of such a position seem clear: she is never an agent, a subject of meaning, or a wielder of power, but rather a figure of negativity" (10). The mother, then, is considered a void, a being that exists to sacrifice. To give to her offspring, she denies herself.

When we think with Rose, however, and her collaboration with O'Brien in this piece, we go elsewhere. Rose's maternal enactment is a specific agential performance of care, vulnerability, and pleasure. But this form of care is particular. It is not about self-sacrifice or shielding the other from danger, but about enabling a more robust and possibly pleasurable form of engagement with the world for both parties. This form of care is about the frictional; it allows us to think about the maternal in relation to boundary production and the labor of containing vulnerability while also giving us a window into maternal agency and desire.

When I describe Rose's care as form of boundary work, I am thinking with Melanie Klein. For Klein, the mother is important because she offers the infant's first opportunity to grapple with otherness through interactions with the maternal breast. The infant understands the world through the prism of the "good (gratifying) and bad (frustrating) breast"; the infant introjects the good breast, which offers sustenance and expels the bad breast (99). This divides the world into interior and exterior, marking the first encounter with otherness as spatial and affective. The split between internal and external can also be understood as a division between the continuous satiated self and the rest of the world over which one does not have agency. The starting position, then, is schizoid and paranoid; the task of the infant is to work through these divisions and ambivalences in order to situate herself within the social world. Ideally this would involve incorporating the maternal as a whole object (good and bad) through reparation and achieving a depressive position, which involves "an awareness of vulnerability, dependence, and guilt" (Zaretsky 143). Though it is the infant's task to process the affective landscape produced by the mother, through Rose's work with O'Brien, we can begin to think beyond infancy to see how much of mothering is about establishing boundaries for what should remain external and what can be incorporated and what being a whole object looks like.

Though the labor of boundary creation is often filtered through the lens of safety, which is to say that it is wrapped up in the task of maintaining the child's bodily integrity, in Rose's work we can see that it might also function less as prophylactic against invading dangers and more as agential exposure to that which might give way to new experiences and sensations. In an interview with Yetta Howard a few months after the performance, O'Brien narrates an intimidation scenario involving Durk Dehner that illuminates Rose's agency within the care relation:

> One thing to note here is Sheree's position in all this as a sort of orchestrator, as someone in charge. One of the things I found interesting was how she positioned herself in relation to different people. She had known him [Dehner] for a long time and she just kind of sat away, laughing and enjoying it, whereas with other people, I felt her really close to me, just a few yards away. For instance, the girl who we didn't really know, who put ginger in my ass. Sheree was quite close at that time, just making sure. . . . But nothing went wrong. I felt Sheree was present in those moments.

In O'Brien's description of the event, Rose facilitates exploration while also making sure that O'Brien is not harmed. This oscillation between hovering close to the action and distancing herself in order to allow O'Brien more space for his experiences is the type of boundary work that I am attaching to the maternal. It requires that Rose be discerning about her involvement so that O'Brien can experience submission in particular ways. In order for the performance to work, Rose cannot simply prohibit or permit; she must consider her own relationship to controlling the scene. In the same interview, Rose describes her anxiety about opening the performance to others: "One of the things you have to do in a performance like this, part of it, for me, was having to give up a certain amount of control and trust that the things that were going to be happening would be all for the good" (Howard). In Rose's reflections on the event, we see that maternal care requires not only the establishment and maintenance of boundaries for the other/the child but also the act of giving up the ruse of control. This is a different form of mothering from that of the ideal of strict domination that Rose and Flanagan practiced during their collaborations.[1] It allows us to see both O'Brien's and Rose's vulnerability and agency in coming together to face a reality in which omnipotence is impossible, but care functions as boundary work.

In her reading of the Kleinian subject, Eve Sedgwick focuses on the vulnerability that this self, who understands herself to be capable of violence, experiences. Sedgwick writes:

> For the Kleinian subject, however, unlike the Freudian one, omnipotence is a fear at least as much as it is a wish. [. . .] The problem is that the infant's desires are passionately experienced but intricately self-contradictory. The Kleinian infant experiences a greed—her own—whose aggressive and envious component is perceived as posing a mortal threat both to her loved and needed objects and to herself. This perception of oneself as omnipotent is hardly less frightening than the perception of one's parent as being so. (290)

This abandonment of omnipotence is an explicit part of O'Brien's performance in this collaboration, but Rose's vulnerability, which is activated through her boundary work, is also at play. This produces a vision of the maternal that is vastly different from descriptions of the mother as self-sacrificing void; instead we begin to see the maternal as whole object. Focusing on the insertion of ginger into O'Brien's anus by a woman who was unknown to them, Rose highlights the array of feelings at work. She describes wanting to provoke, but being uncertain of the outcome: "I wanted him to be distressed. I wanted that danger, that unknown quality of what was going to be happening. I wanted that. I was excited about it, too. That kept our energy up, I think: the unknown quality of it and not knowing" (Howard). This uncertainty, which sits alongside boundary work, is central to the work of care and mothering. Rose's positioning of it as a form of excitement, however, gives us insight into modes of fusing care with desire and agency. Here, Rose wants to push O'Brien to explore his boundaries with the knowledge that these sensations will challenge, even if they do not harm.

Given that this particular moment hinges on anality, it provides an easy segue into sodomitical maternity, which Maggie Nelson, working

---

1. I described Rose and Flanagan's collaborations through the lens of the maternal in *Sensational Flesh: Race, Power, and Masochism.*

through Susan Fraiman, argues "is . . . meant to indicate the mother with a sexuality that's in excess of the procreative capacity" (Doerr). In *The Argonauts*, Nelson connects this surplus sexuality to anality as she discusses both her enjoyment of anal sex and her desire to be a mother. In this formulation, anality in relation to the maternal body is considered excessive in that it is tied to the possibility of pleasure outside of the reproductive. This hole is not a substitute but rather another space that offers its own deep pleasures and excesses. This anality is about experiencing the body as body in a multitude of ways. While Rose's own anal sensations are not at play in this moment, she makes it clear that she shares a stake in this form of bodily pleasure. Boundary work and care are infused with pleasure for her because of her own negotiations of agency and selfhood.

Though Rose is explicit that this form of pleasure is not sexual in relation to O'Brien, this should not make us dismiss it. In *The Art of Living*, Rose parses some of the textures of her relationship with O'Brien. She says, "As a gay man, Martin's relationship to me is not sexual, it's something else, and this is made more pronounced by the age difference between us. There's something maternal in my relationship to Martin, which I felt very strongly when I spanked him that first time in London. I think I'm always expressing a love/hate aspect in my relation to Martin, like the ambivalence of a mother to her child, who loves but also resents him—these feelings are heightened" (Johnson 125). The resentment Rose describes might have to do with the labor she has to perform to allow O'Brien to explore submission and the boundaries of his body, but this ambivalence, I argue, is foundational to the work of care in which one has to give up aspects of the self for the other while simultaneously grappling with admitting the overarching loss of control that comes with being. Rose, however, gives us a space to read this loss of control as potentially pleasurable. It is not only O'Brien, then, who experiences pleasure through submission in their collaboration. Rose's submission is more subtle because it emerges through an erotics of care, control, and vulnerability.

In *Do with Me as You Will*, Rose and O'Brien focus on the ways that this double bind comes through within the semibounded space of performance, but Rose, herself, indicates that she is also thinking about the lack of control in relation to mortality. She tells Howard, "Obviously the issues are still there, for me, the issues of aging. . . . Death seems to be hovering. . . . So issues for me of mortality and illness and my own mortality . . . my own body that is not what it used to be" (Howard). In a sense, then, the vulnerability of Rose's own body is made as visible as the vulnerability of O'Brien's, and this, too, alters what we can imagine about care and mothering. Beyond the image of the maternal as disciplining and pedagogical, we see that care work produces a maternal that is insistently corporeal and vulnerable, a maternal that is strong and demanding, but also one that is multifaceted, agential, desiring, and ambivalent. This is a maternal in relation to a void, but still imaginable as a Kleinian whole object.

Rose and O'Brien's performances highlight the work of care and the erotics of vulnerability for both. By working through the particular corporeal and agential stakes for Rose, we can come toward a nuanced understanding of the position of the maternal, which Rose claims in relation to O'Brien. This mother does not hew to the ideals of discipline nor does it produce the mother as empty space. Instead, the mothering that she performs reveals ambivalence and the work of maintaining boundaries. Through this labor, we also see vulnerability and pleasure.

Works Cited

Beauvoir, Simone de. *The Second Sex.* Translated by HM Parshley, Penguin, [1949] 1972.

Doerr, Jennifer. "Making Space Around the Beloved." *Brooklyn Quarterly,* no. 8 http://brooklynquarterly.org/making-space-around-the-beloved.

Firestone, Shulamith. *The Dialectic of Sex: The Case for Feminist Revolution.* Farrar, Straus and Giroux, [1970] 2003.

Howard, Yetta. "Obliquely Chronophilic: An Interview with Sheree Rose and Martin O'Brien on *Do with Me as You Will,* a 24-hour Performance." *Fiction International,* no. 47, Fall 2014. http://fictioninternational.sdsu.edu/wordpress/catalog/issue-47-phobiaphilia/obliquely-chronophilic-a-dialogue-with-sheree-rose-and-martin-obrien-on-do-with-me-as-you-will-a-24-hour-performance/.

Huffer, Lynne. *Maternal Pasts, Feminist Futures: Nostalgia, Ethics, and the Question of Difference.* Stanford UP, 1998.

Johnson, Dominic. *The Art of Living: An Oral History of Performance Art.* Palgrave Macmillan, 2015.

Klein, Melanie. "Notes on Some Schizoid Mechanisms." *The International Journal of Psychoanalysis,* vol. 27, 1946, pp. 99–110.

Musser, Amber. *Sensational Flesh: Race, Power, and Masochism.* New York UP, 2014.

Sedgwick, Eve Kosofsky. "Melanie Klein and the Difference Affect Makes." *After Sex? On Writing since Queer Theory,* edited by Janet Halley and Andrew Parker, Duke UP, 2011, pp. 283–301.

Zaretsky, Eli. "'One Large Secure, Solid Background': Melanie Klein and the Origins of the British Welfare State." *Psychoanalysis and History,* vol. 1, no. 2, 1999, pp. 136–54.

"You Always Hurt the One You Love"

Transference, Pain, and Endurance

CHELSEA COON

Love and pain are terms as elusive to universal definitions as they are experientially intense. The various interpretations of these sensations also describe corporeal limitations. Love is synonymous with intimacies made real through time and can become pain. We might be reminded here of the expression *love sickness,* but more as a sensorial infliction of emotional or physical pain caused intentionally or unintentionally and generated or transferred between bodies. These felt but intangible forces can profoundly determine both physiological and psychological states observable in the collaborative works of Sheree Rose and Bob Flanagan as the interplay of love and sickness manifest themselves as lived experience in their practices. As a performance artist, I have been deeply influenced by the power of Rose's work (both with and after Flanagan), mostly in how it pushes boundaries of the body through processes of endurance that describe the act of living as art in and of itself.

The shared role that masochism plays in both my work and Rose's is demonstrated through repetition and duration in the transference of actions to the audience. This transference also enables audiences to reciprocate through relational encounters. In such encounters, pain heightens experience, a neurological rush analogous to love. Further, love may or

---

The title of this essay references the last line of Bob Flanagan's poem "Why."

may not implicitly relate to the acts of pain. Amber Musser notes that "pain caused by S&M is part of a performance, and as such it has a beginning and an end. Masochism's relationship to pain is one of control and subversion; pain is manipulated and enjoyed" (127). The manipulation of pain can be understood as a point from which a shift in perspective of self is possible. This shift is the crux of my work. As an audience member at one of my previous performances noted, "suffering for your art is one thing; suffering as your art is another" (Sadi). Indeed, in my performance works, pushing physiological and psychological limits is a persistent theme, as reflected in my *No One Thing Is the Root of All Anything* (2014). This work is presented as an annihilation of self that is made manifest in filing away a tooth that I lost sixteen years previously onto sheets of sandpaper—leaving behind traces of faint white lines that marked my erasure. The accumulation of my airborne dust particles was inhaled by the audience. Structuring the viewers as active participants in this way touches on a critical interest of the power of performance in that it structurally "shifts between loss and control" via a necessity to responsively react because outcomes cannot be known in advance (Coon 58).

As suggested above, transferences positioned as relational physiological and psychological proximities can be thought of in terms of endurance. In reciprocal-erotic exchanges through their Mistress-slave BDSM relationship where pain equated with pleasure, Flanagan took the pain inflicted by Rose, and Rose gave this to Flanagan (O'Dell 77). Here, pleasures are the result of pain and are, in turn, enacted in the temporal and spatial dimensions of performance. As Chris Kraus describes, "the furious contradiction [existed] between [Flanagan's] lust for physical pain as a masochist and his rage at the involuntary pain that he was now subject to" (7). Along these lines, cycles of life and death communicate through BDSM in their eroto-performative connections. The work of desire, then, was a rehearsal for death, with Rose as director helping Flanagan feel pleasurable pain as he prepared to die. As the cystic fibrosis progressed, the concern was to exceed the pain, to surpass it.

But then there was the psychological pain—the pain of loving. In one of his last entries in *The Pain Journal*, Flanagan articulates the transference of love and pain: "Sheree comes home" [. . .] "loving me to pieces and telling me how she wants to grow old together" [. . .] "This breaks my heart more than anything, the pain I'm putting her through" (161).

Transcending this type of pain may be navigated between performers and between performers and their audiences. As I have stated elsewhere, "Mental and physical risks taken to realize the work" can form expansive interrelationships through transference in performance (Coon 39). The investment in risk that characterizes Rose and Flanagan's collaborative work is similarly apparent in *Phases* (2014), a six-hour performance in which I explored proximities between the body and the cosmos through a physiological wearing down of myself via a slow, repetitive action involving walking barefoot on a sandpaper circuit until the skin on my feet completely wore away and the flesh broke. Consisting of traces in the form of two circular paths made from the accumulation of my skin over the six-hour duration, the work spoke to the way that everything has to come to an end so that it can begin again. In response to the repetitive nature of this action, an audience member noted that "[the] temporal nature of her action created within itself a vacuum of space around her" (Bacon 2). This perceptive response speaks to the way that the intensity of actions can affect time in performance structures. The accumulative experience of time was marked as lines of my feet being stripped on the coarse sandpaper circuit. A similar temporal framing can be detected in the repeated overlay of razor-blade incisions Sheree cut into Flanagan, her iconic mark of *S*. In these contexts, performance extends across time through bodily documentation as well as in the memories of both primary and secondary audiences. Implicit contracts with the audiences who enter the atmosphere of pain are something I have also directly addressed. What we are giving, receiving, or projecting determines outcomes; traces of an action, always referring back to the body and the marking of its erasure.

The shared contemplation of mortality that exists in our respective performance practices is further reflected in Rose's *Corpse Pose* (2012).

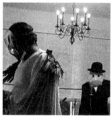

p. 278

Here, Rose invoked sensorial responses in her audiences by addressing lived experience through the flesh, by conceptually speaking of time, the body, and impermanence. In one version of this performance, Rose lay on a table and invited the audience to view her still body and drop rose petals on her. Rose explained, "Partly I'm trying to invite the audience to consider what it feels like to view me as if I'm dead. [. . .] I'm completely passive in these pieces, and vulnerable" (Johnson 124). The marked shift from dominance to passivity in this work speaks to the way that roles can shift as time shifts. What is particularly apparent in my process is that the longer the duration, and the more repetition that takes place within the work, the more vulnerable I become. As durational practices may advance methods of passivity in performance, for me this strategy essentially becomes a mode of survival.

Rose's, Flanagan's, and my performance practices necessarily incorporate vulnerability and the unpredictable nature of the body through transference, pain, and endurance. I wish to conclude with the performative possibilities of Rose's words in her essay that concludes Flanagan's *The Pain Journal*, "In Semi-Sickness and in So Called Health, I'm Still in Love with You": "Together, we transformed shame and sorrow into a transcendent state that defies logic and reason and death" (Rose 178). In these words, love can be understood to permeate experience beyond pain and death. Perhaps in this way, the flexibility of these terms encapsulates something that is generated through the body in performance but that ultimately exceeds it and rivals it with the complex unknowns of the cosmos.

Works Cited

Bacon, Thomas John. "Introduction." *No One Thing Is the Root of All Anything: Phases and Performance of the Imminent*, by Chelsea Coon. Not a Cult, 2018, pp. 7–19.

Coon, Chelsea. *No One Thing Is the Root of All Anything: Phases and Performance of the Imminent*. Not a Cult, 2018.

Flanagan, Bob. *The Pain Journal*. Semiotext(e), 2000.

——. "Why." *Sick: The Life and Death of Bob Flanagan, Supermasochist*, director Kirby Dick, producer Sheree Rose, 1997.

Johnson, Dominic. *The Art of Living: An Oral History of Performance Art*. Palgrave Macmillan, 2015.

Kraus, Chris. "Foreword." *The Pain Journal*, by Bob Flanagan. Semiotext(e), 2000, pp. 7–9.

Musser, Amber. *Sensational Flesh: Race, Power, and Masochism*. New York UP, 2014.

O'Dell, Kathy. *Contract with the Skin: Masochism, Performance Art, and the 1970s*. U of Minnesota P, 1998.

Rose, Sheree. "In Semi-Sickness and in So Called Health, I'm Still in Love with You." *The Pain Journal*, by Bob Flanagan, Semiotext(e), 2000, pp. 174–78.

Sadi, Mahmood. "Dhaka Live Art Biennale," *Dhaka Tribune*, 3 Feb. 2017, https://www.dhakatribune.com/feature/2017/02/03/44332.

Artist's Statement for *An Illegal Operation for Mary Toft*

RHIANNON AARONS

See *An Illegal Operation for Mary Toft* image gallery.

This artist's statement originally appeared with Rhiannon Aarons's performance and collaboration with Sheree Rose on April 23, 2017; minor changes have been made. Aarons and Rose were assisted by Aliza J. Bejarano, Dulcinea Circelli, Kayla Tange, and Sona Lee.

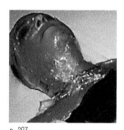

p. 297

The performance titled *An Illegal Operation for Mary Toft* addresses issues of female matriculation into mainstream art practices, and the way that female sexuality and the female body have historically been exploited by the art institution while female artists continue to be disenfranchised. In collaborative works made by married teams such as the Oldenburg/van Bruggen, Kienholzes, and Christo/Jeanne-Claude, the female collaborators in the equation have only recently been credited and in some cases remain uncredited. The title of the performance references Edward Kienholz's *The Illegal Operation*, a sculpture on abortion made before he met his partner Nancy Reddin Kienholz, with whom he later collaborated on all work.

Motherhood itself is still heavily stigmatized within the art world, resulting in an astronomical number of female artists over sixty who were forced to obtain illegal abortions in order to maintain validity during their early careers; in this sense, the illegal abortion became a rite of passage for many women within the art world. This backward ideology still maintains an iron grip on the community and is only thrust upon female artists. Male artists such as Jeff Koons, John Baldessari, and Ed Ruscha remained free to procreate at will without judgment. Through the 1980s and 1990s, women were advised by art professors at various institutions not to have a child if they wanted to be taken seriously as an artist. I personally faced being blacklisted from studio-assisting after having my child in 2011 and returned to working as a professional Dominatrix, as it was the only viable avenue; I had to support my child and practice while holding down a job.

As Sheree is yet another largely unappreciated driving female force within a partnered collaboration, as well as a mother and artist, we found it fitting to utilize actions she traditionally performed on Bob Flanagan with my body to expand the existing discourse established by their earlier practice. These are not BDSM activities for sexual pleasure brought into a gallery space but the utilization of marginalized methods preserved by BDSM to discuss the politics of the body, catharsis, transformation, personal trial, and gender roles. The performance is designed to address how these artmaking techniques can only be learned through direct experience, providing a foundational knowledge base that will allow performance art addressing extreme body politics to be advanced; in the same way that students are expected to put their experimental endeavors on hold to learn Cartesian perspective, my submission in this context represents a willingness to learn fundamental and established cornerstones of a rarified creative dialogue.

When the often-singularly credited Edward Kienholz can acceptably discuss illegal abortion—which is unarguably a woman's issue—it points to the continued oppression of cis women and our ability to speak about our own issues directly. It is solely misogyny that makes it acceptable for Paul McCarthy and Mike Kelley to slice an orifice into the lifecast of a female vulva with a Swiss Army knife, then graphically sodomize it with a packaged sausage dipped in mustard with complete cultural acceptance in *Heidi* (1992). Yet as a woman in 2017 I'm still expected to defend the creative validity of having an inanimate object safely and consensually removed from my vagina to discuss illegal abortion in response to current legislation that is immediately threatening to defund Planned Parenthood. That I am in a position to have to write this defense at all illustrates the dangers of cultural amnesia and the lack of foundational acceptance and cultural integration of established feminist practices developed by works such as Carolee Schneemann's *Interior Scroll* and Barbara T. Smith's *Feed Me.*

The performance is framed in the context of series of prints created from composited versions of Tenniel's illustrations for *Alice in Wonderland* and *Through the Looking Glass.* Throughout the exhibition, I appropriated this and other male-dominated narratives in order to speak about my personal experience—infused with the collective narratives of powerful female artists preceding me—in gaining traction as an artist, in establishing a safe place in the world where I—and others—can exist without lying by omission. The passage Alice takes from red to white on the chessboard in *Through the Looking Glass* parallels the literal bloodshed from female artists in their attempt to gain recognition within the white cube.

Sheree Rose, Martin O'Brien, and Rhiannon Aarons on *Philosophy in the Bedroom* and *The Viewing*

YETTA HOWARD

See *The Viewing* and *Philosophy in the Bedroom* image galleries.

October 29, 2017

YETTA HOWARD: We're going to start with *The Viewing,* if that's OK with you?

SHEREE ROSE: The thing is, we got the idea to use the CCTV from *Philosophy in the Bedroom.*

RHIANNON AARONS: Yes, for *Philosophy in the Bedroom,* we started using the CCTV because it was a necessity. I was talking to Luka [Fisher] and said, "I want to record all 24 hours of this performance" because prior to that, I would look at footage of Sheree's performances and Martin's performances and there's little bits but with those durational performances, there's no way to get the whole thing. I wanted 4 channels and the original intention with that when we installed it was to project it on 4 different walls. It was an after-thing: we didn't intend to use it as part of the performance but that was just how it evolved. The CCTV was the only recording equipment that could record for that duration. It was originally motivated by just a tech problem.

MARTIN O'BRIEN: *The Viewing* came from Bob and Sheree's original version of *The Viewing,* which was supposed to be a posthumous piece where Bob

135

is buried with a video camera in the coffin. So the idea of CCTV was born out of necessity with this project but has a conceptual relationship with the original idea of *The Viewing* where it's a body buried with a single camera.

YH: . . . where the audience is supposed to watch his body deteriorate.

SR: Exactly; he was buried in a Jewish cemetery because he converted to Judaism on his deathbed, so you don't have any embalming, the body's just there: a very natural process of the decomposing. It was Bob's idea conceptually. There's a piece in the movie *Sick* where he talks about being buried with the camera but couldn't get a rich-enough collector to pay for it, but I don't think back in 1996 the technology was capable of doing it and the Jewish cemetery would never have allowed it.

RA: Didn't the Guggenheim give Bob money to execute that project and then revoked it after his death?

SR: He got the Guggenheim but they took it back after he died. They said they couldn't give it to a dead person.

MO: That was one of the things that struck me when I had the residency in 2015 in Sheree's archive at ONE. Sheree and I were going through the archive and there was this idea of the death trilogy and only one of the performances was realized, and that's when Sheree and I started talking about how we might find ways of trying to make the overdue pieces that were missing. In the archive, it felt like a gap, where two performances were planned, *Dust to Dust* and *The Viewing*, that should've been in there but it wasn't possible because Bob died too early and the Guggenheim revoked the fellowship, so it seemed like quite a significant thing to go back and think about how we could make these things that are missing from the archive happen.

SR: The germination of all these pieces was all Bob Flanagan. It was his concept. He was obviously very obsessed with death. But for many years after his death, I did not do much about it. I could not bring myself even to think about it. But once I started working with Martin, it seemed to fall into place because we were doing all these pieces that had to do with Bob in one way or another. He's a very strong presence in my life and Martin's as well. But they evolved: what we did with *Dust to Dust* was not really what Bob had in mind. He had a different idea. It was just going to be a coffin in a room with millions and millions of little photographs of him. No body, no ritual, nothing else. But because I love doing rituals and I had done a ritualistic performance [*Corpse Pose*] with Michael [Griffin], we expanded it.

MO: It was a beautiful thing to be involved with, the realization of performances that didn't get to happen. Finding ways, even in different forms, to try to make something happen out of those original ideas that could otherwise be lost.

RA: I found an extra layer of pressure created creatively because so often when you're making work, you're making work for yourself, but in these situations you have an obligation not only to the people you're collaborating with but [to] someone who's gone. [Bob] doesn't have that voice anymore.

SR: When Bob and I first starting doing work together, he was the performer. I did a few pieces with him, but basically he loved doing as much wildness and craziness as he could do for an audience. He loved it. I really feel that we honored his wishes and even took it to greater depths of experience. I always feel that Bob's spirit is around everything that I do. I sort of check in with him and ask, "do you think Bob would have liked this?" And I think, yeah, he would've. Now the trilogy is coming to an end but I have one more piece [*The Ascension*] I'm doing with Martin that will be a culmination of everything that we've talked about and done in the last few years.

Part of this is Jeffrey Vallance. I give Vallance credit for a lot of this since he was the one who came up with the idea for the St. Bob Flanagan S&M Chapel. But I ran with it as soon as I heard him do that. Everything just worked out. I have Martin here; I didn't think, "what should I do with Martin?" It wasn't like that. Everything was organic in how it developed. Martin is his own person but he is also a manifestation of Bob in the spirit. And what we're doing now, especially [*The Ascension*] I'm doing with Martin in December [2017]—and what I did with him at Spill—is raising that whole idea of Bob as a spiritual presence. The "St." wasn't really a joke. He wasn't a saint, believe me, but the idea was that we're sanctifying him and what he did and his way of seeing life, which was in the face of terrible adversity. Most people would go to bed and not come out again. You overcome whatever the physical and mental limitations are and you create art out of it. Martin, of course, has done that. It is sort of religious but I'm making fun of the religion a little bit. What do you think, Martin, especially with *Sanctuary Ring*?

MO: Over in England, we had this commission from Spill, and [Vallance] took me to places to do the performance and he took me to this church and I thought, "oh my god, this is the place where we have to do it!" I told Sheree that there was this church we might be able to get. And Sheree said, "yes! yes!" As we started working on it, we found out that the church was still consecrated. They said we could do anything we want but we can't be blasphemous.

[Laughter]

SR: Fucking him in the ass in the bathroom of the church is not blasphemous! We had to take off "St. Bob Flanagan." We could not say that; that was what they objected to.

MO: It was really a strange process. That space is already imbued with these ideas of the religious and of spiritual beings. We gave the audience these hymn books, and there was a kind of call and response every time something would start at one end of the church and move toward the altar. There'd be these different stations and actions along the way and, each time we did one, we had a call and response between Sheree and I, and then the audience joined in as well. It went something like, "in honor of Bob, I obey," "in honor of Bob, I submit," "in honor of Bob, I fight sickness with sickness" and everyone said "keep breathing" together. And it became this beautiful catchphrase, "keep breathing," just keep going. It's all about survival. Taking another breath and another. It's the mantra of the St. Bob Flanagan Chapel. You just keep breathing. And it brings a different idea to these BDSM actions we're doing. It's not about violence and aggression but it's life-sustaining.

SR: Life-affirming. Even though Martin doesn't do SM, Bob definitely did, and so we're keeping that aspect of it alive. So it was sexual, yes definitely, but it also had a very big spiritual component.

RA: Martin doesn't practice SM in his life but he does practice durational performance art. In a certain way, I think that's how you got to that elevated state that Bob got to with lifestyle SM. That was your way of compensating to get that adrenaline rush to help deal with the CF. Do you feel like that's accurate? I felt that watching you.

MO: I see performance through ideas of endurance and the acceptance of endurance. The pain-based stuff that we're doing might not necessarily have anything to do with sexual pleasure for me but it's more about enduring these things, going through these things, which is an act of claiming agency over your own body. The idea of submitting to somebody else is a way of taking ownership over bodies. And acceptance of monsters has always been a big thing to me. Disease turns you into a monster of some kind and, often, trying to act normal and be like everybody else is to accept and overly perform.

SR: You embrace your monster.

RA: Everything we do is so much about transvaluation, and I feel that domination, in general, as a woman being in that dominant space, there is a lot of agency in reclaiming your sexuality, your body but also the mechanics of what one's body can do on either side of the SM spectrum.

YH: BDSM eroticism is definitely all about transvaluation and really breaking down what are positive and negative sensations. It's not even about making the negative positive or the positive negative. It's about breaking down the very categories. But what you were discussing earlier makes me think about agency and autonomy and how you're situating illness within that framework because you're all at once in control and losing control. You're in control of not being in control. Can you talk about how you harness that in relationship to performing?

MO: I think submitting and giving control of my body to Sheree or Rhiannon—it's a really different experience than submission to medicine, for example. In submitting to illness, there's no agency, really, where you have to submit in order to survive and stay alive, submit to a medical regime. And illness at any time can burst through and demand that I submit to it. So the act of saying "I'm choosing to submit"—we always begin the performances with a contract that says "I'm choosing to give my body to these people to do whatever they want with"—is where the politics sits, is almost in that contract, in the signing [of] the contract. This is choice, this is this co-created thing as being consensual in relationship to the politics around agency. This is a very different relationship to pain and submission than it is in everyday life for me.

SR: For Bob and I that was an important part of our relationship from the very beginning. We were big fans of Leopold von Sacher-Masoch, who gave the name to masochism. When we read his book *Venus in Furs,* he was very adamant about having contracts. It was important that the contract was there: no one was coercing. It wasn't forcing; it wasn't subterfuge. Everybody knows what's happening and you voluntarily do this because there's a higher purpose to it: whether it's sexual or whether it's just transcending the normal bounds of behavior. But the fact that it is consensual and it is contractual gives it some kind of gravitas in a way that you wouldn't have ordinarily. Bob and I used to think that all relationships should have contracts. We used to have three-month temporary contracts and both people adhere to those rules for three months and, if that doesn't work at the end of the three months, then both parties renegotiate and then maybe go on to a six-month contract. But I think in "normal life" and "normal relationships" that doesn't happen. People go into it and don't really know what they're agreeing to and what they're not agreeing to. And they have fights about that, which causes a lot of disharmony. So for me, personally, it was very political to have these contracts, because otherwise I would never be able to do what I was able to do to Martin if I didn't know if he was fully wanting to do this and agreeing to it.

RA: I also think in the current political atmosphere that that raises very important issues about consent and how straightforward and how easy in certain ways consent can be in situations that aren't sexual necessarily but are still intimate, and I think that statement in terms of how we interact with each other sexually is something really important to be making.

MO: The other thing that the contract does not bullshit around is victimhood. "Oh, poor Martin, victim." This is consensual.

YH: It's a choice. It's also choosing for things not to be scripted, even though the contract does kind of script things in a sense. So there's another reversal there.

SR: It's definitely more complicated at first. It's very political, and Bob even wrote a poem about that. The reason I got into SM in the first place was that it was more political than anything else. I felt as a feminist, as a woman who had been in a normative heterosexual marriage, I saw the flaws of that and I wanted to see it changed, change the whole context. And with Martin, because it's not sexual, it takes it to an even higher level than just sex because we're transcending even the sexual boundaries. I do very sexual things to him sometimes but . . . don't worry, Martin, you're going to be in a bathtub in the gallery and I'm not sure what's going to happen yet.

MO: I remember the last time I was in a bathtub with you. "I'll only thrust up against you." And then, the thrust was her shoving a strap-on straight up my ass.

[Laughter]

SR: Well you have a story you can tell your grandchildren, Martin.

YH: Why don't we talk about some of the specifics of *The Viewing*. All of these pieces are transgressive resurrections. But, just to begin with, I'm interested, how you set it up and some of what went into that because so much about even doing a performance has to do with the idiosyncrasies and quirks of the space, the setup, and everything involved with that.

SR: Rhiannon had a lot to do with that in terms of putting the proposal in for that space. But we didn't really know what that space was going to look like.

RA: Martin did the proposal. I brought the tech.

YH: Can you describe the space?

MO: We had two spaces: one that the audience would inhabit, a black box theater space essentially. A black box space with four walls, and on one wall there was a CCTV screen, which was one big projec-tor screen split into four small screens, and, then, on the other three walls we had six-foot-tall photographs of Bob's corpse that Sheree took, which were close-ups of different parts of his body: his penis, his face, and his chest. And we were in another room completely, which was a very small room—I think it was a changing room

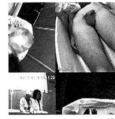

p. 292

or a green room—and we decorated it the way we wanted it. We placed the four cameras—we changed them around quite a lot in the days leading up to it. So we had a coffin, which I lay in for the whole time, and we had a table with all the implements that Sheree and Rhiannon were going to use on me, and we had the four cameras that were fixed in position, looking at different angles on my body, some of which took in the entirety of the coffin and my body, some of which took in the space around as well so they could see the way Sheree and Rhiannon were operating, and some of them which were more close-ups of particular areas. There was one down low near my feet where you can look up and see my ass and scrotum. So that was the physical setup of it, and there's no sound going through. It was just a separate soundtrack playing that the audience heard the whole time. It was Luka who did the soundtrack.

SR: Luka Fisher and Peter Kalisch.

YH: Wasn't it noise-focused?

SR: The video was a zombie and other weird things that Peter did, and Luka took Bob's poem "Why" and added distortion to it. It was quite an elaborate setup. We worked it out so that the 24 hours was in 15-minute segments. Only one 15-minute segment per hour did we actually do something to his body, we did actions to wake him up from being dead. It started out that he's absolutely dead in the coffin. During one 15-minute segment there was nothing—we all had a rest in that time. The other time, the audience could see his body in there and videos going downstairs. Even explaining it is elaborate. People could come as they wanted downstairs and stay as long as they wanted. For each 15-minute segment out of an hour they would see something new that was live. But three quarters of the hour they did not see any live action.

RA: The three-hour stretch when Martin is sleeping is actually quite beautiful. I've been working with the footage in post-production. When we're doing this, you can't really see what's going on to a certain extent. I could

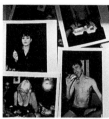

run out and check to make sure that everything was going OK at certain points, but something I noticed that was interesting was [that] with *Philosophy in the Bedroom,* we had the same four channels but it functioned in a very different way with that footage and that mediation. *Philosophy* had more of a sexual, voyeuristic quality behind it, but when you look at the same application in

p. 289

The Viewing, it's very procedural and almost kind of cubist in that it's four ways of breaking down this one procedure. I just felt that, for whatever reason, the way of looking that's related to *Philosophy* in that footage is just something else entirely. Watching that footage of Martin sleeping, there was something eerie about it but also something amazing in that you have that stillness and that black-and-white footage because it drops to the infrared in the dark and just kind of sitting with the body, it is very much like sitting shiva or a traditional idea of a wake, and you just see this little bit of breath every now and then or the clock glowing from the air-conditioning vent and there's a moment where you [speaking to Martin] open your eyes in the morning and the camera has it so that you absolutely look like some undead creature: your eyes are glowing this weird silver color. But that level of mediation adds so much to the piece in a certain way. And I think in some of the pieces, like in *The Viewing*, the work we did on you [speaking to Martin] was quite heavy, and just for Martin's safety that mediation is important because we can't have 250 people breathing on him after he's been cut or pierced or everything else that many times.

SR: Like most of the pieces that I do, it was pretty improvisational. I had all the tools—everything I thought I might need—and I wrote out 24 procedures. I had a basic outline. We started with him being dead, and we took off the shroud that we had on him and sort of woke him up with a little whipping and cutting: it got heavier as we went on but I felt that, often, it was as if we really were doctors. We had our masks on, of course, and our surgical things and gloves, so we were very careful as far as all the hygiene was concerned. So it had that very medical, sterile quality. We're waking him up: the idea was that he's dead but we're doing all these things to him to bring him back to life, which we did and he bit us— you [speaking to Martin] became a vampire.

RA: You bit my boob [speaking to Martin].

[Laughter]

MO: It's 24 hours and, as Sheree said, it's just these one-hour cycles, so for 15 minutes things [are] happening to me and then for the other 45 minutes I'm just lying in the coffin.

SR: Thirty minutes in the coffin, then for 15 minutes you got to get out for a little bit.

MO: Thirty minutes in the coffin and 15 minutes of the video that Peter Kalisch made that interrupted the segments where the audience didn't see me anymore, just this video and 15 minutes of the interactions. It's quite interesting just seeing the body because the body becomes this living corpse where you're simultaneously presenting yourself as a dead body. These moments of seeing me breathing or opening my eyes as both dead and alive or pretending to be dead. I might fall asleep and then I might wake up and I might yawn or cough. For a while you see stillness and then you see something that breaks the deathly image, the cough, the sign of life. The other thing I wanted to mention was when they dressed me up as a zombie.

RA: Oh, yeah, the Dynasty wig!

MO: And there's this thing about Bob: performing this thing that Sheree and Bob conceived of and I felt myself as "Zombie Bob" or something like I am Bob but a younger, zombie version of him. The animation of his corpse.

YH: That's part of what's striking or even terrifying. When I was watching the footage, you'd be dead still and, all of a sudden [speaking to Martin], your arm would move, just slightly. You're breaking the audience's concentration on those kinds of mournful moments. I think that really speaks to some of the fragmentary qualities that you all were talking about earlier in what we're experiencing visually. These fragments of the body operate in terms of how you as the performers are interacting with the audience/viewer for a disruptive—productively disruptive—event.

SR: I think because we're mixing all these different elements: the morbidity of someone who's dead, and the fact that we're sort of desecrating his body, and the voyeuristic aspect of being curious, "What's going to happen to what part of his body next?" And, I think that was why we spent so much time trying to get the angles the way we wanted them so that when you saw this, it wasn't just a straight-on four things: the angles were different, it was very disorienting. We played it at Rhiannon's MFA thesis show and people were really interested in it because it's a way of seeing and viewing that you don't normally do.

RA: There's something that happens in the space of *The Viewing* that I was thinking about when you were talking about the fragmentation of the body, Yetta, in that context when Martin coughs, it's a sign of life, so that in terms of transvaluing that really critical element of CF into something that is affirmative: you're still coughing, you're still breathing. That I found very poignant.

YH: Rather than associate the cough with mortality, it becomes associated with living. There's an exteriority to it, too—the cough is something that [speaking to Martin] you're enacting but itself is ephemeral as a bodily object, beyond what's physically coming through. [Speaking to Sheree and Rhiannon] What were some of the more intriguing things that you did to Martin?

SR: Well, most of it was stuff I had done to Bob or to Martin before, such as the piercing. The stapling was new. At first I was a little frightened of it, but it turned out to be one of the easier things that we did. How did it feel when you were stapled, Martin? Did it hurt a lot?

MO: No, it didn't hurt that much. It wasn't that painful at all.

RA: [Speaking to Martin] You were anxious about it. With everything else, there was no anxiety but when I got that stapler out . . .

SR: Well, this was a medical stapler. People in SM have done stapling before, and a friend of mine, Diana Torres—Diana Pornoterrorista—did a performance where she used an actual stapler, not a medical one. She would staple little notes to her body, all over her body in the performance, so I always remembered that, how intense that was. And there was another video that I was involved with where Luka Fisher stapled something to someone's chest, so it's been done; it's not so unusual. But it's different because it's not like a medical procedure, but we mixed everything into it. It was mostly whatever felt interesting to me as long as I had my toolbox there. It was almost like doing an abstract painting: I just spontaneously figured out what I wanted to do.

YH: So the stapling was something you didn't do with Bob. What were some of things you did do with Bob, and what would you say were the distinctions or similarities when doing them with Martin?

SR: The piercing with needles. That was a big thing that Bob and I were very into and the cross-dressing, which was lovely.

RA: You did cut an *S* into him.

YH: What about some other memorable procedures from the performances, unexpected moments?

RA: Well, this was the first time I had ever sutured anyone. And that was the first time you had ever been sutured, right, Martin? Or had you tried it on your own?

MO: In *Sanctuary Ring*, it was the first time we sewed up my scrotum.

SR: That wasn't very successful [laughs]; I remember we had some trouble with that . . .

RA: I was able to get one stitch in. Bob was so stretched out from having to use the parachute all those years, so it was probably an easier stitch. Martin's body is not the same. Learning to suture on the fly was a fascinating experience for me. But also this was the first time I had ever done any heavy medical SM on someone with CF. The CF body is a very different body; the tissue structure is different. The bleeding is not as excessive in a lot of ways, and I noticed, Martin, that you clot a lot faster than anyone else I've ever worked on. I came to the realization that that's what enabled Sheree and Bob do such extreme things is that the CF body is an extraordinary body.

SR: The CF body is very accustomed to extreme medical intervention. Many of Bob's SM activities stem from things he remembered having been done to him when he was a child. It became normalized in a way for him, and that's how he sexualized a lot of it, because he had no choice but to endure the medical procedures for his health. Bob would talk about being in tubs of cold water to bring down his temperature. Did you have to deal with that, too, Martin?

MO: They didn't do that to me. But during the performance, particularly in the morning, I had these really strong memories of being a kid in a hospital: a similar fear of just lying in this bed with these horrible lights on me and waking up with the sound of nurses and doctors outside the room clattering around, and Sheree and Rhiannon took on that role in trying to figure out what to do next. I was just waiting for it to happen: knowing that they're going to come into the room but not knowing what they're going to do to you and just waiting . . . I had this strong . . . I can't really explain it: just a feeling of that space, the smell of it: being in that hospital space, that medical space and it was similar. The idea of waiting for something to happen.

YH: You're never alone and in this sterile environment. You're never waking up in a comfortable space; you're waking up in an anticipatory space and your entire being might seem crowded out in a sense.

SR: That's what makes the performance so intriguing, though, is the spontaneity. I don't know exactly what I'm going to do. I can change my mind in the moment. As a performer, that's how I like to work. If I had to work with a strict script, I would probably get nervous. I like having the freedom instead. The medical context and uncertainty of it made it more poignant, I think.

RA: You did have a pretty structured list of what you wanted to do to him, and I remember in hour 14 or something, you said, "Scrap it all, we're going to start again," and Martin had a whole new element of surprise to contend with, listening to us hatching our plot from the coffin and trying to stay really still.

MO: When I was awake, I would be able to hear them say things like, "Should we do this?" "No, no . . ." "OK, let's staple and then . . ."

SR: And he had no say in it whatsoever.

YH: Martin, did you almost want to know what they were going to do next, or . . . ?

MO: The anticipation is always worse when you can hear what's going on and the stapler, for instance, looked so dramatic. It's not actually very painful when it's being done to you but it looked really scary. The worst was being woken up by it. It was like a horror film. [Laughter]

SR: Well, it was a horror film!

YH: They were nice enough to do that rather than just prod you with the tools!

RA: I remember that look of terror you had when we were testing the stapler. Until I got it into your arm and we squeezed the trigger you had a look of shock that that's all it was. As a professional Dominatrix who lived a double life for most of my life, being in this art space that was also an SM space but that was desexualized in a certain way and that transactional element that is usually in my Domination was taken away, I found that performance space was extraordinary for all of those reasons. It is impossible to replicate a normal world.

YH: What about the audience?

SR: We had no idea. We were so isolated. Rhiannon, you went out a couple of times to see what was happening. People wrote things about it, but to this day I don't really know what they thought about it. Very few people stayed the whole 24 hours.

RA: We got the audience metrics back and I did go over them. We did have that one from the director of *Assisted Suicide: The Musical,* who said, "This doesn't address disability as well as *Assisted Suicide: The Musical."*

MO: I never heard anything about this . . .

SR: She got more money for her piece than we did.

MO: She's kind of a celebrity in the UK.

RA: One of them went something like, "It talks about disability and sexuality in a very important way, that the disabled body could still be desirable." I think our total audience count for that was close to 200 because the trains were cancelled the second day, so it did drop the attendance quite a bit from what they anticipated.

YH: People could just come in and out and stay as long as they wanted, kind of like Christian Marclay's *The Clock.*

SR: I think, too, that it wasn't easy to be there. There weren't enough chairs to sit around, or comfortable chairs. Thinking about it now, the audience setup would have made it more conducive to people staying longer. But we didn't do that.

RA: Well, we did it when we did the screening [of the CCTV footage at California State University, Long Beach]. I spent months looking for those chairs and had to source them from 6 or 7 Targets to get enough for the audience, but that was something discussed quite extensively: how does the viewer's body function in this space.

YH: I sat in one of those chairs at the screening and they were very conducive to staying. Can you describe the chairs, again?

RA: They were the bungee chairs. Octagonal disc chairs.

SR: We did not have that in the audience space in Liverpool. Those were just for the screening. If we had had those kinds of chairs or thought about that aspect, we might have had a larger audience, maybe.

RA: Those chairs were selected because I looked at one and sat down in it in the store and thought, oh man, it's really hard to get out of this chair. It's kind of like a quiet bondage method almost, and I've been doing a lot of thinking and some writing about how mainstream commercial culture is co-opting a lot of the BDSM aesthetic: you go into Target and you see these black chairs made out of knotted bungee cords. I have other things in my toy chest at home that are not a chair that look exactly like that.

SR: Let's talk a little bit about *Philosophy in the Bedroom*. Bob and I talked about this very early on in our relationship of doing performances. Privately, we liked to do 24-hour things where Bob would be in bondage for 24 hours, for example. But we had the idea of being in a bed—just the two of us—and people would come and go and they would bring us food and we would fuck or do whatever we wanted to do, but not get out of the bed, not even get up to go to the bathroom. We'd just stay in the bed for 24 hours. We wanted to get a rubber sheet and that would be the piece and we'd do it in a hotel or something like that. Why we never did it, I don't know. We talked about it a lot but we never realized it. I love the idea of it: being that vulnerable for 24 hours and inviting people to come in and see that.

RA: After I met Sheree, she said that she had been looking for someone to do this piece with her and no one would do it with her and would I do it with her and I said, of course, because coming out of the sex industry and pro-Domination industry, that interaction of inviting people in after some negotiation for an hour to do whatever it is they wanted with me was something that was really part of my daily life that I wanted to talk about on a creative level. We started working on it and heard that Martin was coming in to town, so we moved the date so that Martin could come, too. The first time that Martin and I had ever met was when we made this piece together, which was a very intense first meeting—I think we pioneered some kind of speed-dating process: just lock them in a room together for 24 hours and expose them to massive amounts of flying Cheetos and piercing [laughter].

SR: The genius of it was the fact that we had people write to us and tell us what they wanted to do for the hour. That wasn't exactly my idea. That was Dawn Kasper, who did a piece several years ago in which she invited people to come to her Santa Monica hotel room for one hour and you had to tell her what you wanted to do. If you were admitted, you were one of the 24. I loved that piece. I took a bubble bath with her. We had such a good time. It was all videotaped but I never saw the footage of it. So when I got together with Rhiannon, we talked about SM, and I thought this is going to be perfect, let's do it. I'll give Dawn that because I saw her do it. Bob and I weren't planning to invite people to come do things with us. We were just going to stay in the bed, sleeping, watching television, fucking, and just never leave the bed while people could just come and go.

SR: *Philosophy in the Bedroom* turned out to be far less sexual than we thought it was going to be.

RA: The only people who did anything remotely sexual was when Cassils came in with Trinity and others and dominated us. Someone fucked me with a strap-on.

MO: This one was interesting because you keep forgetting that you're being watched. There was a lack of live audience in the space.

SR: I'm turned on by the whole idea of being in motels, but I really wish the whole thing were sexier.

RA: At a few points we became the audience for some of the people who came in. Dulcinea Circelli, who came in with a very large man who had used breast pumps and penis pumps, wearing a Trump mask. Dulcinea proceeded to stab him, and fake blood splattered everywhere, and then to castrate him.

YH: This was on the bed?

RA: Yes, a lot of these blurred the dynamic between audience and performer.

SR: A lot of people were on the bed throughout the 24 hours.

YH: Any final statements you want to include about the performances?

MO: It all feels bigger than the performances, a way of connecting with the lineage of illness and Sheree, Rhiannon, and I making work with the specter of Bob hanging around.

The Viewing

Supermasochism and Sanctification

RHIANNON AARONS

See Breathing Space, *The Viewing*, and *Dust to Dust* image galleries.

This excerpt is taken from the program that attendees received for The Viewing, *commissioned by DaDaFest, and has been edited for this volume.*

Prior to his death, Flanagan and Rose conceived of three major pieces that were designated the *Memento Mori* death trilogy, "involving three different casket installations—*Video Coffin, Dust to Dust,* and *The Viewing*— (grappling) with Flanagan's own mortality through technologies of representation that produce his body in relation to ours, projecting his image / his body outward to those who engage with the piece. In *Video Coffin* (1994) the head of a casket (decorated with icons of death such as bullets and body parts) is laid open to show a text ('I was promised an early death but here I am, some forty years later, still waiting') and to expose a video monitor with a loop of Flanagan's face" (Jones 703).

After Flanagan's death Rose took a lengthy hiatus from her performance practice in order to grieve the immense loss of her partner and collaborator. The *Memento Mori* death trilogy lay fallow until 2015, when O'Brien acted as the catalyst for its completion. *Dust to Dust* emerged from O'Brien's residency at ONE National Gay and Lesbian Archives, Los Angeles. During this time he worked with Sheree Rose, going through her archive. The performance was a response to this process and involved staging the second part of the death trilogy originally conceived by Rose and Bob Flanagan. They were only able to realize the first of the trilogy, and so *Dust to Dust* became an addressing of something missing from the archive (O'Brien).

The Viewing is the last installment of this trilogy. Described as "almost impossible to fathom in its original formulation, [. . .] the piece was to document the decomposition of Flanagan's body through the placement of a video camera in his coffin underground. The camera would be hooked into a monitor placed in a gallery or other public place, to be accessed at will by visitors apprised of its 'contents'" (Jones 704). It could not be completed in its original format because of intense logistical obstacles. However, in fundamental concept, "*The Viewing* [. . .] proposes an nth-degree interrogation of the relationship of the body to the self: for it is only in death that the body is stripped of its inexorable role as instantiation of the cogito. [. . .] At the same time, we might also become acutely aware that Flanagan does still 'exist' in and through the others who have engaged him (in particular, Rose), marking the contingency and embeddedness of the self on/in the other" (Jones 704).

While Flanagan and Rose's BDSM performances "focused on eroticism" (Johnson 111), with O'Brien and Rose the relationship is "purist."[1] Their interaction speaks to the relevance of BDSM as cultural necessity and a vital component of learning to renegotiate the predominant cultural programming related to pain in allopathic medicine. While BDSM is typically portrayed as sexual in mass media, the actual reasons that people gravitate toward BDSM can be anything from strictly meditative practices to acclimating to life after cancer. "In this context the sexual gratification usually associated with s/m is removed as the body is examined, treated, mutilated, humiliated, laughed at and cared for. Sufferance is used as a way of examining the sick body as a body negotiating its position at the limits of human corporeality" (O'Brien).

Several critical principles of BDSM mirror holistic medicine tropes that have been historically overlooked in conventional allopathic medicine: fighting like with like, building a controlled relationship with pain, and use of the biofeedback loop (Lamaze breathing is the most common example of using the biofeedback loop for pain management). The technique of "fighting sickness with sickness"—or treating "pain with pain," "like with like"—is a core tenet in many holistic techniques that are gaining legitimate traction within the medical community. Andrew Weil and Peter

---

1. Within the SM community, individuals who participate in SM for reasons other than sexual gratification are known as "purist players."

Fields fight inflammation pain with controlled inflammation—through the more conventional bee sting, apitherapy (Weil), or the more modern prolotherapy regime (OrthoRegen). The science behind this rests on causing temporary inflammation, which triggers the body to send additional platelets and other healing compounds to the injury site in response to the artificial stimulation; once the apatoxin or proliferent is absorbed by the body, the healing elements remain to treat the pre-existing injury. This also supports the metaphor used by Burroughs in *Junky*, in which he cites experiments where worms forced to constantly regenerate pieces removed from their body attain greater longevity.

Another primary focus of allopathic medicine is the denial of pain. Tylenol, Advil, OxyContin, Vicodin—the list of painkillers available in contemporary civilization is virtually endless. Native American, African Tribal, Shia Muslim, and Hindu cultures all possess ritualized mechanisms for enduring pain. Hook suspension, ritual scarification, self-flagellation, and ritual piercing (respectively) have sanctioned niches within these cultures (Musafar). Learning to endure, process, and transvalue pain is given proper space as a process of enlightenment and prospective source of compassion for the suffering of others. For those with chronic pain, one could imagine that heavy BDSM is likely to have the same impact on physical pain that exposure therapy has on posttraumatic stress disorder (US Department of Veterans Affairs). By fully engaging with pain, rather than avoiding it, it is possible to learn methods by which it can be better managed.

While people participate in BDSM for a variety of reasons—from sexual to cathartic—the ultimate goal of any BDSM encounter is to obtain the meditative space that occurs during the act and then reap the positive benefits of the endorphin rush that follows; one cannot come about without the other. The meditative state—termed by the community as "sub space"—occurs as the body begins to acclimate to systematically increasing levels of pain as administered by the top.

On the hour and for a period of twenty-four hours total, Rose, assisted by artist and Dominatrix Rhiannon Aarons, performed a series of consensual BDSM acts on O'Brien. Through this meditative space of controlled pain and endurance, O'Brien became enabled to experience intense personal and spiritual transformation—a metaphorical death—in a touching tribute to his creative influence and muse, Bob Flanagan.

Works Cited

Johnson, Dominic. *The Art of Living: An Oral History of Performance Art.* Palgrave Macmillan, 2015.

Jones, Amelia. "Dispersed Subjects and the Demise of 'The Individual': 1990s Bodies In/As Art." *The Visual Culture Reader,* edited by Nicholas Mirzoeff, Routledge, 2013, pp. 696–709.

Musafar, Fakir. "Suspensions and Tensions." *BME/Modblog,* 15 Jan. 2005. https://news.bme.com/?s=suspensions+and+tensions&submit=Search

O'Brien, Martin. https://www.martinobrienart.com/

OrthoRegen. n.d. http://www.drfields.com/Articles/Prolotherapy-Research/Lower-Back

US Department of Veterans Affairs. http://www.ptsd.va.gov/public/treatment/therapy-med/prolonged-exposure-therapy.asp

Weil, Andrew. n.d. http://www.drweil.com/health-wellness/body-mind-spirit/autoimmune-disorders/rheumatoid-arthritis/

PART 3

PERFORMATIVE WRITING

Oatmeal and Shit

Some Notes on Mundanity

MARY ANN DAVIS

> Ordinary, commonplace. Hence: prosaic, dull, humdrum; lacking interest
> or excitement.
>
> —"mundane, 1. c." *Oxford English Dictionary*

> The dull bill paying and office filing
> can't compete with my rubber underwear
> but it needs to be done to organize
> and make life smooth like my shiny black ass.
>
> —Bob Flanagan, poem, February 27, 1985, lines 13–17

> In this performance, Martin will live in the cage for twenty-four hours.
> There will be specific actions at various times, some dictated by the audi-
> ence, some prearranged by Rose. The actions range from the bizarre to
> the mundane. There will be time for resting, eating, and bodily functions.
> There will be periods of boredom.
>
> —description of "*Do with Me as You Will / Make Martin Suffer for Art,*"
> Los Angeles, June 23–24, 2013

Down at the ONE Archives—hot as fuck—un-autumn of October in Los
Angeles. City on fire, you think, and fall in love and pleasure just a little
bit more with it all, the sprawl. Like being held in a god's open hand, you
think.

You have history with the ONE: You were here in 2005 for a graduate conference, on your own; you were here, with the person you called "Daddy," in 2010, maybe 2011, to attend a roundtable featuring Gayle Rubin (you spoke to her about your writing on erotic power in Victorian novels, she gave you her card, which you carried around in your wallet for a while, then it went into a file, then you lost it when you took too much time to leave the person you called "Daddy").

You were here, on your own again, in 2015, to see a performance with Sheree Rose and Martin O'Brien. *Dust to Dust*, you remember. You were moving on from the person you called "Daddy," immersing yourself in a daily-ness of your own making. Now you're here looking for signs of the mundane in the infamous, the death-defying relationship between Sheree Rose and Bob Flanagan. Because you know the depths of the tension between reality and fantasy in BDSM practice, and you've been ruminating on how the mundane circulates between the two.

*

> July 13, c. 1970s, one of Bob Flanagan's many journals:
> *It's not just the pain I want, there has to be an atmosphere
> of eroticism, of decadence, of meanness, of sincerity, of
> understanding, of control. Without some of these things it's
> more like having a headache or toothache.*[1]

Those everyday, annoying pains. Take an aspirin; go to the dentist. What does eroticism bring to pain? An attention to sensation, to sensuality—suffering with intention. And further: eroticism brings a consciousness to relationality (even if to the self)—someone to be mean, sincere, and understanding, someone to exercise control.

Karmen MacKendrick, in *counterpleasures*, describes the relationality of topping and bottoming as one of "responsive receptivity" (127). In the ethics of this relation, bottoms exercise their power by being radically open to ceding control and responsive to the attention from Tops. Tops exercise their power by being radically open to taking control and receiving responses from the bottom. Tops give attention and bottoms give response; Tops give commands and bottoms give control.

---

1. I have corrected all spelling errors in the quotations from materials in the Bob Flanagan and Sheree Rose collection at the ONE National Gay and Lesbian Archives at the University of Southern California Libraries. Many thanks to the folks at the ONE, especially Loni Shibuyama, Bud Thomas, and Michael C. Oliveira.

Both sides of the power exchange are a giving, even in the taking. And so does the giving render the pain less mundane?

*

Finally—there—first mention of the Mistress:

> November 28, 1980. *Sheree. Mistress Sheree. I think about her all the time. . . . . I am totally submissive to her. She is the kind of woman I have fantasized about all my life. But this is no fantasy. This is no game. It's the real thing. I am giving myself to her completely. I want to do whatever she wants me to do . . .*

Followed by, in swift, unsurprising succession, the erosion of, the impossibility of fantasy:

> November 30, 1980: *I want to put all the fantasies in here. And then I want to put the real life in here also. I'm at a point where the real life is becoming more important than the fantasy. I think I mean more exciting.*

> January 1, 1981: *Gotta take the good with the bad. It's not real otherwise.*

> January 15, 1982: *[S]he wants me to do the laundry but she was even ambivalent about that, about telling me to do it. I hate her ambivalence more than anything. I'll do anything she says to do. I'll accept anything I have to accept—but ambivalence is the hardest thing of all.*

About seven years of more or less consistent journaling, through which Bob struggles to reconcile his fantasies of living in a 24/7 Mistress/slave (M/s) relationship with the realities of living in romantic partnership with someone. The mundane enters hard, here, painfully, here.

You know the abyss that exists between fantasy and reality for BDSM practitioners, more than for relationships without consensual eroticized power exchange. A harder reality-check. So you're generalizing. But you've read too much, seen too much, been to too many munches and roundtables. And you lived with the person you called "Daddy" for close to eight years, with too few moments of BDSM fantasy made flesh. Something was always in the way, usually involving paying bills, raising her kids, getting chores done, getting a PhD.

You remember thinking, at the time, the many times, a chorus in your head: *Just call me babygirl and I'll be fine.*

Bob writes, February 26, 1985: *Being referred to / as slave is enough for me.*

At clearer, angrier times, you think: *You promised consistency in control and guidance, but where is it?*

So you don't give a fuck about generalizing. Reality is hard to face when you're attempting to make fantasy real.

*

MacKendrick's *counterpleasures* is dedicated to Bob Flanagan.

And this—which causes your laugh-out-loud pleasure in the archive— this discovery, many file folders later: Karmen MacKendrick has written a card to Bob Flanagan and Sheree Rose.

Oh, the small circles of our intentional, intensive pleasures.

*
*
*

Reality. Fantasy. Where does mundanity fit, in relation to this dialectic?

Erotics *of* the mundane; eroticizing *the* mundane. Yes—the mundane can be seen in BDSM performances and scenes (it can be eroticized). N.B. all the mundane elements of Bob Flanagan's *Visiting Hours*, the deliberate invocation of the mundane and of tedium in Sheree's construction of the performance-scene with Martin O'Brien. Yet focusing on the mundane (as in the everyday and ordinary) also draws our attention beyond the exceptional/spectacular moment of scene/performance.

*

Beginning to realize Bob's own boundaries around his journals were permeable. Yes, of course, with *Fuck Journal* (1982) and *The Pain Journal* (2000). But here is 1985, where he writes a poem nearly every day. Many of these will get reworked and published the next year, in *Slave Sonnets*.

And everywhere the ordinary and the everyday. These poems of 1985 are often about writing, serving, staying alive, the struggle to do all of these at once. They tread an abyss between the Mistress's inconsistent attention and her consistent expectation that he take care of their everyday life, her everyday comforts.

January 5, 1985:

> *I want to make sense;*
> *at least I don't want to lose sight again:*
> *my writing, my servitude, work and health.*
> *Speaking of that, hey, listen, Babes, I'm off.*
> *Gotta make my Mistress some tea and breathe*
> *some medicine for a while, pound my chest,*
> *spit up green slime and put this day to rest.*
> (lines 22–28)

This poem begins as "a strictly journalistic approach / without passion and without imagery / but still maintaining proper discipline" (lines 1–3). The discipline described in the last lines, above, is one of balance. It is a discipline vectored through mundane imagery: making tea for the Mistress (servitude) and performing breathing treatments (health, which is also for the speaker a sort of enslavement to the illness, self-servitude). So the discipline through attending to the mundane gets him closer to his writing and his submission? Or the mundane, the daily-ness, is a place to begin? Or it grounds, because it is always there?

*

January 12, 1985:

> *What I have to say today will be said*
> *with couplets, two line summations of thought.*
> *Disciplinarian that I yearn for*
> *force me to eat oatmeal and nothing more.*
> . . . .
> *The words don't even matter anymore*
> *it's the act I care about, and the form.*
> *The content is: I'm content to be here,*
> *a vessel to be filled with your liquid.*
> *Goddamn it, no one can understand this.*
> *A man who wants to be your furniture?*
> . . . . *and what about the shit?*
> *Could Shakespeare describe a plate of your shit*

any better than I, and if so, why?
To take what is thoroughly disgusting
to most folks and make it acceptable.
Waste, all of a sudden, is savable.
What you give up to me I will savor.
(lines 1–4; 25–30; 32–38)

Oatmeal and shit. Mundane and extreme. The speaker invokes "force" to describe eating nothing but oatmeal (4). And this is in fact what Bob does for four months. Nothing but oatmeal. Other restrictions are repeated, such as sleeping in a tiger cage that the Mistress acquired. But eating oatmeal and eating shit are running themes, handled with two different tones: forced to eat oatmeal, allowed to eat his Mistress's shit.

What food is more mundane than oatmeal? The food of the people, the grain that fed livestock before it started to feed peasants. Mild, even bland, lacking in shape but not texture, prone to turning to mush or to congealing, slick, even slimy. Fed to children and the elderly. Full of fiber, ideal for regular shits. What an interesting mouthfeel.

*

January 25, 1985:
While it's true that sometimes I eat her shit,
I'm always the one left who gets the shit.
And boy, do I . . . .
no matter how much work I've done for her
there is no joy or appreciation.
Ah, shut up and shove oatmeal down your throat
before you get yourself into trouble
saying something you'll regret, a lifetime
of oatmeal for you if you don't watch out.
(lines 11–20)

Two kinds of shit, here: the physical gift from the Mistress and the affective shit of the Mistress's lack of acknowledgment.

Really, you think, Bob should know better: a Mistress is only obligated to give attention, which may sometimes take the form of an acknowledgment, but not always and not guaranteed. The heart of service must not be sustained by the desire for acknowledgment.

*
*
*

Thinking of intensity and intensifications, today. Here are threads you have gathered, in your endless reading:

1886: Austrian sexologist Richard von Krafft-Ebing, who coined the terms 'sadism' and 'masochism,' describes sadism as a process of "react[ing] on the object with the greatest intensity" (84).

1999: Karmen MacKendrick, again in *counterpleasures*, describes the pleasures that bottoms experience as "not gratification . . . but intensification" (126).

2008: Andrea Zanin, on her blog *Sex Geek*, describes BDSM practices as "an intensified form of communication, trust, and intimacy."

2015: Sinclair Sexsmith's boy, rife, while discussing the fantasies and realities of a 24/7 Dominant-submissive relationship, states: "But when I imagine that kind of intensity every day, I kind of lose my boner for it."

Intensity, intensified, intensification—day after day of poems full of oatmeal and shit, much more of the former than the latter. You understand that intensity in BDSM is not necessarily a relinquishment of the mundane, but sometimes an intensification of attention *to* it.

The dialectic between the mundane and the extreme loosens. Does not the mundane act of only eating oatmeal become extreme, when carried out over the course of four months? Is not shit mundane? Certainly it is sublunary—all of those things under the moon, not celestial. "Characteristic of this world and its concerns; mundane; material; temporal, ephemeral" (*OED*). But as something abject it approaches the sublime (Kristeva, you believe, talks about this). As something emerging from his Mistress's body, it is always treasured.

Desire for the extreme—and delivered by someone with authority and attention—transforms anything, including the ordinary and everyday, into the sublime. Or not transformation, but sublimation of the ordinary and everyday. Or not sublimation, but eroticization. Because a key pleasure of BDSM is the mundane *as* mundane.

*
*
*

You, you're realizing, are deeply biased. Everywhere in the journals you see pieces of the person you called "Daddy" alongside threads of your own anger.

Your desires were so different from Bob's: never the extreme pain or humiliation, pushing the body to its edges of living in order to laugh at death. You, you wanted consistent training in how to be a girl, how to properly serve, someone to say *good girl* or *bad girl* from a place of clearly enumerated expectations and proper evidence in support of any infractions. But like all s-types, the core desire is the same: attention from the one to whom control is ceded. *Don't ignore me, don't forget me, don't leave me.*

So you are deeply predisposed to read Bob's dissatisfaction as a problem with the mastery exercised by the Mistress. You forget that, even with attention, sometimes submission is just a struggle.

> January 26, 1985:
> *Enough with this silly putty, butt plug,*
> *cock ring, oatmeal, penises and movies.*
> *I've got to get some sleep. Work tomorrow,*
> *and a growing list of things to be done.*
> *And the day was blank and nice with Matthew*
> *away watching the Super Bowl, his mom fucking me in the ass with a*
> * dildo*
> *after we fuck, me not allowed to come.*
> *. . . . . The Moustache*
> *Café where I get to watch everyone*
> *scarfing down food but I'm still on oatmeal.*
> *And I'm getting cranky about it too,*
> *even though I'm supposed to be submissive,*
> *I want food. Tuesday in Vegas, maybe.*
> *Now I need sleep. No oatmeal. No nothin'.* (lines 1–8, 10–16)

Yes, even with attention, sometimes submission is just hard. Thus the lack of shit, the blankness of things. Not even oatmeal at the end, that mundane sublimity. *No nothin'.*

*

You still cook oatmeal the way the person you called "Daddy" directed: a cinnamon stick and a splash of vanilla extract, slowly boil down, stir frequently, remove from heat and let stand covered for the last five minutes.

You could never get the eggs right, however. It's a wonder you can still eat them.

*

> February 26, 1985:
> *Napping after a few chores and oatmeal*
> *til the Mistress calls and pokes me a bit*
> *about 'publishing' the sonnets as is*
> *but I'm not ready and there's yet more work.*
> *Cleaning; laundry; take it personally*
> *when the Mistress talks about how mundane*
> *it all is. While I'm working up a sweat*
> *she just wants to get away from it all.*
> (lines 17–28)

Bob is always doing laundry. Did the Mistress pay attention?

You remember a phone conversation with peri, who tells you about the beginnings of her Master/slave relationship with Ma'am: An evening, some really good play. peri's omnipresent laugh turns low, pleasure-ful. *Really* good play. She calls Ma'am the next day, asks to come over. Ma'am assumes for more play (those insatiable s-types) but peri says, *No, that's okay. I just want to do your laundry.* Such laughter over the phone line.

*

Someone to pay attention. Someone to give attention, to be more accurate, if you are breaking from the pressures of productive pleasure, the give and take. Just giving and giving, even in the taking.

Tonight, for example. You left the archive early, exhausted from immersion in someone else's emotional life, familiar yet not. Too familiar. You've been holed up in your rented room, shades drawn against the relentless light, fan whirring, boxes of Thai food spread around you.

Your davey-boi awaits an email from you, to arrange your quarterly extended play, to occur upon your return from LA. So different from Bob and his Mistress, this relationship: you are lovers and housemates, 24/7. You have a rich BDSM switching relationship at varying levels of intensity and varying periods of time—most certainly not 24/7—detailed at length in your eight-page contract, which has taken you over a year to write together and which you still haven't signed.

Too much life has been in the way, of late. Too much reality. Your boi needs attention, he needs your firm and exacting tone over email, as you lay out your expectations for a scene. The details are intensely mundane: *. . . You will take a shower first, then retire to our room to complete getting ready. No earlier than 10:45 and no later than 11:00 am, you will knock twice on my door when you are ready, then retreat downstairs, sit on a cushion on the floor, facing the couch. Cross your legs, keep your eyes closed, and remember to sit up straight. . . .*

But the pleasure of writing out these instructions lessens the hold of reality. The pleasure of spending time with the mundane details, drawing them out to exacting degrees that demand the attention of your boi—an attention that you then turn to your boi, in scene, to see how well he follows your direction, accepts your random and somewhat arbitrary control . . .

Your focus, your sustained attention:

The way you hold your hands clasped in front of you, waiting for your boi to complete some task.

The effort to turn your body away after giving direction, trusting that he will complete the task, ready to respond if he doesn't.

The way you step up close to him, telling him to avert his eyes, to stand erect, arms folded behind his back, and proceed to question him about a flaw in his response or his carriage.

The way you pace pain, slow down and drawn back your own eagerness to inflict, to generate response, run your hands over the flaming wings you have given him on his back, once, twice, thrice, feeling for his temperature, subtle shaking, the general state of his flesh.

There is no sleep quite like the sleep after being dominant.

So you write to your boi.

*
*
*

You're beginning to think that the journals of others should never be read by others.

Because you can't hear from the others invoked within the journals of others. And so you don't know what's real, what's true.

You realize, in encountering the journals of others, that questions of reality or truth miss the point. The point can only be what is on the page.

In this case, Bob struggled again and again with the Mistress's feelings of ambivalence and her sometimes-absent attention, struggled with a reality/fantasy dialectic.

The other dialectic, extremity/mundanity, shit and oatmeal, does not align with reality or fantasy.

*

March 15, 1985:
Padlocks and oatmeal.
(line 4)

March 16, 1985:
Darkness, thunder, rain, lightning, lots of sleep
for a change, touching myself, my nipples,
wishing someone else would—but excited
too cause no one does—the life of a slave.
Mild sadness today. Because it's Sunday?
Because it's raining? Because she's not here?
(She's never here, even when she is here.)
Cause I'm lost in the midst of these changes?
All this deprivation's gone to my head.
Nothing in there anymore but oatmeal.
Sad oatmeal. Lonely oatmeal. Oatmeal that
wants something but it ain't gonna get it.

This is your favorite of Bob's poems from 1985. Nearly a sonnet. Bob alone. Bob without shit. Bob alone with himself, alone with the months of sleeping in a cage, penis padlocked, only oatmeal. Bob the slave who has transformed into the materials of his submission, into oatmeal.

*
*
*

Time to leave this place of extremes, your Los Angeles, to head back to the Midwest. You're bored, there. It's tedious, there.

You read *Slave Sonnets* on the plane ride home. They have nothing to say about oatmeal, and only the last two mention eating shit. You're not surprised, given what seems to be a tendency to present the most extreme forms of their M/s relationship to the public.

It makes for a good show, you know.

You can't help but to return to an obsession:

A line from anthropologist Margot Weiss's *Techniques of Pleasure: BDSM and the Circuits of Sexuality*, which comes after she has described a demonstration scene enacted during a workshop on "Playing with Taboos": "I suspected that [the scene] was too mundane to make good erotic drama" (213). The scene itself is not important, right now. Rather the reminder that BDSM play tends to be viewed through the framework of drama or performance, which does not quite capture the fullness of BDSM scenes. You suspect it is a perspective too embedded in the position of outsiders to a scene, outsiders to *the* scene. Too invested in beginnings and endings, in the proscenium of normative desire. The recurring question: *From inside the scene, would the mundane be "too mundane"?*

*
*
*

Works Cited

Flanagan, Bob. "Journal Entry." 13 July 197?. Box 1, Folder 1. Bob Flanagan and Sheree Rose Collection. ONE National Gay and Lesbian Archives, University of Southern California Libraries, Los Angeles, CA. 19 Oct. 2017.

——. "Journal Entry." 28 November 1980. Box 1, Folder 12. Bob Flanagan and Sheree Rose Collection. ONE National Gay and Lesbian Archives, University of Southern California Libraries, Los Angeles, CA. 19 Oct. 2017.

——. "Journal Entry." 30 November 1980. Box 1, Folder 12. Bob Flanagan and Sheree Rose Collection. ONE National Gay and Lesbian Archives, University of Southern California Libraries, Los Angeles, CA. 19 Oct. 2017.

——. "Journal Entry." 1 January 1981. Box 1, Folder 12. Bob Flanagan and Sheree Rose Collection. ONE National Gay and Lesbian Archives, University of Southern California Libraries, Los Angeles, CA. 19 Oct. 2017.

——. "Journal Entry." 15 January 1982. Box 1, Folder 13. Bob Flanagan and Sheree Rose Collection. ONE National Gay and Lesbian Archives, University of Southern California Libraries, Los Angeles, CA. 19 Oct. 2017.

——. "Untitled Poem." 5 January 1985. Box 2, Folder 2. Bob Flanagan and Sheree Rose Collection. ONE National Gay and Lesbian Archives, University of Southern California Libraries, Los Angeles, CA. 19 Oct. 2017.

——. "Untitled Poem." 12 January 1985. Box 2, Folder 2. Bob Flanagan and Sheree Rose Collection. ONE National Gay and Lesbian Archives, University of Southern California Libraries, Los Angeles, CA. 19 Oct. 2017.

——. "Untitled Poem." 25 January 1985. Box 2, Folder 2. Bob Flanagan and Sheree Rose Collection. ONE National Gay and Lesbian Archives, University of Southern California Libraries, Los Angeles, CA. 19 Oct. 2017.

——. "Untitled Poem." 26 January 1985. Box 2, Folder 2. Bob Flanagan and Sheree Rose Collection. ONE National Gay and Lesbian Archives, University of Southern California Libraries, Los Angeles, CA. 19 Oct. 2017.

——. "Untitled Poem." 27 February 1985. Box 2, Folder 3. Bob Flanagan and Sheree Rose Collection. ONE National Gay and Lesbian Archives, University of Southern California Libraries, Los Angeles, CA. 19 Oct. 2017.

——. "Untitled Poem." 5 March 1985. Box 2, Folder 4. Bob Flanagan and Sheree Rose Collection. ONE National Gay and Lesbian Archives, University of Southern California Libraries, Los Angeles, CA. 19 Oct. 2017.

——. "Untitled Poem." 11 March 1985. Box 2, Folder 4. Bob Flanagan and Sheree Rose Collection. ONE National Gay and Lesbian Archives, University of Southern California Libraries, Los Angeles, CA. 19 Oct. 2017.

——. "Untitled Poem." 15 March 1985. Box 2, Folder 4. Bob Flanagan and Sheree Rose Collection. ONE National Gay and Lesbian Archives, University of Southern California Libraries, Los Angeles, CA. 19 Oct. 2017.

——. "Untitled Poem." 16 March 1985. Box 2, Folder 4. Bob Flanagan and Sheree Rose Collection. ONE National Gay and Lesbian Archives, University of Southern California Libraries, Los Angeles, CA. 19 Oct. 2017.

Krafft-Ebing, Richard von. *Psychopathia Sexualis: A Medico-Forensic Study.* Introduction by Ernest van den Haag. Translated by Harry D. Wedeck. Putnam, 1965 (1886; English trans. 1903).

MacKendrick, Karmen. *Counterpleasures.* SUNY P, 1999.

"mundane, *adj.; sense* 1 c." *The Oxford English Dictionary.* 2nd ed. 1989. *OED Online.* Oxford UP. 10 Sep. 2015. http://dictionary.oed.com

rife. "Submissive Fantasy vs. Submissive Reality: Guest Post by rife." *Sugarbutch Chronicles,* edited by Sinclair Sexsmith. http://www.sugarbutch.net/2015/01/submissive-fantasy-vs-reality/

Rose, Sheree. "Making Martin Suffer for Art: Sheree Rose and Martin O'Brien." 23–24 June 2013. Box 4. Bob Flanagan and Sheree Rose Collection. ONE National Gay and Lesbian Archives, University of Southern California Libraries, Los Angeles, CA. 19 Oct. 2017.

"sublunary, *adj.; sense* 3." *The Oxford English Dictionary.* 2nd ed. 1989. *OED Online.* Oxford UP. 10 Sep. 2015. http://dictionary.oed.com.

Weiss, Margot. *Techniques of Pleasure: BDSM and the Circuits of Sexuality.* Duke UP, 2011.

Zanin, Andrea. "Kink and Campus Controversy." *Sex Geek,* 6 Mar. 2008. https://sexgeek.wordpress.com/2008/03/06/kink-and-campus-controversy/. Accessed 5 Apr. 2018.

Bob Flanagan Sentenced

HAROLD JAFFE

> Eat shit or die.
> —Bob Flanagan

While teaching in Brunei, the novelist Anthony Burgess was diagnosed with an inoperable brain tumor and given a year to live.

Wanting to provide for his widow he began to write madly producing his best books, including *A Clockwork Orange.*

The diagnosis turned out to be wrong and he lived another forty years.

Bob Flanagan had cystic fibrosis and was not expected to survive his teens. Instead he lived, with severely increasing health difficulties, until age forty-three.

Like Burgess, death's seeming proximity energized Flanagan to imagine venturesomely, break through limits.

Death is

In his performances Flanagan at his best transformed his torment into a principle of conquest.

The principal conqueror was his penis, which refused to die.

Flanagan and his dominatrix-partner Sheree Rose tormented his penis into outlandish theatrics.

To Sheree Rose's accompaniment, Flanagan nailed his penis and testicles to a board; ate his own excrement; displayed his naked wasted body in chains and shackles to audiences; suspended that same wasted body from pulleys.

His body was wasted; nonetheless he was virile. His virility was the crucial actor in his project.

"These are bona fide boners and they feel good. When all else fails at least I know the plumbing is still functional."

Bob Flanagan's virility signaled the murdering back of the virulent disease that was murdering him.

Outdeathing death.

Was Flanagan aware of how his erotic masochism interfaced with his cystic fibrosis death sentence?

He was, he claims, playing sexual masochist games as early as seven years old with his nine-year-old male cousin, and enjoying the feeling without understanding why.

Not just enjoying the feeling but finding it "sweet."

That dialectical-seeming sweetness Flanagan invoked his entire brief life whenever he and the other BDSM participant or participants "melded," as he put it.

His theoretical understanding of what he was up to became clear while he was with Sheree Rose, from 1980 to 1996.

He responded to an interview question in *RE/Search* about his impending death:

"There are shamanistic cultures that believe in 'little deaths' . . . [that] prepare you for the 'big death.'

"Once I'd had enough sensation and gone far enough [in a performance], there was an immediate release afterwards, and I felt peaceful, calm and sharp—like I could do anything."

In her generous afterward to *The Pain Journal,* Sheree Rose mused on her love for Flanagan: That "brave and heroic heart."

That she could pay him such a compliment after his affectionate, but also critical, even cruel, pages about her in his journal, says something.

What does it say?

Cystic Fibrosis is

Reading Flanagan's *Pain Journal,* which records his last tormented year on earth, is not to respond to his art.

His constant complaints, peevishness, paranoiac fantasies about his friends' and family's neglect or betrayal.

None of that seems brave or heroic.

But his suffering was ceaseless and increasingly unendurable; even so, he was able to joke and mock himself, mock the pain journal he was in the process of dying while writing.

If Bob Flanagan had been thirty-five or forty years old in, say, 1960, would he have been forging art out of his body's fatal illness?

Unlikely.

It seems necessary for culture to have passed through the AIDS panic, when every aspect of the pleasuring body was under institutional assault.

When a generation of young people were forbidden to engage in traditional sexual practices for fear of contamination.

One unanticipated result of that repression is that the body was turned into a site of struggle, a "canvas," on which artists inscribed their pain, angst, new-found pleasures. Paper, wood, stone, metal, glass, sand, whitewashed walls, the soil of the earth.

Why not the flesh-and-blood body?

Artists in various countries were using their bodies in dramatic ways: Orlan in France; Chris Burden; Carolee Schneemann; Karen Finley; Fakir Musafar; and many others in the US; The Viennese Actionists; Hannah Wilke; Marina Abramović; VALIE EXPORT; Shigeko Kubota; and, irrepressibly, Bob Flanagan.

We are all sentenced to die, but for most of us death is a metaphor.

For Flanagan, death was his dominant; it could happen at any moment, and it encouraged him to expand, stretch, dare, explore the precipitous edges of consciousness.

"I'm getting Demerol. But all that is is a kiss on the cheek. I want . . . some dick, some analgesic dick down my throat or up my ass . . . just as long as you make like you love me and take away the pain."

Fibrosis is the mother

Death is the mother of the imagining heart-mind that seizes, explores the outermost reaches, farthest perimeters.

With death looming, what is there to lose?

Bob Flanagan was sentenced to death at age two, at ten, at twenty. Just two cystic fibrosis sufferers on record had lived longer.

With his body under nonstop assault, every lived day was a gift with decidedly mixed blessings because of the extreme ongoing pain.

Flanagan's art attempts to regain possession of a body that is no longer his.

Erect an artistic prison which mocks and out-extremes the actual prison of his fatal illness.

"Shitty lungs filled with shit and I feel like shit."

That he habitually presented his art with charm and humor testifies to his art's transformative, shaman-like potency.

The condition out of which Flanagan created his art is, in extremis, our own condition. Nor is our death sentence any longer deferred.

Global warming has suddenly brought death much closer. The body is our agent but ultimately our prison.

Towards the end, Bob fantasized about castrating himself and presenting his testicles to Sheree.

Mad, *n'est-ce-pas*?

If, though, the world one inhabits is itself mad, or maddening, or, finally, insupportable, then deviations, radical deviations, can be viewed as dialectical affirmations of one's own sovereignty (Bataille), however short-lived.

Cystic Fibrosis is the mother of beauty

The Duchess of LA

JANE DELYNN

My friend Linda used to be an ordinary housewife married to a professor in Westwood, but she had artistic aspirations, and when she and her husband split up she began to hang around with a hip LA crowd, people who went to poetry readings, art openings, clubs. She met a poet named Jack, who moved in with her and her cats and her two kids. Jack was nice and a good poet, but sexually he had his quirks. He had been immobilized in a full body cast for six months because of a car accident in his childhood, and the memory of that bondage held him in all. He liked— "needed" is perhaps a better word—to be tied up, spanked, suspended, insulted. Although Linda had begun to make assemblages, she was still pretty much the same nice Jewish housewife she had always been, and she tried to oblige him. Paddles, collars, handcuffs, and restraints of various kinds, even a cage for Jack to sleep in, soon made their appearance in the Westwood house. Some of it she kept locked up in a little room where Jack had his desk, but the cage was too large to hide from her children. Her daughter began to spend nights at her father's house; her son quit the high school soccer team and began to indulge in the standard drugs. For

---

"The Duchess of LA" originally appeared in DeLynn's *Don Juan in the Village* (Pantheon, 1990).

brief moments Linda would be very upset about this, then she would dismiss it as one of those things you grow out of in time. One time the fetish closet was broken into, and after that, pee began to appear in the morning all over the son's bathroom, which was also the guest bathroom. Her son said it was because if he turned on the light to pee he couldn't get back to sleep; Jack told her it was because of the fetish objects. I kept wondering when Linda would cut it out and find a nice lawyer to marry and take care of the mortgage payments, but one year passed, then another, and Jack was still there.

It is impossible to know human beings. You think you know them and most of the time you do, but then they will do something to surprise you and you can't fit this in with anything else you know about them, and the fact that you have been able to predict with near certainty their actions in the past only adds to this puzzlement. But I still felt like I really knew Linda, that she was only pretending to be this other person and any day would revert back to the one I knew. I was supposed to be the hip person in our relationship, and this change irritated me. Thus, although when I was with her I pretended to admire her new life, I didn't. I had enough friends who wrote, painted, danced, sang; I had been glad to have a friend who was basically just a nice Jewish girl. She now said things like she couldn't feel complete unless she could build objects that expressed the things that had been hidden inside her for years. I suppose everyone has stuff hidden inside them, but the world would be even more cluttered if everyone felt like they had to convert it into bits of metal, wood, and plastic. Nonetheless, I was in the habit of being her friend, and I saw her and Jack whenever they came to New York.

One time I was in LA, and I stayed for a few days in her house. The son was still peeing all over the bathroom; Linda warned me to be sure to wipe off the toilet seat before sitting on it. Or maybe I should just squat over it, the way you did in Africa or Asia. At night we went to punk clubs, where people looked like people had in New York a year or two before—but more so.

"What happened to your furniture?" I asked. We were sitting on cushions in her living room, just as if it were 1968.

"It's kind of a long story. . . ." said Linda. She looked at Jack.

"Just tell her the truth," said Jack. "It was our night for the club, and things got a little out of hand."

"What club?"

"Oh, just a club that meets sometimes at our house."

"What kind of club destroys the furniture?"

It turned out to be a kind of liberation organization to protect the rights of people to beat, bind, give enemas to, and urinate on each other, as well as perform other similar such acts. Although the focus of the meeting was usually on theory rather than praxis, sometimes things got out of hand. Linda was the chairwoman.

"You're kidding!" To my knowledge, Linda had never run anything bigger than a yard sale.

"Jewish women," said Jack. "They're used to ordering people around."

"Yeah. Everybody wants to be a slave but me." She sighed.

During my stay Linda and Jack had a lot of squabbles. Most of these seemed to revolve around Jack wanting Linda to order him to do things, and Linda refusing to do this. "You're crazy," I told her. "Why don't you make him go shopping and clean up the house? Do the laundry. Wipe up the pee in the bathroom. Give you a massage. Or won't he do stuff like that?"

"He'll do anything I tell him," she assured me smugly. "We have a three-month contract."

"What does that mean?"

"He has to do whatever I want for three months, and if he doesn't I have the right to punish him."

"If I were you I'd take advantage of it. You're always telling me how you can't stand housework."

"I know. But it's not that simple."

"So you lock him up in the dog cage at night to make him happy. So what?"

"I can't explain it;" she said. "It's very complicated. You really should read this thing I wrote." She went to her desk and pulled out some xeroxed sheets that were stapled together. So Linda had become a philosopher. That night we went over to the house of a woman who was Linda's main slave. She was skinny and pale, as if she hadn't been in the sun in years, and it was obvious Jack was jealous of her. After dinner Judy cleared up and then Linda told her to go into the bedroom and get things ready.

"Can I join you?" asked Jack

"No. But if you want, you can kneel outside the door on your knees and listen to us."

"On my hands and knees or just my knees?"

"On your hands and knees. Don't move. Be sure to tell me if he moves," she said to me. "He'll be punished very severely if he does."

"How?" I asked.

"I'll probably tie him up outside the house all night with a gag in his mouth. It's supposed to rain and he'll catch a cold. Jack hates colds."

"Nobody likes colds," said Jack.

Linda got up to leave the room, then stopped. "If you'd like, you could come inside and watch us," she told me. "It would give you a better sense of what I'm into."

"Judy wouldn't mind?"

Linda gave me a somewhat patronizing smile. "It doesn't matter. After all, she's my slave."

I wasn't really interested in what they were doing, but I felt Linda would be insulted if I told her that, so after a few moments of watching Jack kneel like a dog, I followed her into the bedroom.

Judy was dressed only in her underpants. A number of objects, some of which I had never seen before, were lying on the bed: a whip, hand restraints, a paddle, several metal devices that looked like those things we held the remnants of joints with in the late sixties, short chains with pieces of lead on the ends. Linda told Judy she was going to perform something called "breastwork" on her. She took the things that looked like roach clips and put one on each breast. "Ow," said Judy. Linda pulled on these a bit and asked Judy how she liked it. "It hurts," said Judy. Linda nodded and with much seriousness told her that was good. Then she took several of the lead pieces and attached the chains to the roach clips. "Ow," Judy said again. Then Linda told Judy to take off her pants. Judy stepped out of the pants and laid herself across Linda's lap. Linda picked up the paddle and began to spank her. But for some reason she wasn't pleased with this and told Judy to get the hairbrush that was lying on the bureau. Linda explained to me how you couldn't use your hand to spank someone because it hurt too much—not the person you're spanking but your hand. The spanking was done in a slow and rather desultory fashion, as if Linda were performing a somewhat tedious but necessary task. Occasionally I peeked out the door at Jack. As commanded, he was kneeling like a dog on all fours. It was hard to sense the connection between these acts and sex, though I don't know exactly what else you could call it.

When the spanking was done, Linda told Judy to put on a pair of latex panties. They were a hideous thick green rubber. Linda told me the point of them was to keep Judy's ass hot, in order to prolong the pain and memory of the spanking after Linda was gone. Then she asked Judy to please make some coffee for herself and me.

"What would you like in it?" Judy asked.

"Just bring everything in on a tray. I think we'd better have some milk, and cream, and sugar—or maybe honey, if you'd prefer that?" she asked me.

"Sure."

"And some cinnamon. Please use the silver tray. And cloth napkins, please. Not paper."

When Judy opened the door we could see Jack still kneeling there. Jack asked Linda if he could come into the room and join us. She told him no, he had to stay in this position until we left the house, but she said we would keep the door open so he could hear what we were saying.

He could listen, but he was not allowed to say anything himself until we were in the car.

Judy brought in the coffee as ordered. She had added some cookies on her own initiative and Linda reprimanded her for this, saying she should have asked permission first. But I told Linda I was in the mood for cookies, so Linda decided not to punish her after all. Meanwhile, as Linda and I sat on the bed eating and drinking and talking about Judy and Jack, Judy sat in her green latex panties at the foot of the bed. At first I felt self-conscious, but I quickly grew to like it. There was something very leisurely about it all, as if I were a pasha. Soon Judy and Jack became invisible. Oddly, this did not make it harder to be with them later, but easier.

Before we left, Judy asked Linda if she could go to the bathroom.

Linda looked at her watch. "No."

"Please. I have to."

"Judy, you asked me and I said no. I don't like to be questioned when I tell you something."

"I'm sorry."

"That's better."

"When am I going to be allowed to go?"

"I'm not sure."

"But I have to go." One leg rubbed against the other.

"Judy, this is very bad." Linda shook her head sadly. "We're going to leave now. In one hour you may call and ask my permission to go to the bathroom. I may pick up my phone or I may have my machine on, I don't know."

"Couldn't she cheat?" I asked Linda in the car.

"What would be the point of that?"

Jack began to explain poopoo sex to me. Sometimes you wouldn't let someone go when they had to, and sometimes you made them go even if they didn't want to, by giving them an enema. After administering the enema, you would forbid them to go—which of course they would be unable not to do—then you would punish them when they did.

This seemed even less like sex than Jack's kneeling outside the door. "Do you do that a lot?" I asked, in the same tone I would ask them if they had seen the latest Bertolucci film.

"Not much," said Linda. "We have enough bathroom problems with my son."

Linda asked me if I had read her article and what I had thought about it. I said it was interesting but a little murky, as if she had been reading too much semiotics. She rolled her eyes at Jack as if I were some philistine.

"Have you heard of Duchess La Jeanne?" Jack asked me.

"No."

"Well, that's Linda's public name. She's the most famous dominatrix in LA."

That night, despite his docility in kneeling outside Judy's bedroom, Jack was forced to sleep outside in the dog cage. There was a kind of wall covered by ivy around the property, but there was nothing to prevent a neighbor from peeking through and seeing this, let alone Linda's son. I realized that in peeing all over the bathroom he was not just expressing his displeasure, he was acting like a *dog*. It did rain, and Jack was sniffling the next day. By the time I left for New York a few days later, it had turned into a mild form of pneumonia.

"They say people don't die for love," joked Jack. "But maybe they do."

"I nearly died once of a broken heart," I said. "But I guess that's only a metaphor."

"I take love seriously, but sometimes I wonder if it matters that much who I'm with," said Linda. "Like if Jack died, as horrible as this sounds, I'm sure I'd soon be in love with someone else."

Jack did not seem shocked by this, but I was. Not just that she had said it, but that she had thought it. It was the kind of thing I could imagine myself thinking, though probably not saying, but Linda?

"I often think I don't like people, but when they leave I miss them," I said.

"I never missed my husband when he left," said Linda.

Jack told us about a boy in high school he had had a tremendous crush on. He still regretted not having sex with him, even though he had never slept with a man and had no interest in doing so. He didn't like the idea of having to do stuff with a man's asshole; that was one of the reasons he wasn't into enemas. But women were a different matter. He thought it was a very sexy thing to watch women make love together. That was why he had encouraged Linda and Judy, only it had backfired against him because they never let him join in.

"That doesn't seem fair," I said.

"I think I'll renegotiate it in the next contract," said Jack.

"I don't know about any more contracts," said Linda.

"Is something the matter between you guys?" I asked her the next night. We were driving to The Marquis d'O, a sex club that had a woman's night once a month. Sometimes it was good and lots of sexy people turned up; sometimes it was terrible.

"Well . . . I don't know. In a way I think this relationship has run its course."

"You're not in love with Judy?" I asked.

"Maybe," said Linda. "Sometimes I think I am. She needs me so much."

I thought of mentioning that her children, who needed her too, did not seem to receive much of the benefits of Linda's empathy. "What about Jack? He seems to need you too."

"I know," she sighed. "That's the problem." She paused. "Jack'll be okay. I'll always be there for him. He knows that."

"Are you really the most famous dominatrix in LA?" I asked.

"Yes. It's a great way for people like us to make money and not have it interfere with our art. You make a hundred dollars an hour, sometimes more—not including tips."

"What do you have to do?"

"Insults, dressing up, enemas, spankings. You negotiate with the customer. If it's something really disgusting, I won't do it."

"I can't believe it, Linda," I said. "I still think of you as a nice Jewish girl."

"I *am* a nice Jewish girl. Don't you think you're a little naive?" We pulled into the parking place.

"Tsk," Linda said, that sound of the tongue between the teeth. Only ten or twelve women were in the club, which smelled of old liquor and cigarettes. A fat woman dressed in a black leather slip and halter stood behind the bar. She gave Linda and me free drinks. Everyone seemed to know Linda. The women were incredibly unattractive, overweight or unduly skinny, with pale unhealthy-looking skin—unless this was due to the lighting, which seemed designed to make everyone look like heroin addicts. They were dressed in predictable ways: black leather pants, belts studded with silver, metal bracelets around their wrists. The conventionality of style and fantasy with which people into this form of sex expressed their violations of conventionality has always been astonishing to me. A few women were dressed in classic pornography style, with tight little skirts and lacy black camisoles or bras. One had on just a bra and G-string with garters and stockings. Several wore dog collars around their necks attached to leather leashes wound around their mistresses' wrists. They stood by passively with pouty lips and expressionless eyes as their owners opened their shirts and fondled their breasts in public. Sometimes their breasts or buttocks were offered to other women to touch, and when this was done they evinced no reaction either. Linda was popular, and everybody offered her their slaves. As she stroked them she would talk about them in the third person, telling the person who had given her permission to touch them how attractive, how soft, how obedient their slaves were.

"If you'd like, I could ask permission for you to touch somebody too," Linda said.

"No thanks."

"Are you scared?"

"No. They're too ugly." What bothered me even more than their looks was their apparent social class—rather, their apparent lack of social class. They looked like they lived in East LA, or some cheap place in the Valley.

We went into the back room where the action, if any, usually took place. The walls were black, and as it was lit by only a dim red lamp it took me a few seconds to see what was going on. There were several sets of stocks—the kind Puritans used to punish sinners, with holes to secure the head and hands—and some basketlike leather seats hung on chains from the ceiling. On a shelf in the rear was your standard assortment of paddles, whips, riding crops.

A woman was standing on a little platform, her bottom naked, her head and hands held in place by the stock. She was surrounded by several women who took turns swatting her with a whip. There was no urgency to this, minutes seeming to go by between each stroke. One woman always stood by the head of the woman being whipped, stroking her brow, pushing her hair off her forehead, wiping off the sweat, talking to her through the moans and telling her how beautiful and sweet and responsive she was.

We watched for a while, then the woman holding the whip offered it to me. I would have preferred to just watch but Linda had told me that if anyone asked me to do something I should do it; if I refused to participate I would make everyone uncomfortable, perhaps might even be asked to leave. Women were still a little touchy about this kind of sex, it had a very bad name—not just in the world but in the women's and even the lesbian movement. It was the big philosophical issue at the moment. Surely I must have read the articles.

"Actually, I don't buy that kind of magazine."

"You should. This kind of sex is really the last frontier. Dealing with this is just as difficult as coming out."

"I didn't know you were out," I had said to Linda.

Feeling curious, but not the least sexual, I took the whip. It had a nice, balanced feel. I raised my arm, then flicked it rather gently. You could barely hear the whip land on the woman's ass.

"You can do it harder," she said.

I tried again. Again, it was too gentle.

"Do it harder," the other women told me. "Don't be afraid of hurting her." *Harder*: the word sounded odd in their mouths.

After a few more strokes I began to get into it, and the woman I was hitting began to moan and say "ow." It was gratifying, though not immensely so. Soon an empathy—for the pain I was inflicting on her and the connection we were making through it—began to manifest itself in my body, so that I had my first flickerings of arousal. I no longer cared that she wasn't attractive, and the idea of running my hand over her face or caressing her breast no longer seemed so revolting.

After a while I was told to give the whip to someone else. I was about to leave the room when Linda grabbed my arm.

"Now you," she said.

"What?"

"You want to," she said. "I can tell."

"No."

"Ha!" She began to stroke my thighs. I'm not attracted to Linda, but I felt this searing flash go through me. Then her hand moved to my crotch. "I can feel the heat through your pants."

"Linda . . ." I pushed her hand away.

She grabbed my arms and pinned me against a wall near where we were standing. She was strong, but perhaps if I had really tried I could have pushed her away. But I shut my eyes and let her continue to caress me.

"You want me to, don't you?"

"No."

She laughed. "You sure fooled me."

"Not here."

"What's wrong with here?"

I leaned forward to whisper in her ear. "For one thing, the women are so ugly."

"They're not so bad," said Linda. "What about the one over there, you don't think she's attractive?"

"No."

"Or her?"

"No. I can honestly say there's not one person in this place I feel like having sex with," I said. Then I realized I might be insulting Linda. "I mean, not counting you. You're my friend." Then I realized Linda might be thinking I was making a pass at her, so I added. "Not that I'm attracted to you. God, you know what I mean; it's too complicated to explain."

"It's what you do that's important, not necessarily the people you do it with," said Linda. "You have very nice legs," she said, still stroking me. "Why don't you relax and see what happens?"

"I can't. Not in public."

"But you're wet, I can feel it," she said. "Will it be easier if I put a blindfold around your eyes so you don't have to see what's happening?" She touched my breast.

"Okay," I whispered.

"Wait a minute. I'll be right back."

I stood there, self-conscious, as if she were still propping me up, my eyes shut so I could not see the other women who might be looking at me.

"I don't want you to open your eyes, but move your head forward a bit," said Linda. I moved my head forward and she slipped a blindfold over my head. "Is that better?" she asked.

"Yes."

"Now I want you to unzip your pants."

"I can't do that."

"You have to," she said.

I unzipped my pants. I felt foolish with them slightly open and did not know whether I should push them down more or not. I didn't want to ask because that would look too eager. I almost wished my hands were tied so I would not have to worry about these things.

"Now I'm going to take you by the hand and lead you someplace where you'll be a little more comfortable."

"I'm scared my pants are going to fall down and I'll trip."

"Hold my hand and you'll be all right."

We walked a number of steps, then she told me to stop. She pushed my pants down so they were around my ankles. I couldn't remember what underpants I had worn that day and I was worried they had holes in them, or the crotch was pinkish-brown from blood I hadn't quite been able to wash out from my period. I told myself it was dark in the room and they wouldn't be able to see my underpants anyway. Then I began to worry that maybe she had brought me to the other room.

"We're still in the back room, aren't we?" I asked Linda.

"Relax," said Linda.

"I don't want to be up front. People might recognize me."

"This is a very safe environment," said Linda. "Whoever's here is only going to deal with you with love. Now I want you to lean over."

"But I'll fall!"

"No. There's something here. You'll be more comfortable."

I was draped over an object that felt like a pommel horse. It was covered with suede and had many smells in it. My mouth lay against it but I tried not to touch it with my lips so I would not catch the diseases that were surely nesting there. I was scared I was going to sneeze or have to blow my nose or even pee.

Linda began stroking my thighs. She began telling me how beautiful I was, how soft and compliant. I spread my legs a little so she could touch between them, though I did it in a way that I hoped would look like I was just shifting my weight. "Oh, that's nice," she said. She touched the bottom of my underpants. "You're incredibly wet," she said. "Do you know that? . . . I said, do you know that?" I nodded. "Now I want you to lift yourself up a little . . ." She raised me off the horse and pulled down my underpants. She ran her fingers up the backs of my thighs again, then began to lightly touch my ass. "What a pretty ass she has," she said. "Isn't this a pretty ass? See how it moves towards me when I touch it." And it did; I couldn't help myself, although whether it was because I was so turned on or because I was being hypnotized by her commands I was unable to tell. Now that Linda was talking about me in the third person, the fact that I was in a club returned to the forefront of my attention, and I realized there was a hum of voices around us and that they had been there for some time; I had just blocked them out. They were talking about me in the same calm tones they had used a little earlier in talking about the girl who had been in the stocks—how sweet and docile and vulnerable I looked lying there, how pretty my ass was and how it would look even prettier the next day when it was black-and-blue. "Go ahead, touch her, she doesn't mind," said Linda, and I felt the hands of strangers, the different hands of strangers, moving up my thighs and caressing my ass. Occasionally they would just brush by my crotch.

"She's really wet," they said.

"She's cherry," explained Linda.

"Oh, this is your first time," one said to me. I tried to nod, but it was difficult in the position I was in. She put her hand on my neck and gently stroked it. "We know how you feel," she said. It was very soothing. "Don't worry. We won't do anything you don't want. You know that, don't you?" I tried to nod again, but she kept talking, and I realized she wasn't doing this so much to get an answer as to soothe me by the sound of her voice. I felt soothed. It was really very nice to be talked about like that, in such complimentary tones, in a way that I was not usually talked about unless I had done something extraordinarily witty or wonderful. But for once nothing seemed to be expected of me except to lie there.

I felt a sting across my ass. I assumed it was Linda's hand. I said "ow," more out of surprise than pain. My thighs were stroked again, and I trembled, waiting for the stroke. When it didn't come I was almost disappointed. I twitched my ass.

"See how she wants it," said someone.

"Oh yes. She's quite the little femme."

Again I felt the hand. It hurt more this time but I was expecting it and I didn't say anything. A finger tickled the hair in my ass, then slid down to my crotch.

"She's very wet."

"She'd probably beg for it if we stopped."

"You could tell she was that way when she walked in."

"People who act tough are always the biggest femmes."

"Ow!" I said. This time the hand really hurt. Then the spanks began to come more quickly. I realized my "ows" were due not so much to the intensity of the strokes as to their unpredictability. In a way I wanted to keep saying "ow," to let them know they were hurting me, but I didn't want to say it too much, in case they would stop. Then I thought about how crazy it was that even in here, when everything was being done for my pleasure, all I could think about was what kind of response I was supposed to make. Was there never a moment in my entire life when I could just relax?

I don't know whether it was the lecture or the hypnotic rhythm of the strokes, but after a while my mind stopped its chattering, and I was in a different kind of space, the one that exists while you're in a dream or watching a totally engrossing movie, and there's nothing to do but calmly witness the events going on all around you.

It was totally peaceful. I wanted to go to sleep. When they stopped I felt bereft, as if I had been chucked out of paradise.

"You can go on," I told Linda. "I'm okay."

"You've had enough."

She removed the blindfold, and I was forced to look at the women around me. They were still ugly, and though I felt more empathy for them than I had before, I wasn't sure whether this made it better or worse.

The next day I felt terribly depressed. I wanted to expunge my thoughts in water but the blue marks on my ass and thighs made me too embarrassed to go to the health club and swim. When Linda went to visit Judy I realized I was jealous—not of either of them but of the acts that went on between them. I knew on my own that I would not have the courage to do such things. I lay in bed most of the day and slept, then I took the red-eye home.

I hadn't talked to Linda for almost a year when I received a creamy, engraved, stiff card inside a creamy, engraved, stiff envelope informing me that the former Ms. Linda Birnbaum of Westwood and Dr. Henry Goldberg of Beverly Hills were pleased to announce their marriage. The receipt of this note made it safe for me to contact Linda again. In the course of the conversation I asked her if she had shared the details of her life as Duchess La Jeanne with her new husband.

"Oh no," she said. "I stopped that stuff when Jack and I broke up, soon after you were here. I realized it wasn't me at all." She told me that her son had stopped peeing all over the bathroom soon after Jack had moved out and that, as there was currently no extra room in Henry's house, her sculpture was temporarily on hold until they could build her a studio in his garage. One other thing. Henry had no children, and she was trying to get pregnant. At her age this was difficult, and she went into a long litany about bilirubins and luteal phase deficiencies and b.b.t. curves. It was both boring and reassuring and served exactly the same conversational function as discussions of one's latest therapy session had in the old days.

When I hung up the phone I was both relieved and disappointed to discover I had been right, that deep down Linda was, as I had always thought, a nice Jewish girl. I realized also that, for some reason, no matter what I did or did not do, I was not, and this both relieved and disappointed me too.

CONTRIBUTORS

RHIANNON AARONS is a Los Angeles–based interdisciplinary artist, writer, and lecturer. She received a BFA from Otis and an MFA from California State University, Long Beach. She is a recipient of the Marilyn Werby Grant, HOGAR Grant, and Live Art Development Agency's DIY+. Her work has been included in *Senses of Cinema, Rip Rap,* and *Culture on the Offensive.* Rhiannon has exhibited at Jason Vass Gallery, LACE, Bluecoat, The CSULB UAM, Tom of Finland Foundation, and The Situation Room. She is frequently featured on the Dr. Susan Block Show and co-edited Bob Flanagan's *The Book of Medicine* with Sheree Rose.

TANYA AUGSBURG is an interdisciplinary feminist performance scholar, arts writer, and curator who can be occasionally persuaded to perform. She teaches at San Francisco State University, where she is Professor of Humanities and Liberal Studies in the areas of humanities and creative arts. Her research interests include contemporary feminist art and performance, art writing, feminism, and interdisciplinarity. More information about Tanya Augsburg can be found at www.tanyaaugsburg.weebly.com.

CHELSEA COON is a performance artist and writer. She has exhibited internationally at festivals, biennales, and galleries. Coon received her bachelor's degree at the School of the Museum of Fine Arts (2012), master's degree at Tufts University (2014), and Certificate of Advanced Studies in Theatre, Performance and Contemporary Live Arts at the University of Applied Sciences and Arts Scuola Teatro Dimitri, Switzerland (2015). She is the author of *No One Thing Is the Root of All Anything: Phases and Performance of the Imminent* (Not a Cult, 2018) and the chapter "Experiential Traces / Aesthetic of Absence" in *the phenomenology of bloody performance art!*

(Routledge, forthcoming). She is a recipient of the Foundation for Contemporary Arts Emergency Grant and an Australian Commonwealth Government Research Training Program Scholarship. Coon is a doctoral candidate at the Victorian College of the Arts, University of Melbourne.

MARY ANN DAVIS holds an MFA in poetry writing from the University of Michigan and a PhD in Literature and Gender Studies from the University of Southern California. Her chapbook of poetry, *Portrait of a Voice*, was selected for the Robin Becker Poetry series, and published through Seven Kitchens Press. A monograph in progress, *Between the Monstrous and the Mundane: Thinking Erotic Power in the West, 1850–2015*, is a hybrid work that combines theoretical inquiry, literary and cultural criticism, and lyric reflection to trace a different story of erotic power. She is Assistant Professor of Literature at Antioch College in Yellow Springs, Ohio.

JANE DELYNN is a gay Jewish novelist, journalist, playwright, and librettist currently living in Los Angeles. She's the author of the novels *Some Do, In Thrall, Real Estate, Don Juan in the Village, Leash,* and the collection *Bad Sex Is Good*. She was embedded with the military during the first Gulf War, which is not the only reason she has contempt for the US government, mainstream media, the RNC, DNC, PC, and so forth.

LUKA FISHER is a gender-queer transfemme artist, cultural producer, and occasional Russian translator. They began thinking about performance art and its documentation while working as a producer with artists Kayla Tange, Sheree Rose, Tristene Roman, Christopher Zeischegg, and various recording artists courtesy of Records Ad Nauseam to create and promote works that crossed disciplinary boundaries. They are currently developing new performance works with Daniel Crook and Isabelle Sjahsam. They hold an MFA in Photo/Media and Integrated Media from CalArts.

YETTA HOWARD is Associate Professor of English and Comparative Literature and Co-director of the LGBTQ Research Consortium at San Diego State University. Howard is the author of *Ugly Differences: Queer Female Sexuality in the Underground* (University of Illinois Press, 2018) and the editor of this collection, *Rated RX: Sheree Rose with and after Bob Flanagan.* For more information: www.yettahoward.com.

HAROLD JAFFE is the author of novels, short fiction, and essays, most recently *Porn-anti-Porn, Goosestep,* and *Sacred Outcast: Dispatches from India.* Jaffe is editor-in-chief of *Fiction International.*

AMELIA JONES is Robert A. Day Professor and Vice Dean of Research, Roski School of Art & Design, University of Southern California, and is a curator and scholar of contemporary art, performance, and feminist/sexuality studies. Recent publications include *Seeing Differently: A History and Theory of Identification and the Visual Arts* (2012); *Otherwise: Imagining Queer Feminist Art Histories* (2016), co-edited with Erin Silver; and the edited special issue "On Trans/Performance" of *Performance Research* (2016). Jones is currently working on a retrospective of the work of Ron Athey with accompanying catalogue (*Queer Communion: Ron Athey*), and a book entitled *In Between Subjects: A Critical Genealogy of Queer Performance* is forthcoming from Routledge.

AMBER JAMILLA MUSSER is the author of *Sensational Flesh: Race, Power, and Masochism* and *Sensual Excess: Queer Femininity and Brown Jouissance.* She teaches American Studies at George Washington University.

MARTIN O'BRIEN is an artist, thinker, and zombie. He works across performance, video, and writing. All of his work explores illness, death, and pain and uses his own experiences of suffering from cystic fibrosis as a starting point. He is best known for his long-durational solo performances and his collaborations with Sheree Rose. The Live Art Development Agency published the book *Survival of the Sickest: The Art of Martin O'Brien* in 2018. Martin has shown work widely throughout the UK, Europe, Canada, and the US. Venues include Tate Britain, Spill Festival of Performance, Manchester International Festival, Kapelica Gallery, Grace Exhibition Space, and ONE National Gay and Lesbian Archives (Los Angeles), as artist-in-residence. He recently outlived his life expectancy and is enjoying life as a zombie.

SHEREE ROSE has been thrilling, shocking, and exciting audiences around the world, beginning with her collaborative photography and performances with Bob Flanagan in 1981. Their groundbreaking show *Visiting Hours* opened at the Santa Monica Museum of Art in 1992 and traveled to the New Museum of Contemporary Art in New York City. She collaborated with Mike Kelley on the video *One Hundred Reasons* and with Nine Inch Nails on several music videos. She co-produced the Sundance award–winning documentary *Sick.* Since 2011 she has collaborated with British performance artist Martin O'Brien in performances in England, New York, and Los Angeles. Rose is the subject of this collection, *Rated RX: Sheree Rose with and after Bob Flanagan.*

JUDY ORNELAS SISNEROS is a native of Bakersfield, CA. She now resides in Los Angeles where she was a local member of ACT UP, Queer Nation, a Los Angeles Dyke March co-founder and on the board of Tongues, a Latina lesbian arts collective. Currently she practices her activism via documentary photography, particularly preferring to shoot queer underground nightlife, artists, scenesters, activists, and their friends. She plays noisy garage bass guitar, likes her tequila, and is an avid cat lover. *Rated RX's* front cover includes a photograph by Sisneros who has also contributed to the images in the collection.

TINA TAKEMOTO is an award-winning artist and scholar whose work explores Asian American queer history, including the hidden dimensions of same-sex intimacy for Japanese Americans incarcerated by the US government during World War II. Takemoto has exhibited widely and received grants from Art Matters, ArtPlace, Fleishhacker Foundation, and San Francisco Arts Commission. Their articles appear in *Afterimage, Art Journal, Performance Research, Radical Teacher, Theatre Survey, Women and Performance,* and the anthologies *Queering Asian American Art, Otherwise: Imagining Queer Feminist Art Histories,* and *Thinking Through the Skin.* Takemoto is Dean of Humanities and Sciences at California College of the Arts and serves on the board of Queer Cultural Center.

IMAGES

PART 1

1980s–1990s

Commitments, Consent, Contracts

"If there are two consenting adults then any form of sexual relationship is fine. Even if nobody else understands the relationship, it doesn't matter. Sex is not about what anyone else thinks. That is my sexual philosophy."
—Sheree Rose, from 2009 interview with Tina Takemoto

"Bob and I used to think that all relationships should have contracts. We used to have three-month temporary contracts and both people adhere to those rules for three months and, if that doesn't work at the end of the three months, then both parties renegotiate and then maybe go on to a six-month contract. But I think in 'normal life' and 'normal relationships' that doesn't happen. People go into it and don't really know what they're agreeing to and what they're not agreeing to. And they have fights about that, which causes a lot of disharmony. So for me, personally, it was very political to have these contracts because otherwise I would never be able to do what I was able to do to Martin if I didn't know he fully wanted to do it and agreed to it."
—Sheree Rose, from 2017 interview with Yetta Howard

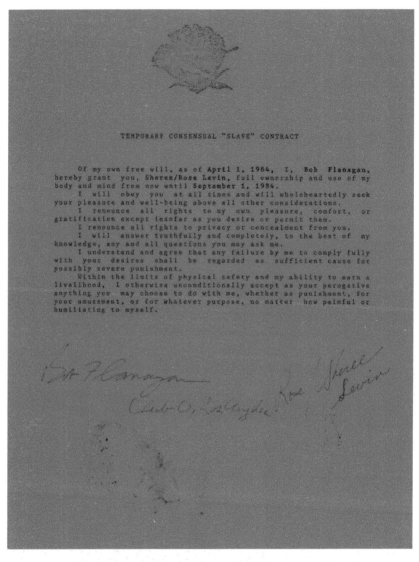

TEMPORARY CONSENSUAL "SLAVE" CONTRACT

Of my own free will, as of April 1, 1984, I, Bob Flanagan, hereby grant you, Sheree/Rose Levin, full ownership and use of my body and mind from now until September 1, 1984.

I will obey you at all times and will wholeheartedly seek your pleasure and well-being above all other considerations.

I renounce all rights to my own pleasure, comfort, or gratification except insofar as you desire or permit them.

I renounce all rights to privacy or concealment from you.

I will answer truthfully and completely, to the best of my knowledge, any and all questions you may ask me.

I understand and agree that any failure by me to comply fully with your desires shall be regarded as sufficient cause for possibly severe punishment.

Within the limits of physical safety and my ability to earn a livelihood, I otherwise unconditionally accept as your perogative anything you may choose to do with me, whether as punishment, for your amusement, or for whatever purpose, no matter how painful or humiliating to myself.

1.1. Slave contract signed in blood by Bob Flanagan and Sheree
Rose (1984). Courtesy of ONE Archives at the USC Libraries.

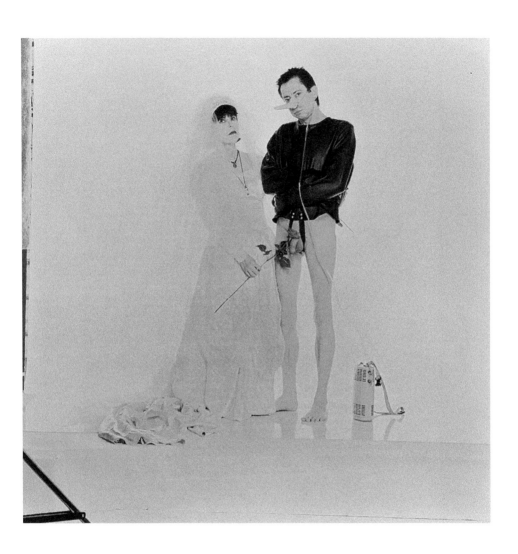

1.2. Sheree Rose and Bob Flanagan, wedding photo (1995). Photo by
Michel Delsol. Courtesy of ONE Archives at the USC Libraries.

Dear Mistress Rose, and/or Sheree,

I'm here at the computer trying to learn the new word
processing program. You're in Santa Barbara, having a good
time I hope. Here's my new project for the New Year: to
write you a letter a day. This has nothing to do with the
other letter wrtiting campaign you want me to undertake.
It's just a way for me to keep a another kind of journal, a
more personal one, directed solely for you. Just think! By
this time next year you shouold have 365 letters from me
(some book that would make).

I hope I can make them interesting for you and manage to
say all that I want to say. Being close to you is the most
incredible high I've ever experienced. But still, typical of
me, I want more. Phone rings. It's you, on your way home.
Oh, boy! But I know you'll be exhausted when you get back
and will probably go right to sleep and I'll be missing
you again. Too bad for me, insatiable me.] I want to be
closer this year and more productive with you and a better
and truer submissive to you. I'm not so good in that
department lately. Bad attitude. Too controlling.
Downright nasty. I want to beg you to beat these things out
of me, really beat me, severely punish me when I'm bad to you
- like yesterday in the car when I refused to admit my
driving mistake, and when I made you feel inadaquate by my
fidgetting and whining in the swing at Antoinette's. What an
asshole I am, despite all my declarations of submission - but
there I go again, trying tyo control you, telling _you_ how to
discipline _me_. That's not my intention nor my desire. I
only wish to illustrate that I know my shortcomings and make
a vow to you that I will change them this year. It's not up
to you to change me, it's up to me. But I will be the exact
slave, to the letter, that you want me to be, for as long as
you want me to be.

Since I'll have 364 more letters to spill my guts to
you, I won't try to cram it all into the first one. But I
have lots more to say to you. If you don't like the style
ofr the content of what I write to you, tell me and I'll
change it. Thankyou for the beating today and the fuck last
night. I'm sorry you were depressed again about your work
this morning. I hope I handled it better than usual,
although I know I got distant afterwards. Sorry. You're
wonderful. Please don't let anyone else tell you otherwiese.
Your happiness comes first. I'll do anything physically and
mentally possible to help you to find peace and fulfillment
and excitement in this life. But I can't do it all. That's
where you _have_ to do some of the work too. Your work is as
important as you make it - So make it.

in servitude and devotion
b.

1.3. Letter to Sheree Rose from Bob Flanagan (1 January 1985). Flanagan wrote Rose
a letter every single day in 1985. Courtesy of ONE Archives at the USC Libraries.

Well, Mistress,

I've been cleaning up your house today but feeling kind of
shitty. I hate the scene I caused last night even though you were
kind enough to understand and forgive me. What a fraud I am.
Isn't that your word? Guess so, but I feel that way now. I
really don't want to be the one in control but much of the time I
am. I push and push until I get it. I could beg you not to let
me do that but in the end that too is controlling. What do you
want? If you'd only tell me. And if I could only believe you if
you did tell me. I love you and need you as always. Even though
you said you understood about last night I'm still afraid you'll
shy away from me as your slave and won't feel it's worth it to try
to dominate me because I'm such a lousy submissive in the first
place. Anyone who only submits when he wants to is a lousy
submissive. Truth is I want to be forced because the untimate,
deepest truth is I want to stay in a submissive state to you
always. Things get so crazy around here sometimes that's a hard
state for me to maintain. But not maintaining is my fault, not
yours, no matter how much I'd like to blame you.

- 1 -

1.4. Letter to Sheree Rose from Bob Flanagan (7 October 1985). Flanagan wrote Rose
a letter every single day in 1985. Courtesy of ONE Archives at the USC Libraries.

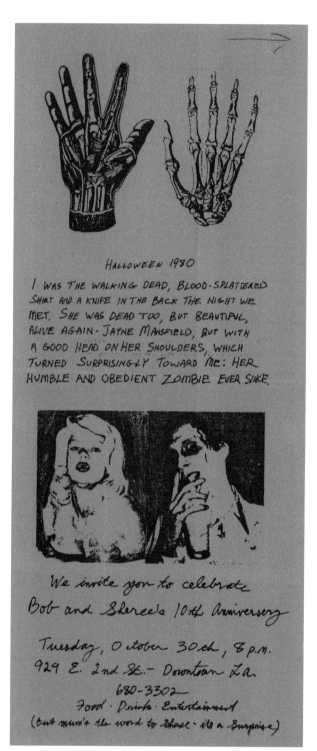

HALLOWEEN 1980

I WAS THE WALKING DEAD, BLOOD-SPLATTERED
SHIRT AND A KNIFE IN THE BACK THE NIGHT WE
MET. SHE WAS DEAD TOO, BUT BEAUTIFUL,
ALIVE AGAIN - JAYNE MANSFIELD, BUT WITH
A GOOD HEAD ON HER SHOULDERS, WHICH
TURNED SURPRISINGLY TOWARD ME: HER
HUMBLE AND OBEDIENT ZOMBIE EVER SINCE.

We invite you to celebrate
Bob and Sheree's 10th Anniversary

Tuesday, October 30th, 8 p.m.
929 E. 2nd St. — Downtown LA,
680-3302
Food · Drinks · Entertainment
(but mum's the word to Sheree · it's a Surprise)

1.5. Bob Flanagan and Sheree Rose's 10th anniversary invitation (1990). Courtesy of ONE Archives at the USC Libraries.

1.6. Handwritten will by Bob Flanagan (1995). Courtesy
of ONE Archives at the USC Libraries.

BEING OF SOUND MIND AND SICK BODY EVERYTHING I OWN I GIVE TO
SHEREE ROSE LEVIN I GIVE ALL MY WORLDLY POSSESSIONS TO SHEREE
ROSE LEVIN OF MY OWN FREE WILL SHEREE LEVIN GETS IT ALL I GIVE
IT ALL TO HER I'M ALL HERS—LOCK, STOCK AND CAGE I AM HER TOTAL
SLAVE SHE OWNS ALL MY SHIT, ALL MY PISS—ALL MY CUM (WHAT
LITTLE THERE IS) ALL MY LOVE—ALL MY DEVOTION—FOREVER AND
EVER—TILL DEATH US DO PART
Bob Flanagan 12/16/95

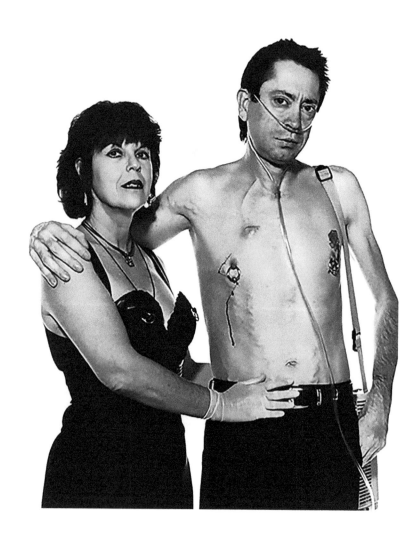

1.7. Sheree Rose and Bob Flanagan. An iconic photo shoot from 1995. Photo by Michel Delsol. Courtesy of ONE Archives at the USC Libraries.

Public/Private Exhibition(ist)s

Sheree Rose and Bob Flanagan's performance art and sexual lives blurred boundaries and blended domestic, subcultural, and corporeal spaces. This section gives a flavor of the range of ways they transgressed notions of such spaces, breaking down distinctions that mark public versus private practices. More specific exhibits and performances are highlighted in the sections that follow.

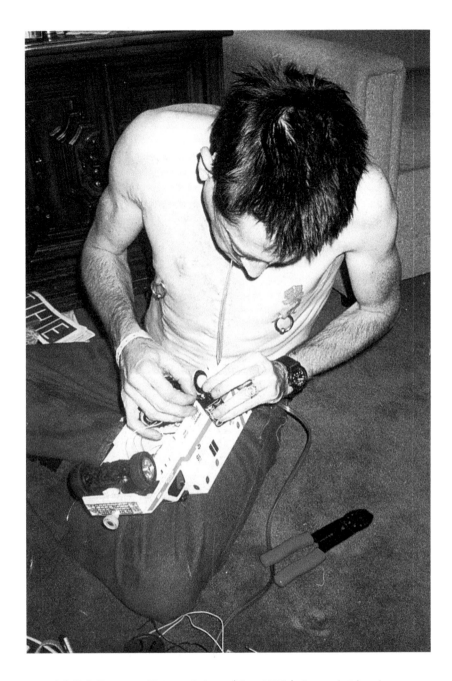

2.1. Bob Flanagan with toy ambulance (circa 1990s). A snapshot from home.
Photo by Sheree Rose. Courtesy of ONE Archives at the USC Libraries.

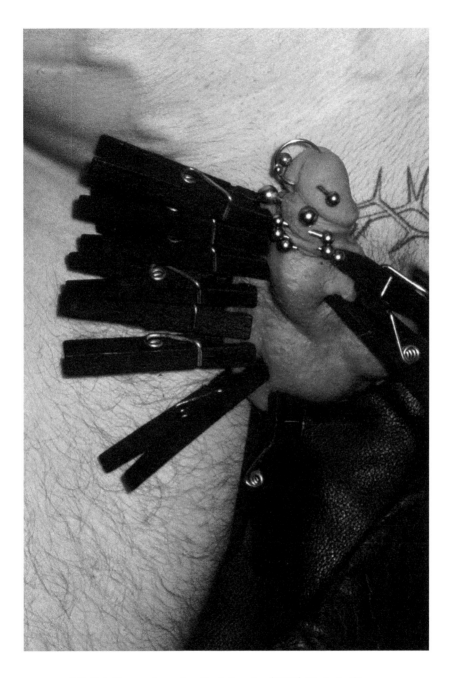

2.2. Bob Flanagan's penis with clothespins (1995). Photo by Sheree Rose. Courtesy of ONE Archives at the USC Libraries.

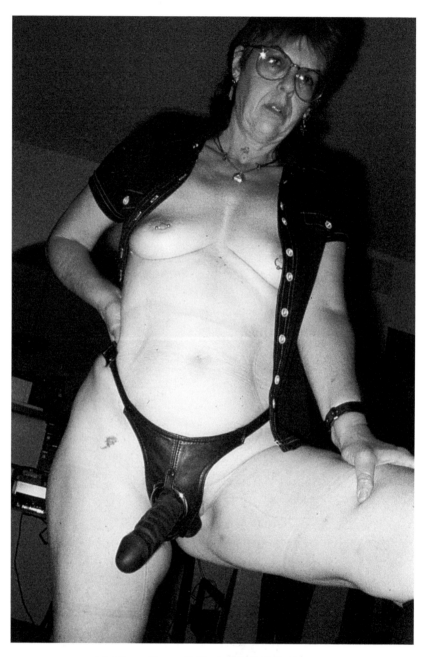

2.3. Sheree Rose with black dildo (1995). Courtesy
of ONE Archives at the USC Libraries.

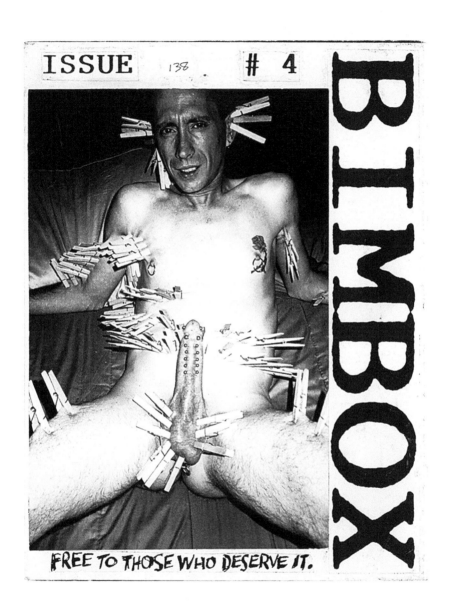

2.4. *Bimbox* zine cover (circa 1990s). Courtesy of ONE Archives at the USC Libraries.

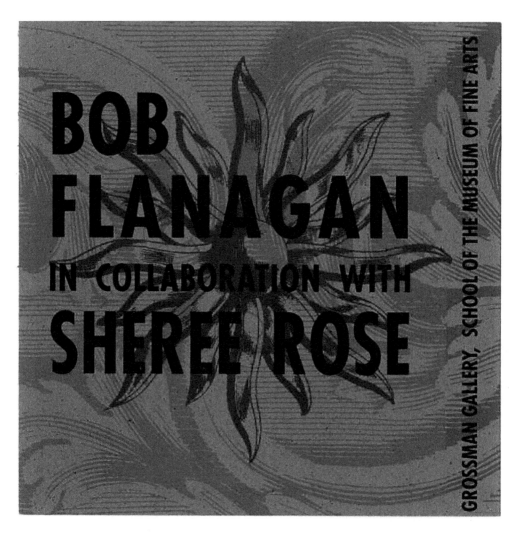

2.5. Bob Flanagan and Sheree Rose exhibition postcard from School of the Museum of Fine Arts, Boston where Rose and Flanagan performed *(Re)Visiting Hours* (1995). Courtesy of ONE Archives at the USC Libraries.

SCHOOL OF THE MUSEUM OF FINE ARTS
GROSSMAN GALLERY
230 The Fenway
Boston, MA 02115-9975
(617) 369-3718

February 10 - March 5, 1995
Reception: February 9, 5 - 7pm

Installation by Los Angeles performance artist and writer Bob Flanagan, collaborating with photographer and companion Sheree Rose.

GALLERY HOURS:
Tuesday, Friday & Saturday: 10am - 5pm
Wednesday & Thursday: 10am - 8pm
Sunday: 1 - 5pm
Closed Mondays & holidays

All exhibitions are free & open to the public.
The School is wheelchair accessible.

Janine Antoni
Nancy Barton
Louise Diedrich
Keith Edmier
Victor Estrada
Bob Flanagan and Sheree Rose
Lyle Ashton Harris and Iké Udé
Richard Hawkins
Larry Johnson
Yayoi Kusama
Jeff Koons
Sean Landers
Yasumasa Morimura
Collier Schorr

Michael Cohen, Curator

narcissistic disturbance

OTIS GALLERY
4 February–1 April 1995

Opening reception Saturday, 4 February 4:00–7:00 p.m.

Audience 0.01
an international video exhibition curated by Helena Kontova

"Narcissistic Disturbance" Panel Discussion
Moderated by Laurence A. Rickels with Nancy Barton, Judith Butler, Michael Cohen,
Lyle Ashton Harris, and David Rimanelli at Otis Gallery
Sunday, 12 February, 4:00 p.m. (Gallery opens Sunday at 2:00 p.m.)

2.6. *Narcissistic Disturbance* exhibit postcard, Otis College of Art and Design
(1995). Courtesy of ONE Archives at the USC Libraries.

TRANCESEX

A STATE OF MYSTICAL ABSORPTION

CURATED BY AMANDA M. OBERING, LES AYRE & ERIKA KNERR

JULY 23RD 12:00 NOON THROUGH JULY 26TH 12:00 NOON, 1993
RECEPTION JULY 24TH 1:00 - 9:00 PM

MONDRIAN HOTEL, 8440 SUNSET BOULEVARD, ROOMS 505 & 508, WEST HOLLYWOOD, CALIFORNIA 90069-1948
FOR INFORMATION CALL: (213) 876-2755

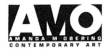

AMO
AMANDA M OBERING
CONTEMPORARY ART

7250 FRANKLIN AVENUE · 804
LOS ANGELES, CA 90046
PHONE/FAX (213) 876-2755

Video Marathon at the Mondrian Hotel

In an age where censorship and sexuality have become the grounds for congressional hearings and the battle cry for breadbasket politics, first amendment rights seem to pale under the spot light of a perceived "common good" of the general population. However, these nefarious forces that government tries to "regulate" and "control" are, ironically, becoming more prevalent than ever. Red light districts are no longer specialized areas of town. Rather, red light districts have become an upper channel on the remote control. Access is the power button. But how will congress regulate the 500 channels soon to be available in each American living room? Is it as simple and effective as initiating an interactive disclaimer a la the N.E.A. reopen's clause?

TranceseX examines the increasing role sexually charged images have played in video throughout the past thirty years and how censorship has affected them. It gathers artists whose works encompass a variety of body issues - issues of love, gender, sexuality, pornography, political satire, documentary illustration, semiotic discourse, power balance. The show functions in the hotel as a "bed" for the survey of videos. Here in the seeming luxury of a Mondrian Hotel suite - moments away from the porn houses that surround it in Hollywood - you are welcome to choose from the large selection of videos. You can comfortably observe or transfix what has at other times been deemed unrespectable. By opening a private room where loneliness is so easily tempted by fantasy, TranceseX offers an alternative for public consumption. The context of the hotel brings to the forefront the obvious differences between sexual content which is privately conjured and publically accepted, versus material which is semi-publically embraced and publically admonished.

VITO ACCONCI	GRAN FURY	BARRY MORSE
EMILY ARMSTRONG & PAT IVERS	GANG	JOHN OBENTLICHER
LES AYRE	STEVE GIULIANO	ALIX PEARLSTEIN
MARIA BEATTY	CHRIS HAMMERLEIN	GENE RASENBERGER
ANTE BOZANICH	MICHELLE HANDELMAN	JONATHAN REISS
KATHY BREW	LYNN HERSHMAN	TRUDIE REISS
KEN CAMP	JANE HUDSON	SHEREE ROSE
MONET CLARK	T. JANKOWSKI	KENNY SCHACHTER
COLETTE - THE HOUSE OF OLYMPIA	JOE JARRELL	CAROLEE SCHNEEMAN
DIANNA COHEN	MIKE KELLEY	SUZY SILVER
JEM A. COHEN	CHARLES LA BELLE	ANNIE SPRINKLE
SHELLEY COOK	SEAN LANDERS	ADRIAN THEAN
DOUGLAS DAVIS	ANDREA LEWIS	AYANNA UDONGO
ANA de PORTELA	ALINE LILITH MARE	HELENE R. VALENTIN
WAYNE DeSELLE	MICHAEL WASCOTT & KIM McKILLIP	VICTORIA VESNA
DEVON DIKEOU	PAUL McCARTHY	ANDY WARHOL
LISA DeLILLO	JO MENELL	LAWRENCE WEINER
SALLY CLENBY	MARILYN MINTER	BRUCE & NORMAN YONEMOTO
ROBERT FLANAGAN	GRAYDON MOFFAT	AND OTHERS!

Special thanks to David Ararch of the Kitchen (New York), Marie Beatty of Vesper Video (New York), Mindy Faber of Video Data Bank (Chicago), Rosamund Felsen Gallery (Los Angeles), Sara Meyers-Kingsly of the Andy Warhol Foundation (New York), Washington Lowe of Electronic Art Intermix (New York), Michael Masucci & Kim McKillip of EZTV (Los Angeles), Andrea Rosen Gallery (New York), Randy Sommer of Food House (Santa Monica), Kathy Brew, Ellen Cantor, Peter Schaaf. D.O. & E.T.

ADMISSION
FREE

2.7 *TranceSex* pamphlet (1993). Courtesy of ONE Archives at the USC Libraries.

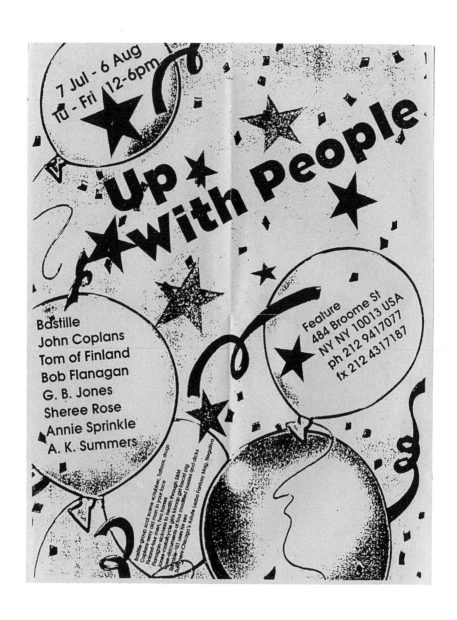

2.8. *Up with People* flier (circa 1990s). Courtesy of ONE Archives at the USC Libraries.

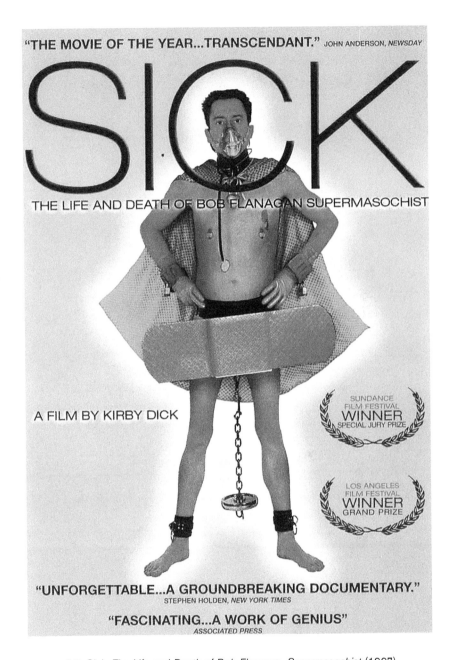

2.9. *Sick: The Life and Death of Bob Flanagan, Supermasochist* (1997)
DVD cover. While Rose is credited as co-producer on the back of the
DVD and in the film credits, her name appears nowhere on the DVD's front
cover. (See Rose's "Why Kirby Dick Is a 'Sick' Prick," page 60.)

Visiting Hours (1992–1995)

Visiting Hours is Rose and Flanagan's best-known collaborative exhibit. It premiered at the Santa Monica Museum of Art in 1992 and then traveled to the New Museum of Contemporary Art in New York in 1994. From there, it was retitled *(Re)Visiting Hours* when it moved to the School of the Museum of Fine Arts in Boston in 1995. Transforming the museum space to hospital space with the text of Flanagan's "Why" poem wrapped around the entire gallery space, the exhibit included a waiting room, a recreation of a hospital room where visitors could sit in the chair next to Flanagan's bed and speak with him and Rose, pieces reflecting subversively cast children's toys as sex toys, BDSM gear, medical equipment, Rose's 1982 hypodermic needles and photography collage of Flanagan's face in various expressions of pain, *Wall of Pain,* and *Video Coffin,* one of three pieces that were to be part of the *Memento Mori* death trilogy (discussed in the "Breathing Space" section, essays by Aarons, Jones, and O'Brien, and the introduction to this volume). One of the key elements of this exhibit was Rose hoisting Flanagan by his ankles so that he would hang suspended indefinitely above the exhibit's visitors.

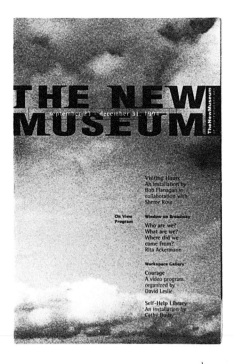

3.1. *Visiting Hours* exhibit pamphlet, The New Museum of Contemporary Art, New York (1994). Courtesy of ONE Archives at the USC Libraries. From the pamphlet: "Rose has described *Visiting Hours* in terms of the idea that, if you pull one thread of a person's life, the rest comes along with it. This image of a life as a tangled skein informs every aspect of the exhibition, from the wrapping text to the complex connections between sickness, death, and sexuality posed by each component work in turn."
—Laura Trippi, curator

VISITINGHOURS
An installation by Bob Flanagan in collaboration with Sharee Rose

Bob Flanagan's Visiting Hours begins and ends with a question: 'Why?' A poet as well as a visual, performance, and video artist, Flanagan has wrapped the perimeter of this autobiographical installation with a prose poem that rhythmically and repeatedly offers answers: 'Because it feels good;... because it makes me come; because I'm sick....' Starting at the gallery's entrance, the poem runs uninterrupted in a single line around the space of display—along the institutional green walls that enclose *The Waiting Room*, various thematic play and display areas, the video scaffolding entitled *Bob Flanagan's Sick*, and the aptly titled *Wall of Pain*. The text flows around odd corners, over doorways, and across a flight of stairs. Relentlessly, 'Why?' works its way into every crease and wrinkle along the circumference of the galleries.

'Why?' addresses the origins of Flanagan's involvement with extreme pain practices as a form of pleasure (sadomasochism or 's/m'); it points to sources as diverse as Cinderella, the natural endorphin high produced in the brain by pain and exercise, and pop culture slogans ranging from 'You always hurt the one you love' to the ever-American 'No pain, no gain!' At the same time, the installation resounds with a disquieting question: what to do with the one on your hands? 'I was promised an early death, but here I am still waiting,' the artist writes elsewhere. Now perpetually hooked up to a tank of oxygen, Flanagan at 41 is among the oldest living sufferers of cystic fibrosis, a degenerative genetic illness affecting the lungs and stomach that usually is fatal by early adolescence.

Visiting Hours stages Freud's strange drama of Eros and Thanatos, in which existence unfolds as a ceaseless struggle between the instinct for life and the instinct for disintegration or death. But this appears to be a version interpreted by Pee Wee Herman. The installation is designed like a crazy stage set of a children's residential hospital, replete with a torture chamber lurking amidst the institutional cheer. Here, the dark encounter between drives for sex and death is framed and buoyed up by a keen wit and a cool sense of the absurd.

But, in terms of masochism, is Bob Flanagan sick? Contemporary pain practices, from consensual s/m to the recent fashion craze for body piercing and tattooing, are fundamentally masochistic. They operate societally as a form of critique, affirming the value of powerlessness within a culture that esteems mastery and domination. Increasingly, death, violence, and drastic social change pervade our society. In the face of AIDS, escalating racial and ethnic violence, the continuing rise of techno-science, the growing instability of geo-politics and the environment, and even the incremental redefining of gender roles, the temptation to respond with a stiffening of the will is almost irresistible. Curiously, though, alternative models to domination are to be found where we least expect them—in the burgeoning self-help industry, where issues of domination and submission emerge under such umbrella concepts as 'addiction,' 'co-dependency,' and 'shame'; in the masochistic excesses of current music cultures that exalt self-surrender to the compulsive pulse of D.J.-driven dance parties; in the dispersion of the self into the fluid group structures of online computer communication; and in the assertion of attitudinal masochism, with the prevalence of piercing and bondage gear, as a postmodern house style for meeting the end of the millennium.

These and other developments do more than attest that a fascination with pain has arrived with a vengeance. They meet the challenge of a terrifying situation with a self that is porous and pliant, embracing an environment in which the self is gradually but radically being redefined. Relinquishing the impulse toward domination and advancing instead the capacity to feel as the ultimate, distinguishing human trait,' such forms of social intercourse can be understood as part of a project to construct an ethics of self-abdication. They evidence a determination, as Flanagan would have it, to fight sickness with sickness.'

And then there is art.

As a poet, but also a stand up comic, Flanagan's performance career began with readings of his own poetry that he soon incorporated into s/m performance demonstrations in the late 1970s and 1980s in the clubs of Los Angeles. In this, he is allied with a loosely affiliated group of contemporary writers and performance artists pushing language, sexuality, and identity to the edge of a violent rupture, from Kathy Acker and Dennis Cooper to Ron Athey and Karen Finley. With the original installation of *Visiting Hours* at the Santa Monica Museum of Art in 1992, Flanagan produced his first major work of visual art, linking him into a sprawling network of artists working with the body in terms of degraded, polymorphous, or socio-disciplinary themes, an approach that has recently been considered under the rubric of 'abject art.'

Various other artistic traditions cross paths in Flanagan's work. Some of these reach back to art of the 1970s: practices of endurance that tested the corporeal body, such as those employed by Chris Burden, Paul McCarthy, and Gina Pane; of performance that explored taboos of eroticism, as in the work of Carolee Schneeman, Barbara Smith, and Hannah Wilke; and of duration that converted the material of lived experience into an art of everyday life, such as the performance activities of Marina Abramovic, Linda Montano, and Tehching Hsieh. But it is finally in terms of the nature of Flanagan's art most clearly emerges. Through the documentary incorporation of intimately personal material, their work together runs the gamut from private to public 'performances,' including college lectures. It rests uneasily within traditional categories, yet in itself is rigorously specific, operating on the border between artistic practice and social work.

Rose has described *Visiting Hours* in terms of the idea that, if you pull one thread of a person's life, the rest comes along with it. This image of a life as a tangled skein informs every aspect of the exhibition, from the wrapping text to the complex connections between sickness, death, and sexuality posed by each component work in turn. Flanagan has commented that, when he first screened the installation, his conversations with visitors often achieved an unprecedented level of intimacy, taking shape as quasi-confessional mini-narratives. Speaking with the artist, visitors gave voice to their own encounters with illness or abuse, or the loss of a loved relative or friend.

Free standing in the center of the gallery, the hospital room is a collapsed and kaleidoscopic emblem of the exhibition in its entirety. Its interior is animated, less by Flanagan than by the visitors' conversations with him and the fast cut compilation video of old cartoons, t.v., and movie clips that plays on the wall-mounted monitor. Flanagan's inner sanctum is ruptured and pervaded by the outside, a pattern echoed elsewhere in the exhibition. Within the 'standing bondage' of the video scaffold, the body is represented as a composite of parts screened independently on seven monitors; but each part is also discontinuous within itself, separate receptors for which 'sensation' (documentary clips of s/m actions) appears interchangeably with 'information' (cartoons and movies, advertisements, home movies of Flanagan as a young boy).

A space of listening and waiting, the core of the exhibition is heartfelt and hollowed out. Along its outer walls, three views of Flanagan appear; each is distinct but partial. Clamped to a light box centered on an otherwise empty white wall are a pair of chest x-rays in which eye-like nipple rings, precisely defined, seem alternately to float through the chest cavity or fuse with the plane of the x-rays themselves. Here, technologies of pleasure and medicine mesh gears, catching between them a spectral image of the human body. When, intermittently, Flanagan slowly and quietly is pulled feet first by an ankle harness toward the ceiling, elevating like the hanged man of the tarot above the hospital room's open walls, this serves as a rending reminder of the authority death holds over life.

But the image of Flanagan suspended further suggests a radical humiliation of the self, a squandering of that precious human capital so conscientiously acquired. Drawing to the surface quandaries, wishes, and fears embedded in the body itself, *Visiting Hours* subtly redirects the will to survive through paths of self renunciation. Death forms a threshold over which all the exhibition's movements are suspended; as in horror films, the nearness of death here solicits from the viewer an almost corporeal enjoyment as well as dread. The complex web of issues raised by the exhibition settles into a layered meditation on the prospect of death. Why? Why? And, in the meantime, the rhythmic repetitions of 'because...'

Laura Trippi Curator

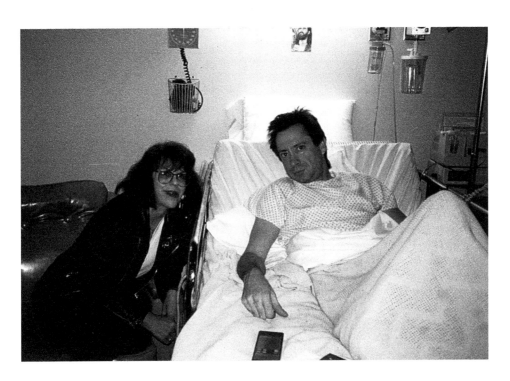

3.2. Sheree Rose and Bob Flanagan in hospital bed at *Visiting Hours,* Santa Monica Museum of Art, Santa Monica, CA (1992). Photo by Molly Shore. Courtesy of ONE Archives at the USC Libraries.

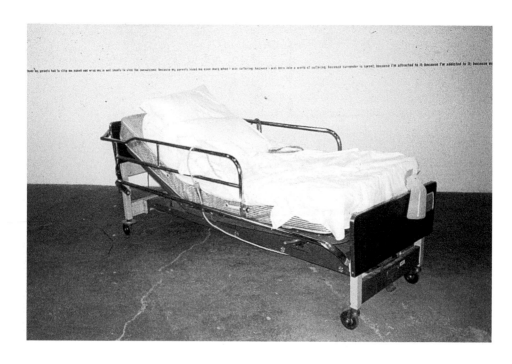

3.3. *Visiting Hours* closing party, empty bed with wall text. Santa Monica Museum of Art, Santa Monica, CA (1993). Photo by Sheree Rose. Courtesy of ONE Archives at the USC Libraries.

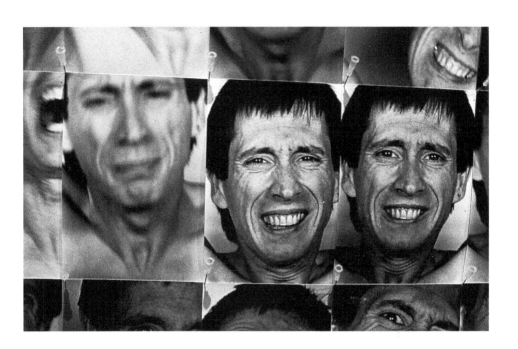

3.4. Detail from *Wall of Pain* collage (1982) by Sheree Rose, exhibited in *Visiting Hours* (1992–1995). Courtesy of ONE Archives at the USC Libraries.

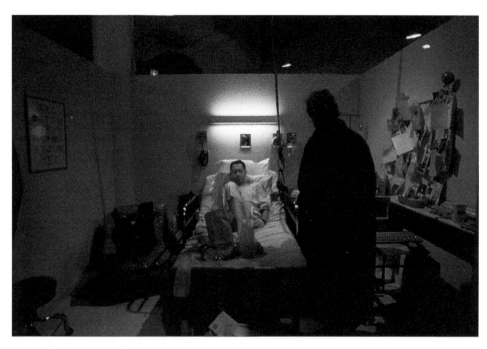

3.5. Bob Flanagan and Sheree Rose at *(Re)Visiting Hours*. School of the Museum of Fine Arts, Boston (1995). Courtesy of ONE Archives at the USC Libraries.

Bobballoon (1996)

Bobballoon was Rose's first piece after Flanagan died in early 1996. *Bobballoon* is a twenty-foot vinyl balloon of Flanagan with a ball gag, wearing nothing but a leather jacket and a pierced, erect penis. It is currently folded up in ONE Archives. It was displayed in Tokyo, Japan, in 1996 but had to be covered with a Sumo-style diaper after viewers complained about its explicitness and in order for Rose to be photographed in front of it with the Japanese Minister of Art. *Bobballoon* is occasionally displayed for special events and exhibits in the Los Angeles area, including at a tribute to Flanagan at Beyond Baroque in 2013.

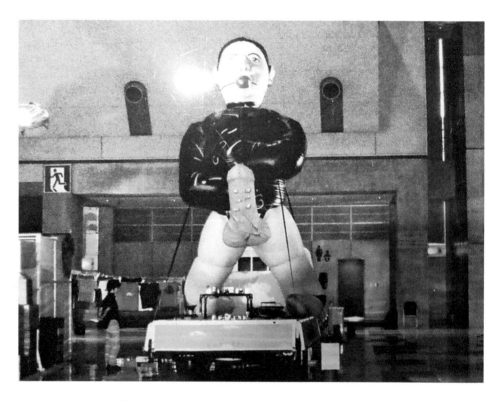

4.1. *Bobballoon* front view. Tokyo, Japan (1996). Photo by Sheree Rose. Courtesy of ONE Archives at the USC Libraries.

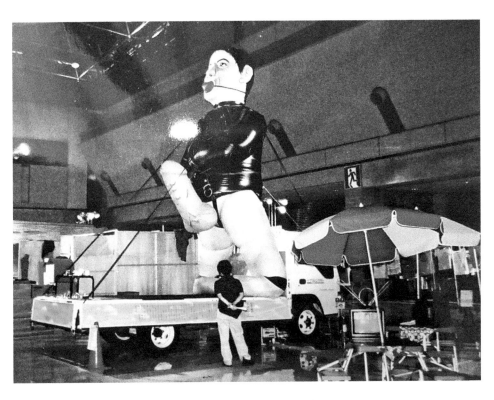

4.2. *Bobballoon* side view. Tokyo, Japan (1996). Photo by Sheree
Rose. Courtesy of ONE Archives at the USC Libraries.

この姿を、なんだか変だ　　これが真の姿だ！©Sheree Rose 1996

「当選しても、会社は辞めません」

東大大学院在学中のフジテレビ報道記者が体験する"小選挙区制"

まず、このプロフィールを見てください。

長島一由・29歳。フジテレビ報道記者（休職中）。東京大学法学部大学院政治専攻在学中。早稲田大学大学院教育学部卒。青山学院大学院卒。国際政治学修士。で、ウインドサーフィン・バルセロナ五輪強化選手（今年度世界大会3位入賞）。

こんな嫌味ったらしい肩書を持つ長島氏が衆議院神奈川4区（鎌倉・逗子・葉山・横浜市栄区）から無党派として出馬表明した。週末にはウインドサーフィンに乗ってビーチと海上からスピーチ。これまた嫌味かって感じ。

チョップ記者（高卒・29歳）は『夏休みに入り、政治活動本格スタート』した長島氏の選挙事務所に行ってきました。事務所は鎌倉のウインドサーフィンショップ。目の前は海。ホントに嫌味かって感じ。

長島氏はホカ弁のカレーライスを食ってました。これ金になってたんですか。

「いえ、実際は40～50歳になったら、と考えてたんです」

かなり早まりましたね。

「2年間の時間ができましたから。去年の11月に東大の大学院に合格。会社で2年間の休職が認められたんです。それで、どうせなら。休職期間中なら選挙に出てもいいと規則があります」

選挙に出ることを睨んで貯金してたんですか。

「最初は1040万円からスタート。最近は週に30万とか平気でなくなっていきますよ」

8,314円」とある。

「とりあえず見てください」『週刊長島』なる1枚のパンフレットを手渡された。「政治資金、残りあと6、66

て。

「後期はあんまり学校に行っ

「夏休みが終わったら活動はどうするんですか。

「反応はいいですよ」波乗り演説は若者にバカにされませんか。

「いいや、わいせつではないとに。でも、こっちスケジュールの都合でNO。あ〜、やっぱりダメなんですよ。

ところが、がっくりと肩を落とす記者を気の毒に思ったのか、ローズさんが1枚の写真を差し出してくれるではないか。

でも、これのどこが"わいせつ"なんだろうか？

それが上の写真。「ボバルーン」のオチンチンは、こういう具合になっているのである。

接、展覧会が終わった後でもいいから見せてくれせつ"なんだろうか？

警告は脅しですから。

「現代美術はすでに価値が定まったものでなく、これから定まっていくものなんです。だから、わいせつという判断自体、作品を見る人たちのこれからの評価を待つべきなんです」

本当にそうだよな。

力をちらつかせて個人の意見を他者に押しつける姿勢は許せない」（アートプラザのキュレーター・岡崎乾二郎氏）

前出の田中さんもこう言う。

これには展覧会関係者も不満を隠そうとしない。「芸術であろうとなかろうと、こんな警告は不当。まるでドラえもんの人形が、わいせつとされたようなもんです」（深川署）

催者側は「できません」（アートプラザ実行委員会・田中藤太郎事業第一課長）のすげないひと言。

じゃあという

ところが、主

だだ〜いとお願いしてみるこ

ローズさんに直

いから見せてく

るということなんです。夏休みで、子供さんもたくさん見に来る時期なんです。だから、夏休みどんなことであろうと許せません。

「あくまでも警告なんで

す」（深川署）

「いやいや、わいせつではないあくまでもその疑いがあるということなんです。

に至るまで—。

4.3. *Bobballoon* covered and uncovered write-up in Japanese erotic magazine (1996). Courtesy of ONE Archives at the USC Libraries.

The translation of the write-up appears as follows in the archive with the magazine:

LOVEDOLL IN TOKIO NOT ALLOWED TO SHOW SHAME
TOKIO 20 August 1996
Japanese police have put a diaper on lovedoll *Bobballoon*. The six-meter piece of art is not allowed anymore to show its erected private part that's pierced with hypodermic needles and rings. For a few days this work has been exhibited in a show in Tokio until the police got complaints. The American artist Sheree Rose who created the work is not surprised, she says that the work is not dirty or aggressive it's just to show that one should not be ashamed about one's sexuality. Rose also questioned the motivation of the Japanese police. "I wonder if a male artist would have had the same problems with a female nude." According the 50-year-old artist, *Bobballoon* exhibits the sexual masochism of her husband performance artist Bob Flanagan. For Flanagan who suffered from CF, this masochism was the way to deal with his pain. He died earlier this year and his paintings were the inspiration for *Bobballoon*. "The penis was a part of my husband's personality," according to Rose. *Bobballoon* is only dressed in a short leather coat and is sucking on a baby dummy. The police were not impressed: "Freedom of speech has nothing to do with scandalizing people," according to the police, "We had complaints and don't see what's wrong with warning the organization." Also, the press in Japan is not shocked by *Bobballoon* while A. P. is criticizing the "inconsistency of Japanese norms." The papers in Japan have different opinions without comment. The first three days the organization put a blanket over the penis; the artist however insisted.

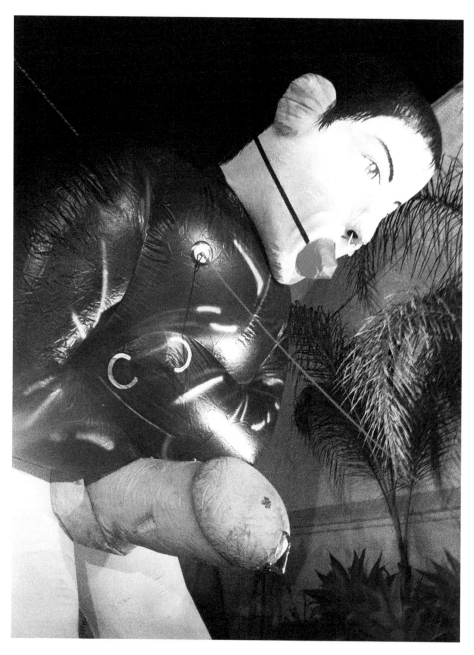

4.4. *Bobballoon* at tribute to Bob Flanagan. Beyond Baroque,
Venice, CA (2013). Photo by Yetta Howard.

Music, Literary, and Sexual Subcultures

While Rose and Flanagan are thought to be primarily associated with performance art, their world included some of the most path-breaking underground cultural contexts. Rose was the staff photographer for Beyond Baroque, a legendary venue in Venice, California, that hosted luminaries from underground performance poetry, literary, and music culture including Dennis Cooper, Amy Gerstler, Patti Smith, and Tom Waits. Flanagan performed his poetry there. In addition to such involvement and redefining sexual, museum, and subcultural space via BDSM practices, the visual presence of Rose and Flanagan's collaborative performances played a significant role in industrial, industrial-metal, and noise music cultural contexts including Rose and Flanagan being featured in videos by Nine Inch Nails, Danzig, and Godflesh.

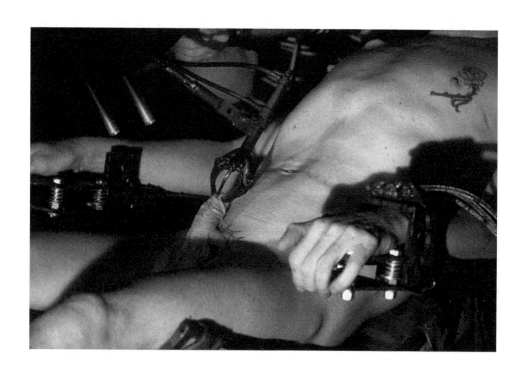

5.1. Nine Inch Nails, "Happiness in Slavery" uncensored music video shoot featuring Bob Flanagan (1992). Photo by Sheree Rose. This video, directed by Jon Reiss, was banned from MTV. Courtesy of ONE Archives at the USC Libraries.

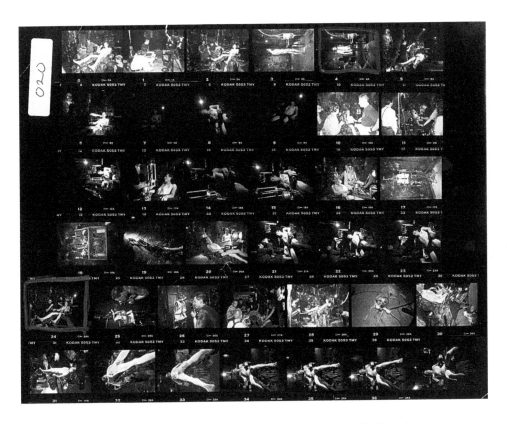

5.2. Nine Inch Nails, "Happiness in Slavery" uncensored music video shoot featuring Bob Flanagan (1992). Contact sheet by Sheree Rose. This video was banned from MTV. Courtesy of ONE Archives at the USC Libraries.

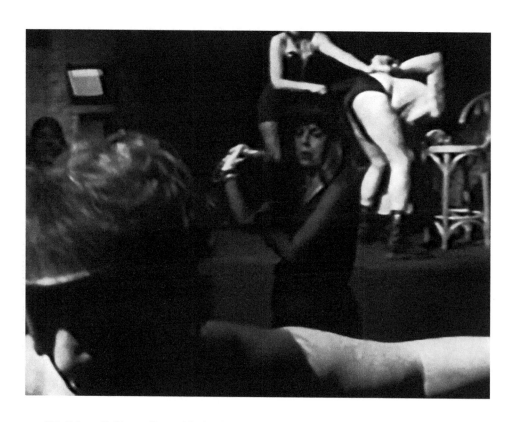

5.3. Video still, Sheree Rose whipping in uncensored Danzig "It's Coming Down" music video featuring Sheree Rose and Bob Flanagan (1993). This video was banned from MTV.

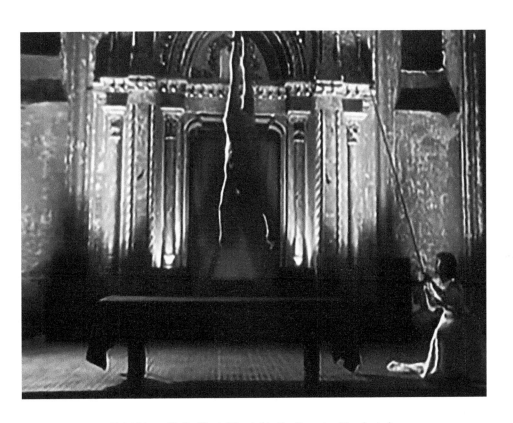

5.4. Video still, Godflesh "Crush My Soul" music video featuring
Sheree Rose and Bob Flanagan (1995).

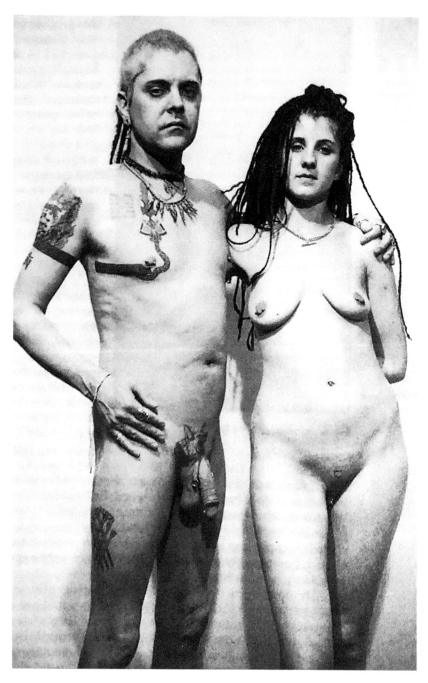

5.5. Genesis P-Orridge and Paula P-Orridge (circa 1987–88). Photo by Sheree Rose.
Genesis P-Orridge is the founding member of industrial group Throbbing Gristle.

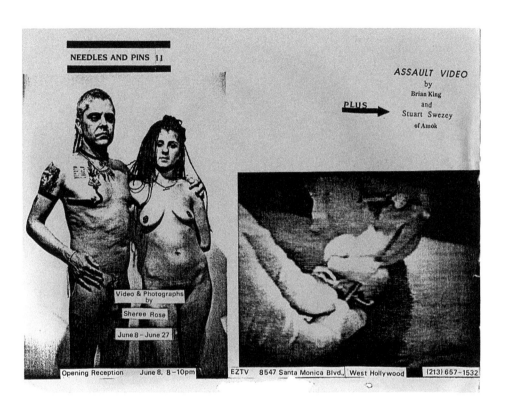

5.6. *Needles and Pins II* flier for event at EZTV, West Hollywood, CA, with reproduction of Genesis P-Orridge and Paula P-Orridge photo by Sheree Rose (circa 1987–1988). Courtesy of ONE Archives at the USC Libraries.

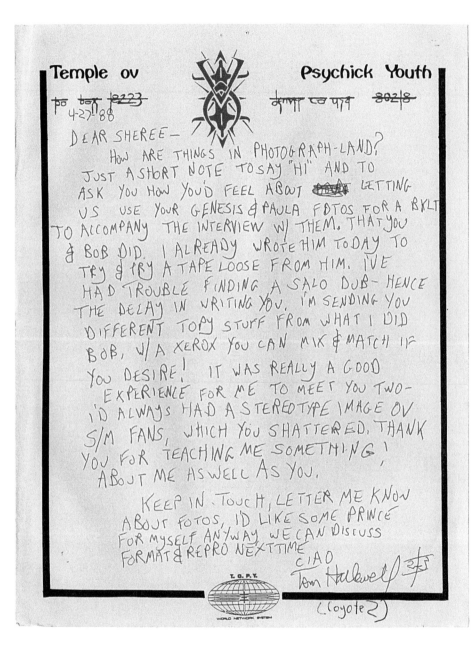

Temple ov   **Psychick Youth**

PO ~~box 19223~~
4-27-88

DEAR SHEREE—
    HOW ARE THINGS IN PHOTOGRAPH-LAND?
JUST A SHORT NOTE TO SAY "HI" AND TO
ASK YOU HOW YOU'D FEEL ABOUT ~~THAT~~ LETTING
US USE YOUR GENESIS & PAULA FOTOS FOR A BKLT
TO ACCOMPANY THE INTERVIEW W/ THEM. THAT YOU
& BOB DID. I ALREADY WROTE HIM TODAY TO
TRY & PRY A TAPE LOOSE FROM HIM. I'VE
HAD TROUBLE FINDING A SALO DUB — HENCE
THE DELAY IN WRITING YOU. I'M SENDING YOU
DIFFERENT TOPY STUFF FROM WHAT I DID
BOB, W/ A XEROX YOU CAN MIX & MATCH IF
YOU DESIRE! IT WAS REALLY A GOOD
    EXPERIENCE FOR ME TO MEET YOU TWO—
I'D ALWAYS HAD A STEREOTYPE IMAGE OV
S/M FANS, WHICH YOU SHATTERED. THANK
YOU FOR TEACHING ME SOMETHING!
    ABOUT ME AS WELL AS YOU.

      KEEP IN TOUCH, LETTER ME KNOW
ABOUT FOTOS, I'D LIKE SOME PRINCE
FOR MYSELF ANYWAY WE CAN DISCUSS
FORMAT & REPRO NEXT TIME
               CIAO
               Tom Hallewell
                   (Coyote)

T.O.P.Y.
WORLD NETWORK SYSTEM

5.7. Letter from Tom Hallewell (Psychic TV promoter) to Sheree Rose (1988). Psychic TV is an experimental group fronted by Genesis P-Orridge. Courtesy of ONE Archives at the USC Libraries.

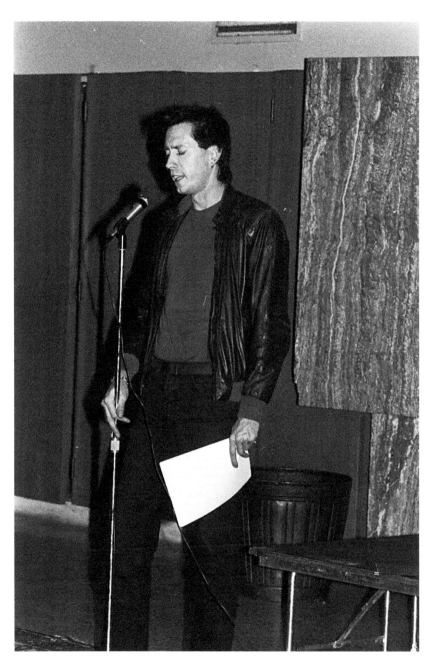

5.8. Bob Flanagan reading at Beyond Baroque, Venice, CA (circa 1980s).
Photo by Sheree Rose. Courtesy of ONE Archives at the USC Libraries.

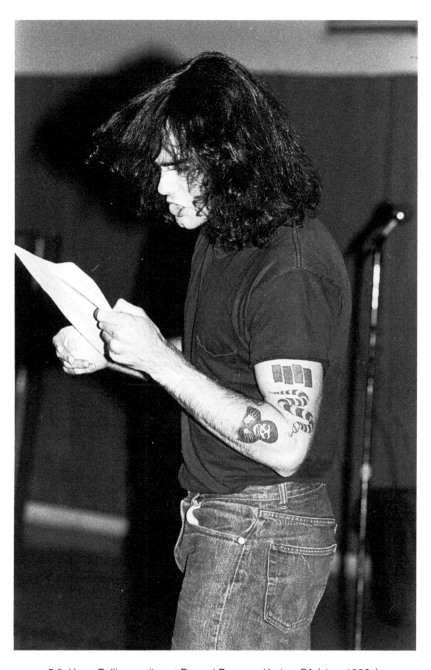

5.9. Henry Rollins reading at Beyond Baroque, Venice, CA (circa 1980s). Rollins fronted the hardcore punk band Black Flag before forming Rollins Band and continues to do spoken-word events and a weekly radio show. Photo by Sheree Rose. Courtesy of ONE Archives at the USC Libraries.

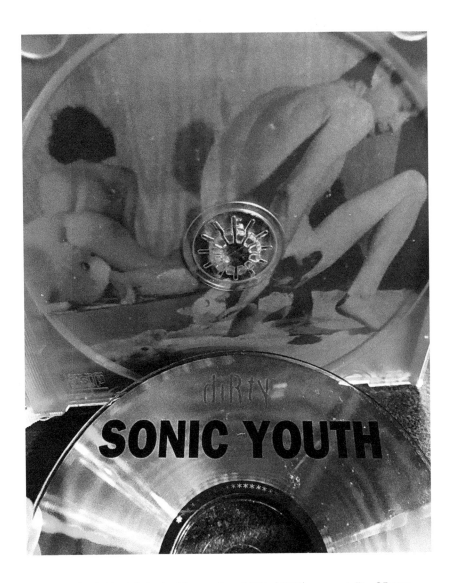

5.10. Sonic Youth limited edition version of *Dirty* (1992) compact disc CD tray, with reproduction of Mike Kelley's photograph *Manipulating Mass-Produced Idealized Objects / Nostalgic Depiction of Innocence of Childhood* (1990). While Kelley did the inner-sleeve artwork for all editions of the album, the version with Kelley's photograph of Rose and Flanagan was only included in the limited edition version of the album. Image capture by Yetta Howard.

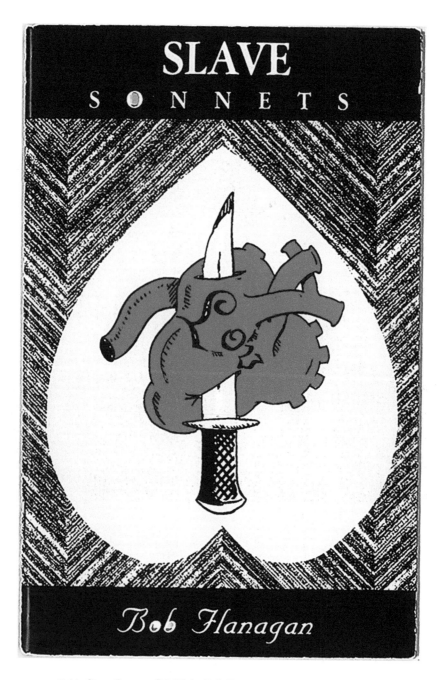

5.11. *Slave Sonnets* (1986) by Bob Flanagan for Sheree Rose. Cover
art by Mike Kelley. Originally published by Cold Clam Press, Los
Angeles. Courtesy of ONE Archives at the USC Libraries.

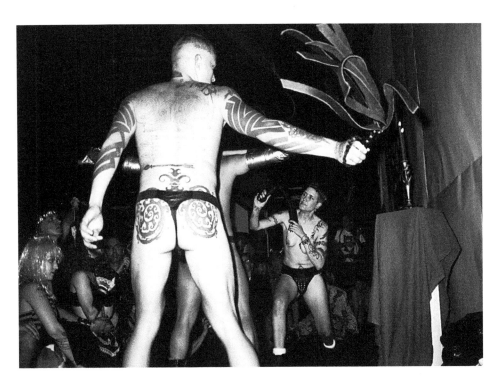

5.12. Ron Athey at Fetish Ball (circa 1990s). Photo by Sheree Rose.
Courtesy of ONE Archives at the USC Libraries.

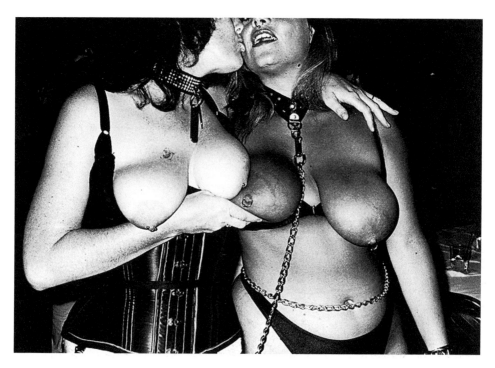

5.13. Two Women at Fetish Ball (circa 1990s). Photo by Sheree
Rose. Courtesy of ONE Archives at the USC Libraries.

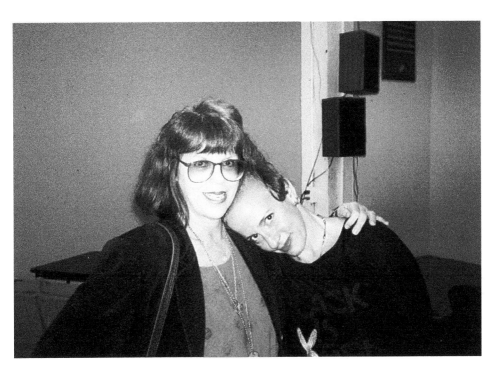

5.14. Sheree Rose with Kathy Acker (1992). Courtesy of ONE Archives at the USC Libraries.

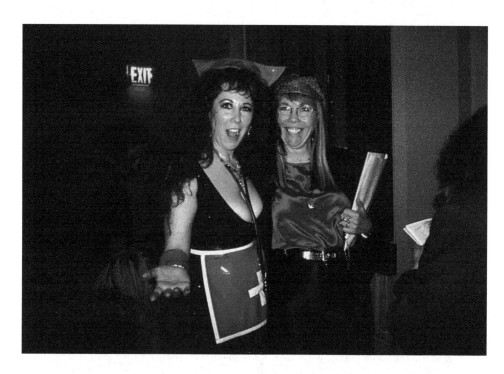

5.15. Annie Sprinkle at Hookers Convention, Van Nuys, CA (1997). Photo by Sheree Rose. Courtesy of ONE Archives at the USC Libraries.

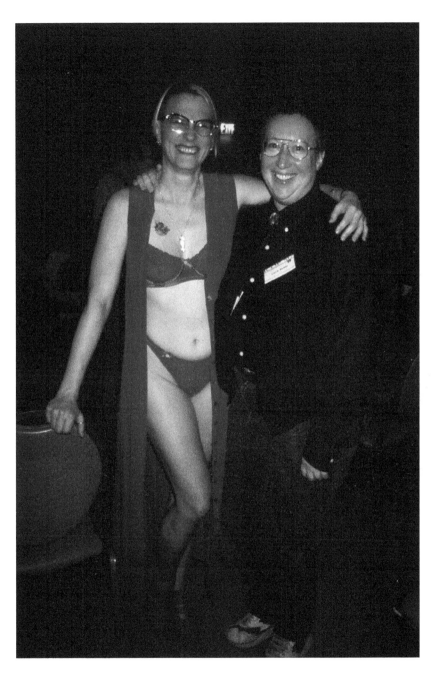

5.16. Carol Queen and Gayle Rubin at Hookers Convention, Van Nuys, CA (1997). Photo by Sheree Rose. Courtesy of ONE Archives at the USC Libraries.

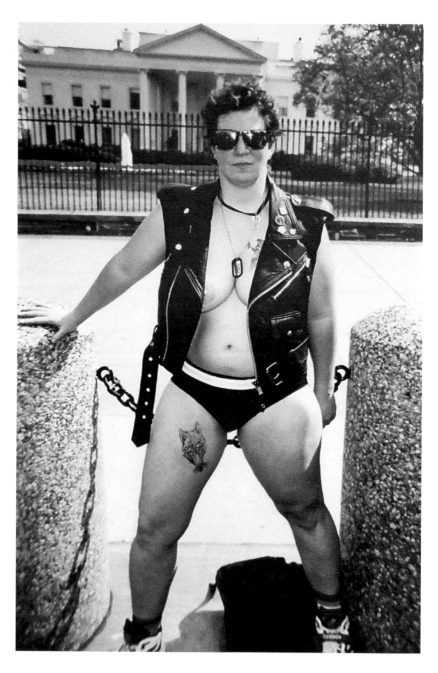

5.17. *Blue Takes Washington* (1993). Photo by Sheree Rose.
Courtesy of ONE Archives at the USC Libraries.

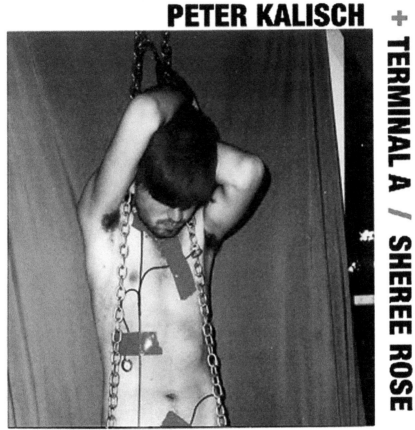

5.18. Peter Kalisch / Terminal A and Sheree Rose, *Denial / Why Not* cover, Records Ad Nauseam, 2016, album cover photo by Luka Fisher. Rose's involvement with underground music cultures continues into the present. Her "Why Not?" piece, reproduced in full in the "Words" part of this book, is her response-version of Flanagan's "Why," which she recorded with postpunk revival synth artist Terminal A on a release with noise artist Peter Kalisch in 2016.

Breathing Space

This section asks those who experience it to take a meditative breath and to keep breathing deeply while closely contemplating explicitly death-related materials—Rose's death portraits of her mother and of Flanagan, for instance—and images that, in their various modes of exhibiting radical temporality, represent re-performance, resurrection, and artistic autonomy such as a photograph by Rose of her iconic *S*, discussed at length throughout the "Words" section of this book. In an interview with Rose, Klare Scarborough includes Rose discussing her portrait of Flanagan on the day of his death and the posthumous carving of the *S* into his chest: "Yes, it was done after his death as part of a private ritual. [. . .] Several months later I got a phone call from the police here. They came to my house, showed me the photographs, and asked me if I murdered my husband? And I said no! Of course not! So I had to show them his death certificate, proving that he did in fact die in the hospital!" (Scarborough 128).[1]

This section isolates *Video Coffin* (1994) from the specific context of *Visiting Hours* where it was exhibited because of its key role in Rose's collaborative performances from the 2010s. The *Memento Mori* death trilogy was intended to be a three-installation, casket-based project that was to encompass *Video Coffin*, *Dust to Dust*, and *The Viewing*. Only *Video Coffin* (1994) was realized before Flanagan's death. It features a coffin with a video monitor of Flanagan's head, where the dead body's head is generally situated, but as viewers approach the piece, their faces appear on the monitor. Embossed in red on the inside of the coffin's cover is "I was promised an early death but here I am, some forty years later, still waiting . . ." *Dust to Dust* was intended to be a coffin filled with thousands of small photographs of Flanagan by Rose—fashioned as "dust." In 2015 Rose performed a reimagined version of *Dust to Dust*, which included a collaboration with Martin O'Brien. In *The Ascension* (2017), several repro-

---

1. Klare Scarborough, "Coffins and Cameras: A Conversation with Sheree Rose," *Performance Research*, vol. 15, no. 1, 2010, pp. 123–30.

ductions of small photographic prints were "dusted" over the participants in the first part of the performance. *The Viewing* was intended to be a post-mortem performance involving a video camera that was to be included in Flanagan's coffin with viewers remotely witnessing the decomposition of his body. In 2016 Rose performed a reimagined version of *The Viewing* as a collaborative durational piece with O'Brien and Rhiannon Aarons.

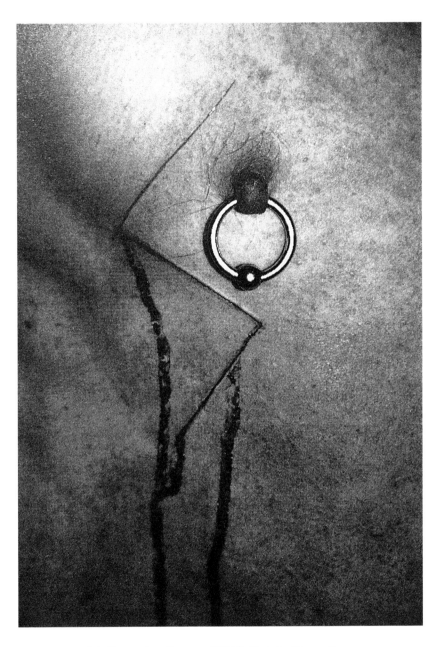

6.1. *S* carved on Flanagan (1991). Photo by Sheree Rose.
Courtesy of ONE Archives at the USC Libraries.

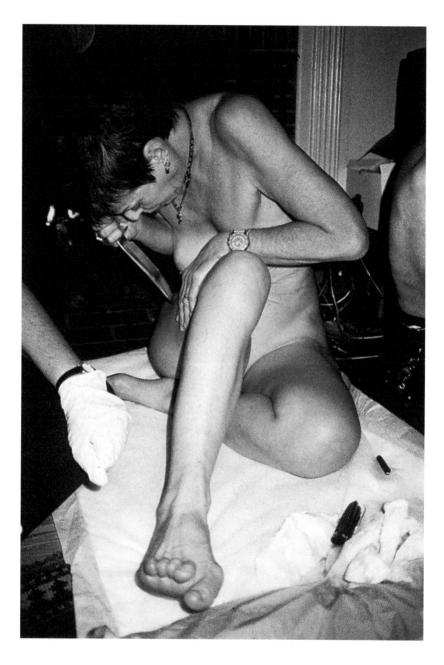

6.2. Sheree Rose's memorial cutting in honor of Bob Flanagan's 44th
(1997). Courtesy of ONE Archives at the USC Libraries.

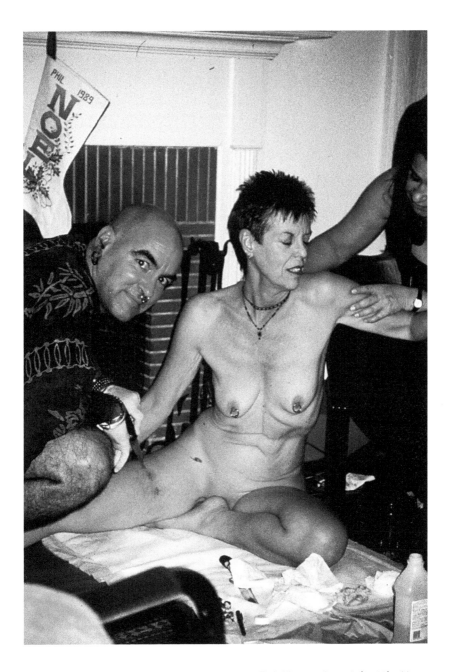

6.3. Sheree Rose's memorial cutting in honor of Bob Flanagan's 44th (1997) with Dragon (left), slave of Mistress Zia. Courtesy of ONE Archives at the USC Libraries.

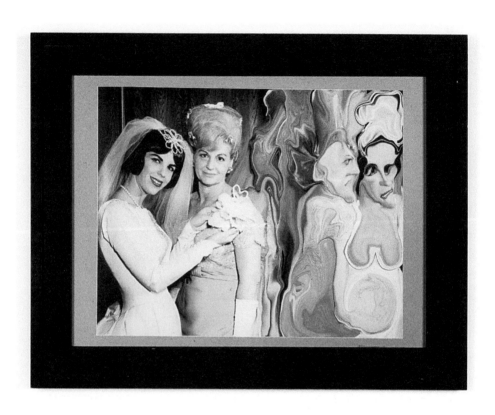

6.4. Manipulated 1964 photo of Sheree Rose on her wedding day with her mother (1995) by Sheree Rose. Exhibited in *Leftovers,* Sheree Rose's University of California, Irvine, MFA thesis show. Image capture by Amanda Majors (2018).

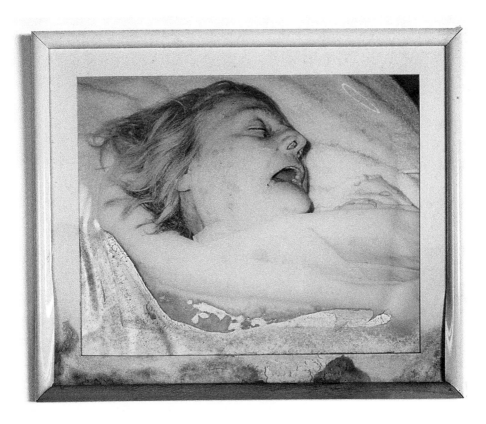

6.5. Death portrait of Sheree Rose's mother (1995). Photo by Sheree Rose.
Also exhibited in *Leftovers,* Sheree Rose's University of California, Irvine
MFA thesis show. Image capture by Amanda Majors (2018).

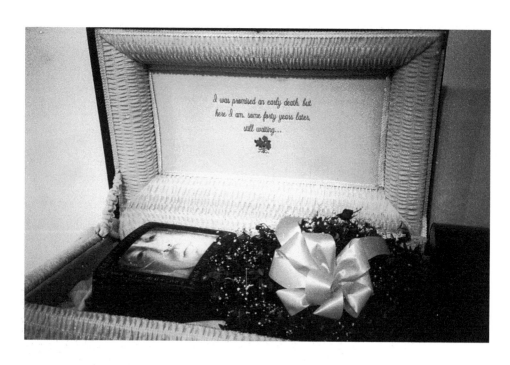

I was promised an early death, but
here I am, some forty years later,
still waiting...

6.6. *Video Coffin* (1994). Photo by Sheree Rose. Courtesy of ONE Archives at the USC Libraries.

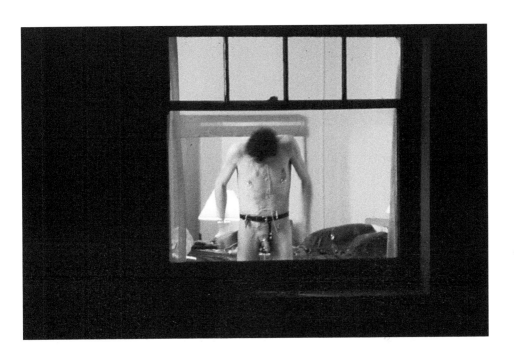

6.7. *In My Room* (1995). Bob Flanagan's final performance. Maintaining voyeuristic qualities associated with Hitchcock's *Rear Window*, the audience watched Flanagan's performance through a window from a hotel across the street. Photo by Sheree Rose. Courtesy of ONE Archives at the USC Libraries.

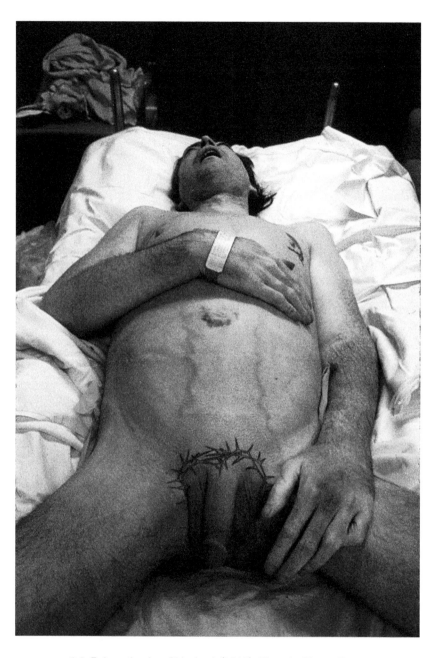

6.8. Bob on the day of his death (1996). Photo by Sheree Rose.
Courtesy of ONE Archives at the USC Libraries.

PART 2

1999–2018

Nailed, Again! (1999–2000)

In 1989–1991 Flanagan performed *Nailed!* and *You Always Hurt the One You Love,* both of which involved nailing his penis to a board. In 1999 Chris Kraus invited Rose to do her own version of *Nailed!*—as *Nailed, Again!*—at Galapagos Gallery in Brooklyn, New York. The following year, in 2000, Tanya Augsburg invited Rose to perform *Nailed, Again!* at a performance studies conference at Arizona State University (see Augsburg's essay about this performance on pages 65–77 of this volume). This involved nailing a phallus piñata in a decommissioned chapel on campus, which followed ritualistic Jewish chanting—Rose was dressed as a rabbi for this part of the performance—and Rose cutting her iconic *S* into herself with a scalpel while a video of Flanagan performing *Nailed!* was screened in the background.

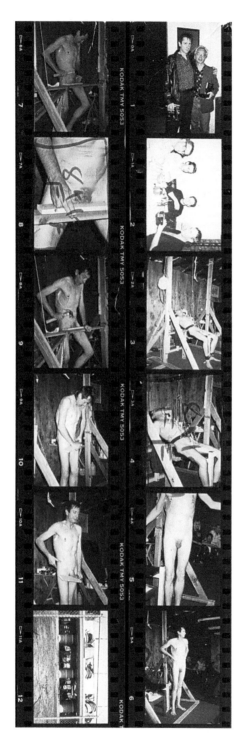

7.1. *Nailed!* (1989). Partial contact sheet by Sheree Rose. Courtesy of ONE Archives at the USC Libraries.

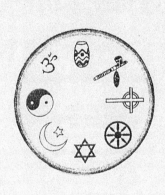

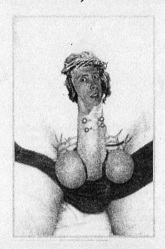

NAILED, AGAIN!

HE IS RISEN

SHE-MA YIS-RA-EL, A-DO-NAI E-LO-HE-NU, A-DO-NAI E-CHAD
LISTEN, THE SOURCE OF ALL OUR BEING, THAT SOURCE IS ONE

7.2. Outside cover of *Nailed, Again!* (2000) program distributed at performance, Arizona State University. Courtesy of Tanya Augsburg.

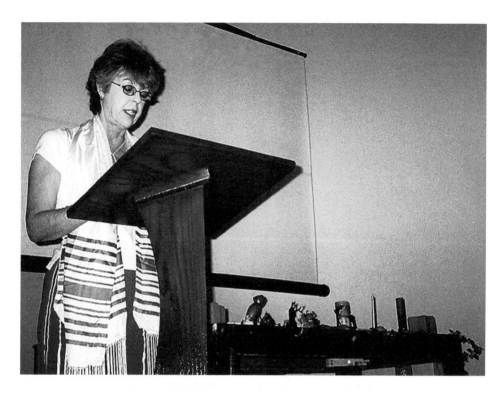

7.3. Sheree Rose delivering sermon at *Nailed, Again!* (2000) rehearsal, Arizona State University. Photo by Tanya Augsburg.

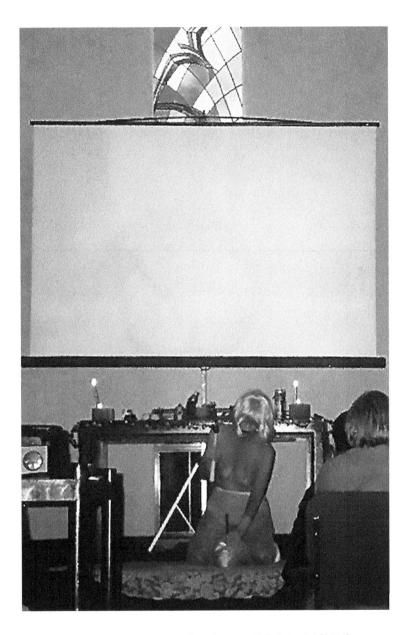

7.4. Sheree Rose nailing phallus piñata at *Nailed, Again!* (2000), Arizona State University. Photo by Tanya Augsburg.

Do with Me as You Will / Make Martin Suffer for Art (2013)

Sheree Rose and Martin O'Brien's *Do with Me as You Will / Make Martin Suffer for Art* took place June 23, 2013, at noon, through June 24, 2013, at noon at Sanctuary Studios LAX, a dungeon near the Los Angeles International Airport. Over the course of twenty-four hours, audience members were permitted to come in at any time during the performance duration and either have Rose orchestrate whatever they wished to have done to O'Brien or fulfill their own requests. Rose made a time-stamp cut on O'Brien's arm every hour. See Amber Musser's and Amelia Jones's essays in this volume (pages 122–27 and 98–109). Also see Yetta Howard's interview with Rose and O'Brien about this performance on pages 110–21.

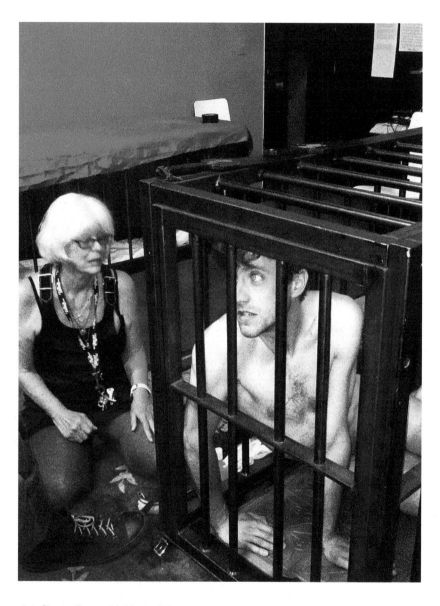

8.1. Sheree Rose with Martin O'Brien in cage at *Do with Me as You Will / Make Martin Suffer for Art,* Sanctuary Studios LAX, Los Angeles (2013). Photo by Yetta Howard.

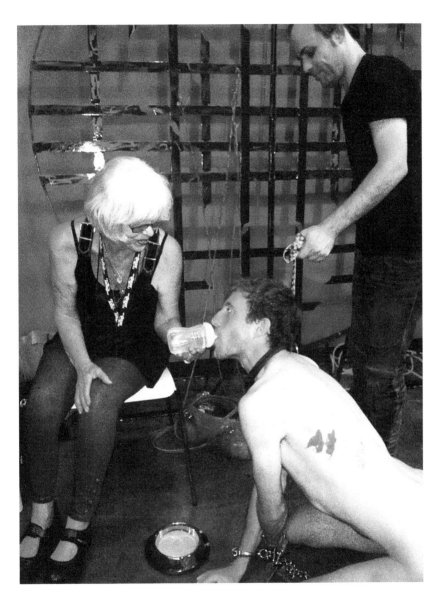

8.2. Sheree Rose, Martin O'Brien, and participant Randy Focazio at *Do with Me as You Will / Make Martin Suffer for Art,* Sanctuary Studios LAX, Los Angeles (2013). Photo by Yetta Howard.

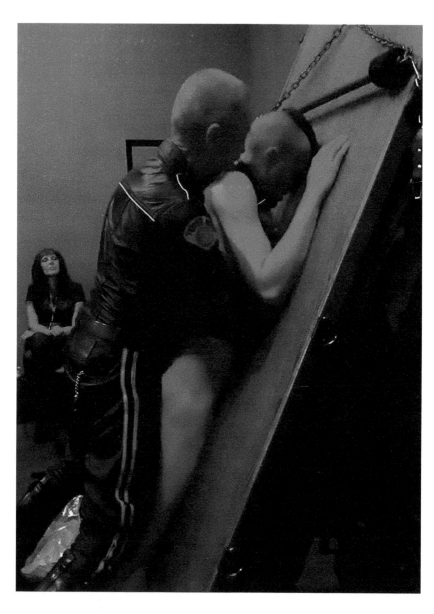

8.3. Martin O'Brien being intimidated by Durk Dehner at *Do with Me as You Will I Make Martin Suffer for Art,* Sanctuary Studios LAX, Los Angeles (2013). Photo by Nancy Popp.

100 Reasons (2014)

100 Reasons is Rose's photography series of 100 individual spanked, slapped, or tortured asses that she shot in the BDSM underground during the period 1983–1993. Mike Kelley's conceivable names for paddles that could go with the ass portraits were used for each one. Rose and Flanagan did a performance inspired by this that included Rose spanking Flanagan 100 times while Kelley read the paddle-names. This version of *100 Reasons* was re-performed as a video piece by Mike Kelley in 1991. In 2014 Rose revived both the photography series and the incarnations of the performance at Coagula Curatorial in Los Angeles, where all 100 images were exhibited, and all 100 spankings and recitations of Kelley's paddle/photography names were collaboratively performed by Rose, Grace Hansmeyer, and Rain Lucien Matheke.

100 Reasons full list:

1. ATOM SMASHER
2. THE CHIROPRACTOR
3. HOMEROOM SERVICE
4. THE REFORMER
5. MASHMASTER
6. REBEL YELL
7. SPINE TINGLER
8. TEACHER'S PET
9. THE SWINGER
10. JUST DESSERTS
11. HISTRIONIC
12. FLANK PLANK
13. MIND BENDER
14. BRUISE BLOOMER
15. RED-EYE EXPRESS
16. NERVE WRACKER
17. WOOD-CRAFT
18. PIMPLE FLATTENER
19. "TRAUMA"
20. THE BUN WARMER
21. MANNER HAMMER
22. RED HANDED
23. THE WHIZZER
24. CRY BABY
25. THE CHEAP PSYCHOLOGIST
26. "THAT SMARTS"
27. THE WILL KILLER
28. ARM OF THE LAW
29. THE LEVELER
30. JOY STICK
31. TARDY TO PROMPT
32. THE WAKER-UPPER
33. ABOUT-FACE
34. FANNY TANNER

35. SWEAT SPRAYER
36. DEEP IMPRESSION
37. HOODLUM HEALER
38. TEAR-WARE
39. BONE CRUSHER
40. THE TENDERIZER
41. THE PROBLEM SOLVER
42. WHITE KNUCKLER
43. WONDER WORKER
44. "WISE YOU UP"
45. RIGHT-REBEL
46. THE SILENCER
47. MEAT BEATER
48. THE PERSONAL TREATMENT
49. LESSON LEVER
50. THE RECTIFIER
51. LET-ER-RIP
52. WOODEN PLATE SPECIAL
53. MOMMY DEAREST
54. LOW SLUNG
55. BOTTOM DWELLER
56. BLIND JUSTICE
57. THE SOCIAL WORKER
58. LEATHER FACE
59. IT HURTS ME MORE
60. PIECE FOR RESISTANCE
61. PRIMAL SCREAMER
62. WHIPLASH
63. GREEK STREAKER
64. I DIDN'T DO IT
65. HAM SLAMMER
66. PALM-AID
67. THE TEAR JERKER

68. PEDALOG
69. ELECTRO-SHOCK
70. BRAT BAT
71. BACK-FIRE
72. PURPLE HAZER
73. TEMPER-A-TANTRUM
74. IMPRESSIONABLE
75. REAR ADVANCE
76. THE DISCIPLANE
77. UP AND AT EM
78. TWAIN MEETER
79. BEAT-IT
80. WHISTLING DIXIE
81. EMILY'S POST
82. THE SWAT BEAM
83. BACK SEAT DRIVER
84. THE ALERTER
85. FRAT FLATTENER
86. REAR ROLFER
87. 'SMOKIN'
88. DADDY'S LITTLE HELPER
89. ASS-ART
90. RED SPREADER
91. SUDDEN INFLUENCE
92. HOT SEAT
93. THE HOWLER
94. WARMWOOD
95. THE BOARD OF EDUCATION
96. FLAT CAT
97. MOONMATE
98. CITY SWITCH
99. VA-VA-VOOM
100. BACKBURNER

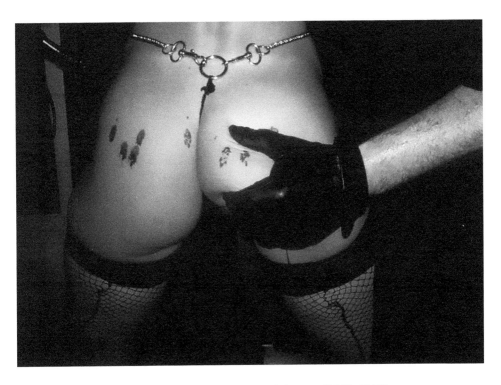

9.1. *Mommy Dearest* #53 from *100 Reasons* (1983–1993).
Photo by Sheree Rose. Title by Mike Kelley.

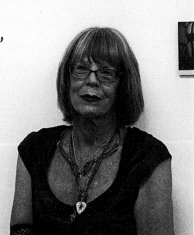

"One Hundred Reasons
as you reap so shall you sow
'One Hundred Reasons'
that's all you need to know"

Photos by Sheree Rose
Words by Mike Kelley

9.2. Sheree Rose in front of Mike Kelley quotation at *100 Reasons*,
Coagula Curatorial (2014). Photo by Judy Ornelas Sisneros.

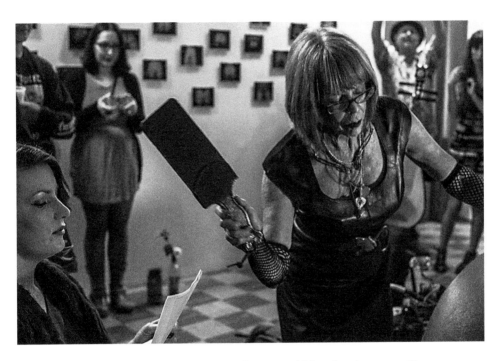

9.3. Sheree Rose performing *100 Reasons,* exhibit and performance with Grace Hansmeyer [reader] and Rain Lucien Matheke [spankee], Coagula Curatorial, Los Angeles (2014). Photo by Judy Ornelas Sisneros.

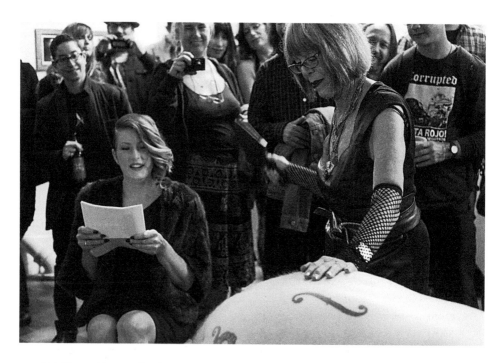

9.4. Sheree Rose performing *100 Reasons,* exhibit and performance with Grace Hansmeyer [reader] and Rain Lucien Matheke [spankee]. *Rated RX* editor Yetta Howard in back, left. Coagula Curatorial, Los Angeles (2014). Photo by Judy Ornelas Sisneros.

Corpse Pose (2014)

A reversal of her usual performance stance, Rose inhabited passivity in performing various versions of *Corpse Pose* in 2011–2012, with the most recent version taking place at Last Projects in Los Angeles in November 2014. The 2014 performance included Michael MP Griffin, Dulcinea Circelli, Daniel Babcock, and Karl Jean-Guerly Petion doing sound. This performance encompassed the naked Rose in an unusually submissive position, as mostly motionless corpse, with Griffin painting her entire body, followed by a range of blood-letting and other ritualistic enactments. In addition to the religious- and mortality-based references, the performance's name refers to *Shavasana*, the resting "corpse pose" that generally ends a yoga session and involves stilling the mind-body. Rose teaches yoga and has been a lifelong practitioner. Last Projects' event description: "A ritual exploration of ancient death rites, and transition of the spirit into the underworld with a focus on the pre-Christianized beliefs of the cult of the goddess such as the idea of life as an imprisonment of the spirit into matter, and death as a liberation of the life force from material constraints of our existence within this earthly flesh. This performance confronts myths and beliefs long suppressed by monotheistic patriarchal religious interests."

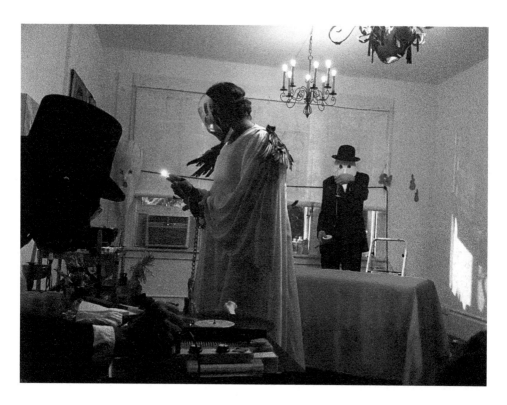

10.1. Daniel Babcock and Michael MP Griffin at start of *Corpse Pose* performance with Karl Jean-Guerly Petion doing sound. Last Projects, Los Angeles (2014). Photo by Yetta Howard.

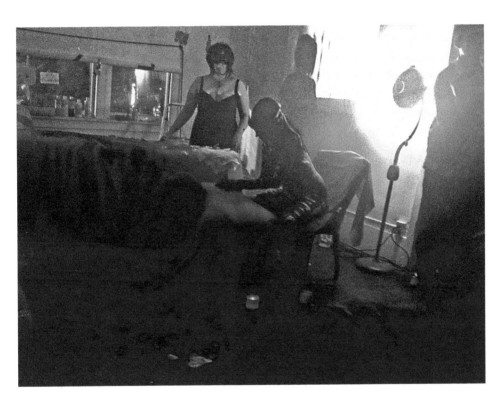

10.2. Sheree Rose carving *S* on Daniel Babcock's back at *Corpse Pose* with Dulcinea Circelli. Last Projects, Los Angeles (2014). Photo by Yetta Howard.

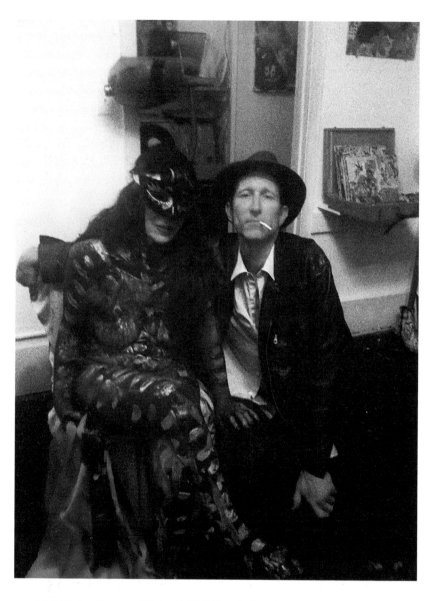

10.3. Sheree Rose and Michael MP Griffin after the *Corpse Pose* performance.
Last Projects, Los Angeles (2014). Photo by Yetta Howard.

Dust to Dust (2015)

Dust to Dust, also called *Goodbye Bob,* is one of the unrealized performances from Rose and Flanagan's ideas for the *Memento Mori* death trilogy, which was to consist of *Video Coffin, Dust to Dust,* and *The Viewing* (discussed in "Breathing Space" section). In 2015 *Dust to Dust* was part of Rose's collaborations with O'Brien that were intended to enact unrealized parts of the trilogy and, by extension, perform gaps in the archive. Taking place at ONE Archives in Los Angeles during O'Brien's residency there, *Dust to Dust* radicalized spatial-archival elements associated with the temporalities of life and death in that it performed a gap in the archive *at the archive.* The performance—and its audience—moved from the main space of ONE ("Invocation") to the gallery ("Flanagan's Wake") to the car park ("Processional") and culminated in the cactus garden ("Transfiguration") before returning from the cactus garden to ONE's main space ("Recessional"). Both O'Brien—into whom Rose carved her iconic *S*—and Rose were naked and painted in white from head to toe. In the "Transfiguration" portion of the performance in the cactus garden, which followed several small photographs from the archive being thrown into a coffin carrying an effigy of Flanagan during the "Flanagan's Wake" portion, the coffin was transported to the cactus garden through the car park, "Processional," and Rose lit the coffin surrounded by the audience, "Transfiguration." Rose, O'Brien, and the audience gazed at the rising flames for an extended period before returning to the main space of ONE. This collaborative performance also included participation by Toro Castaño, Sam Emery, Rafa Esparza, Michael MP Griffin, Rain Lucien Matheke, Grace Marie (Hansmeyer), Dulce Stein, and Albert Vitela. Amelia Jones joined the artists for a post-performance public discussion (see Jones's essay on pages 98–109 and O'Brien's essay on pages 89–97 of this volume for a discussion of this performance and others).

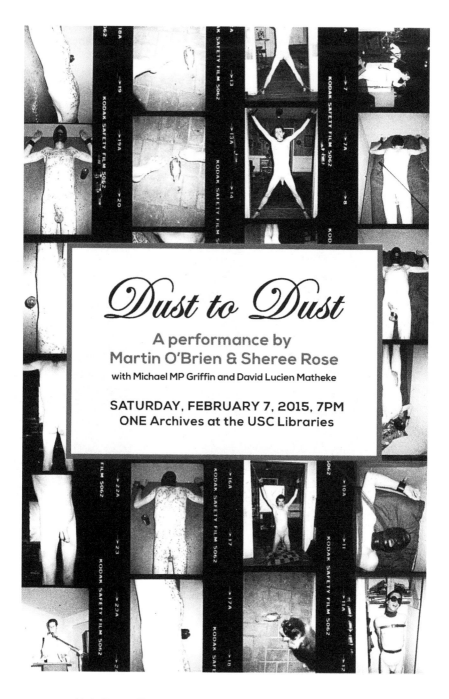

11.1. *Dust to Dust* postcard. ONE Archives, Los Angeles (2015).

11.2. Martin O'Brien with an effigy of Bob Flanagan rising above in "Invocation" portion of *Dust to Dust*. ONE Archives, Los Angeles (2015). Photo by Yetta Howard.

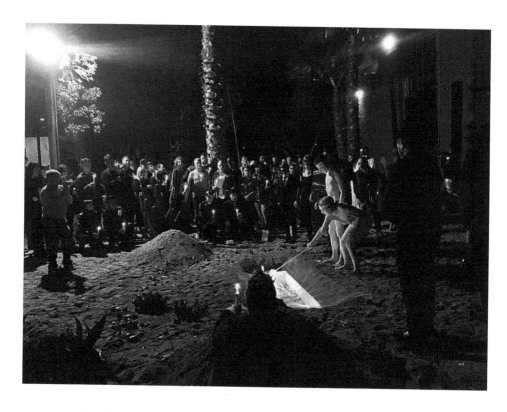

11.3. Sheree Rose lighting grave in "Transfiguration" portion of *Dust to Dust*.
ONE Archives, Los Angeles (2015). Photo by Yetta Howard.

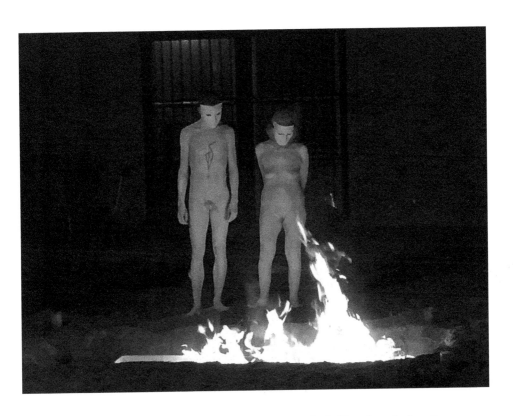

11.4. Martin O'Brien and Sheree Rose observing the fire in "Transfiguration" portion of *Dust to Dust*. ONE Archives, Los Angeles (2015). Photo by Yetta Howard.

Philosophy in the Bedroom (2016)

Philosophy in the Bedroom takes its name from an eighteenth-century book by Marquis de Sade. Inspired by a piece performed by Dawn Kasper, *Philosophy in the Bedroom* was a collaborative, audience-participatory durational performance intended as a celebration of Rose's seventy-fifth birthday. Along with primary collaborators Rose, Martin O'Brien, and Rhiannon Aarons, *Philosophy* included twenty-two participants. It was a twenty-four-hour-long, video-mediated piece that took place at the Royal Pagoda Motel in Los Angeles in September 2016. Rose, O'Brien, and Aarons invited proposals that answered what potential participants would do if they could get into bed with the three artists for one hour. Audience members were also invited to watch the various realizations of the ideas in the proposals via CCTV in an adjacent hotel room. In an interview conducted by Tristene Roman with Rose after the performance, Rose discussed *Philosophy*'s distinctions from *Do with Me as You Will* (another twenty-four-hour-long durational performance discussed earlier) and some of the hour-long participatory actions, which included a séance to contact Flanagan with ONE archivist Cooper Moll, a wine enema, discussions of politics, a piercing, eating Dim Sum, and the exhilarating, outlaw energy when performance artist Cassils came in masked with others and bound up and dominated Rose, O'Brien, and Aarons.

Relics, clips, and images from *Philosophy in the Bedroom* were included in Aarons's MFA thesis show, *Rabbit Hole*, shown at the Gatov Gallery, California State University, Long Beach, where *An Illegal Operation for Mary Toft* was performed in April 2017. The following is an excerpt from Aarons's *Rabbit Hole* gallery statement, which discusses *Philosophy in the Bedroom*:

> Shortly after this I started thinking about female artists whose work addressed issues of sex positivity. The work Sheree Rose had done with Bob Flanagan continued to hold the most relevance for me. The work had always moved me, as it so effectively humanized BDSM

and highlighted its nurturing component in a way left completely unaddressed by pop culture appropriations like *50 Shades of Grey*. I contacted her to talk about the work. We forged a very intense collaborative relationship and produced *Philosophy in the Bedroom* with Martin O'Brien as our first of six pieces together. Based on an untitled and unexecuted work Flanagan and Rose originally created in response to John Lennon and Yoko Ono's *Bed-Ins for Peace, Philosophy* was reworked to encompass a broader spectrum of creative dialogue that accurately reflected the new collaborative configuration. An equipment table was placed within the room in response to Marina Abramović's *Rhythm O* and, instead of guests coming and going freely as in Rose and Flanagan's *Visiting Hours*, participants could submit proposals to do anything with me, Rose, and/or O'Brien for one hour in a motel and were subject to the same screening methods used by Rose and me when selecting Domination clients.

The work subsequently generated within *Philosophy* was effective in hijacking the methods and aesthetics of the sex industry to discuss healing, gender, politics, and loss. The motel room served as an otherworldly space—the other side of the looking glass, what's beneath the hole in the earth. Within this space there is free agency to discuss ownership and control, gender dynamics, age dynamics, disability, and death. This space is a difficult one, and—like any adult bedroom—becomes the stage on which the politics of the body are played out. In our hour with Cooper T. Moll, Rose permanently marks my inner thigh with a scalpel. An act of matriarchal penetration, she is facilitating in disrupting the gestalt of my pornographic objectification. As Mary Kelly in *Imaging Desire* writes, "The art of the 'real body' does not pertain to the truth of a visible form but refers back to its essential content: the irreducible, irrefutable experience of pain. The body, as artist-text, bears the authenticating imprint of pain like a signature" (93). Sheree once told me she followed Bob down the rabbit hole when they started the life that subsequently generated their practice. Living creatively and honestly was my rabbit. I encourage you to find your own.

See Howard's interview (2017) with Rose, Aarons, and O'Brien on pages 135–51 of this book.

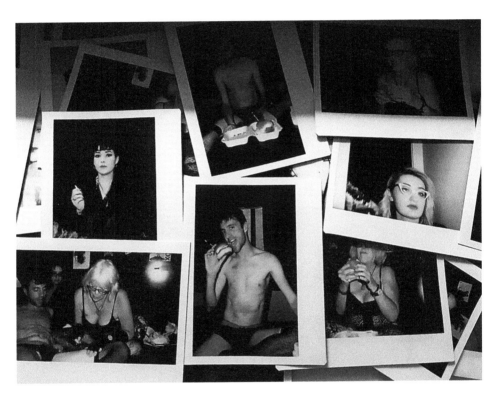

12.1. Photos and collage documentation of *Philosophy in the Bedroom* (2016) by Luka Fisher

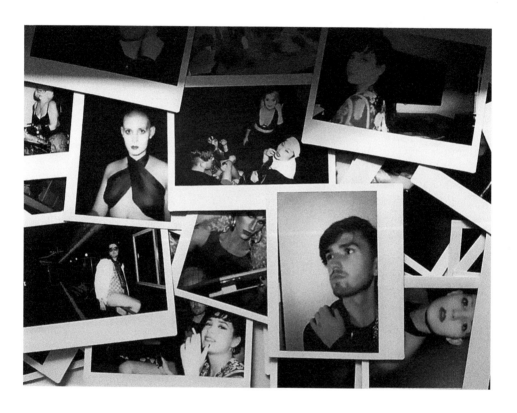

12.2. Photos and collage documentation of *Philosophy in the Bedroom* (2016) by Luka Fisher

The Viewing (2016)

The Viewing is the other of the two unrealized performances from Rose and Flanagan's ideas for the *Memento Mori* death trilogy, which was to consist of *Video Coffin, Dust to Dust,* and *The Viewing* (discussed in "Breathing Space" and in "Words"). The original idea for *The Viewing* was to have a camera included in Flanagan's coffin after death and have viewers watch Flanagan's body as it decomposed. In 2016 Rose, Rhiannon Aarons, and Martin O'Brien performed a collaborative version of it in Liverpool, England, where, through a four-channel CCTV feed, audience members watched O'Brien, who was in an open coffin for twenty-four hours (see their discussion of this performance in their interview with Yetta Howard on pages 135–51). Rose and Aarons came in once per hour and, for fifteen minutes at a time, performed a range of sadistic and medical-style acts on O'Brien. The performance included sound and video art by Luka Fisher and Peter Kalisch. It was commissioned by DaDa Fest. In 2017, the twenty-four-hour CCTV footage from all four channels was screened prior to Aarons and Rose's *An Illegal Operation for Mary Toft* performance at Gatov Gallery, California State University, Long Beach, as part of Aarons's MFA thesis show.

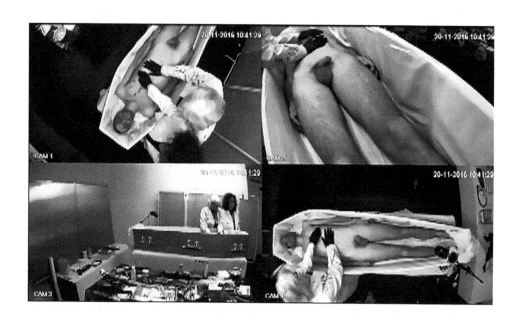

13.1. Video stills from raw footage of *The Viewing* from all four channels.
Liverpool, England (2016). Raw footage courtesy of Rhiannon Aarons.

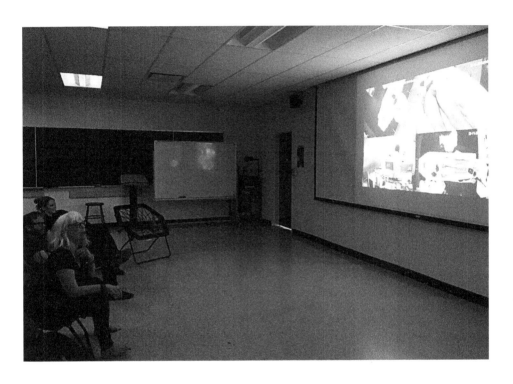

13.2. Sheree Rose viewing *The Viewing* footage before *An Illegal Operation for Mary Toft*. Audience included performance artists Paul Waddell and Chelsea Coon, also pictured here. California State University, Long Beach (2017). Photo by Yetta Howard.

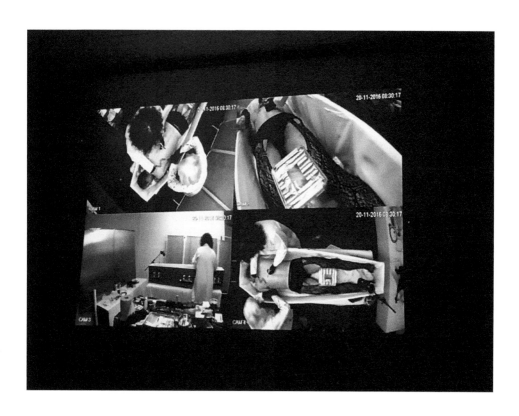

13.3. Viewing *The Viewing* footage as audience member before *An Illegal Operation for Mary Toft*. California State University, Long Beach (2017). Photo by Yetta Howard.

An Illegal Operation for Mary Toft (2017)

An Illegal Operation for Mary Toft was a collaborative performance primarily between Sheree Rose and Rhiannon Aarons with Dulcinea Circelli, Kayla Tange, Jungmok Sona Lee, Aliza J. Bejarano, and Peter Kalisch and functions as a commentary on *Roe v. Wade* via a radicalization of *Alice in Wonderland*. It was performed as part of Rhiannon Aarons's MFA thesis show, *Rabbit Hole,* at the Gatov Gallery, California State University, Long Beach, in April 2017 (see excerpt of Aarons's artist's statement on pages 132–34 of this volume). Against the auditory backdrop of Kalisch's distorted-noise version of "White Rabbit," by Jefferson Airplane, and surrounded by experimental video, Aarons's work from *Rabbit Hole,* performance relics and clips from *Philosophy in the Bedroom,* and audience members, this ritualistic-medical performance involved Aarons being wrapped in plastic with a masked Rose anointing the body and performing a range of masochistic practices including whipping Aarons before and after cutting through the plastic. It culminated in Rose extracting a stuffed-animal rabbit—compactly wrapped in a condom—from Aarons's vaginal cavity and placing it in a medical dish. According to Aarons, an excerpt of the performance was banned from Vimeo even after it had received over 1,000 views in forty-eight hours.

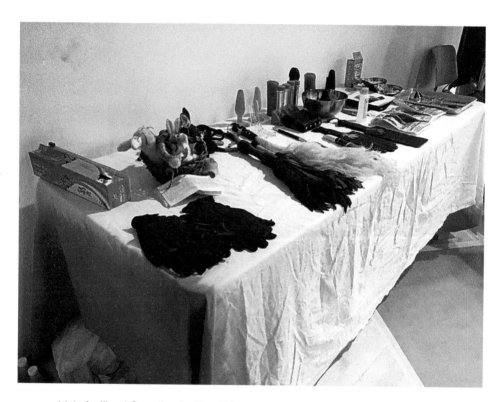

14.1. *An Illegal Operation for Mary Toft,* pre-performance table of instruments. Gatov Gallery, California State University, Long Beach (2017). Photo by Yetta Howard.

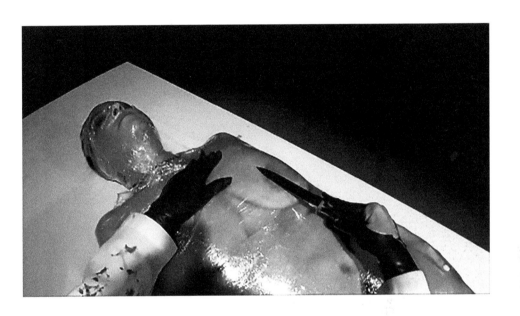

14.2. Video still from *An Illegal Operation for Mary Toft,* Sheree Rose cutting through plastic-wrapped Rhiannon Aarons. Gatov Gallery, California State University, Long Beach (2017). Footage courtesy of Rhiannon Aarons.

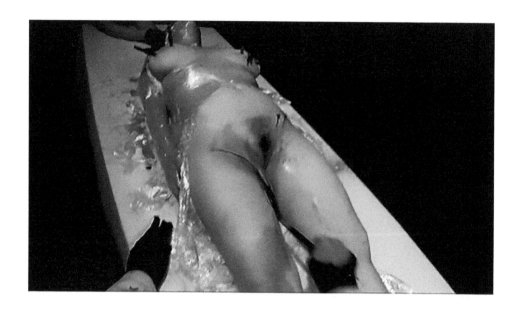

14.3. Video still from *An Illegal Operation for Mary Toft,* Sheree Rose whipping Rhiannon Aarons. Gatov Gallery, California State University, Long Beach (2017). Footage courtesy of Rhiannon Aarons.

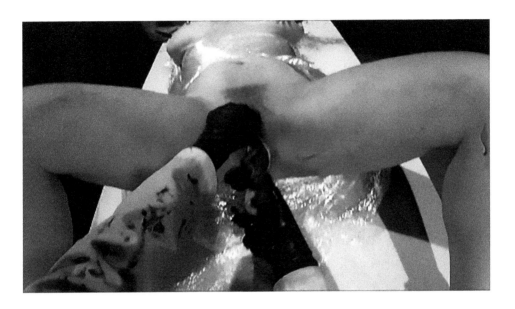

14.4. Video still from *An Illegal Operation for Mary Toft,* Sheree Rose extracting stuffed-animal rabbit from Rhiannon Aarons. Gatov Gallery, California State University, Long Beach (2017). Footage courtesy of Rhiannon Aarons.

The Ascension (2017)

The Ascension was part of the *Every Breath You Take* group show at Jason Vass Gallery in December 2017 in Los Angeles, which, along with Rose's work, also featured work by Rhiannon Aarons, Martin O'Brien, Jeffrey Vallance, Victoria Reynolds, Simone Gad, and Michel Delsol. The December 30, 2017, performance was intended to be a culmination of the resurrected *Memento Mori* death trilogy performances that channeled the spiritual presence of Flanagan via a range of sacrilegious religious rituals. Description from Jason Vass Gallery: "*The Ascension* combines practices of Hinduism with Sheree Rose's Jewish heritage along with her take on Christianity. The performance is announced by the blowing of the shofar, the Jewish start of the new year celebration. The main component of this performance is the Puja, the Hindu form of worshiping the gods and goddesses. Sheree Rose identifies with Kali, the mother who destroys evil by cutting off heads. Martin O'Brien personifies Shiva, the creative force. The performance finishes with Martin ascending to a higher realm. These concepts are referenced as a way to honor Bob Flanagan's, Martin O'Brien's and Sheree Rose's own hybrid belief system."

The performance began in the main gallery space with the Rosh Hashana (Jewish New Year) ritual named above and participants including latex-clad nuns "dusting" O'Brien with several small photos of Flanagan (in reference to the *Dust to Dust* performance concepts) as he crawled around the gallery. Performers then traveled to a back room in the gallery and the audience followed. Accompanied by the performers from the first part, O'Brien delivered "A Sermon on Sickness" (see reproduction of this sermon in O'Brien's essay in this volume, pages 94–96). Sheree Rose along with Ron Athey baptized O'Brien in a bathtub, and audience members were invited to sprinkle glitter as part of the baptism as well. Members of Chaos Suspensions pierced O'Brien's back with hooks in order for him to ascend. Rose embraced O'Brien once he descended and the two were briefly pulled back up together (see O'Brien's essay on pages

89–97 and Amelia Jones's discussion of this performance in her essay on pages 98–109). The performance included collaborators Ron Athey, Peter Kalisch, Madison Jones, Jane DeLynn, Luka Fisher, and Kayla Tange.

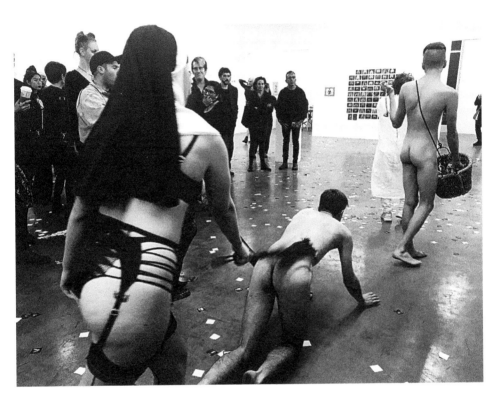

15.1. Martin O'Brien being led around gallery. Jason Vass Gallery,
Los Angeles (2017). Photo by Yetta Howard.

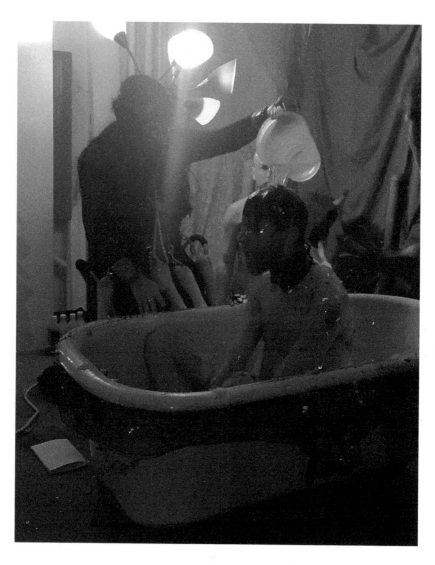

15.2. Sheree Rose baptizing Martin O'Brien. Jason Vass Gallery, Los Angeles (2017). Photo by Yetta Howard.

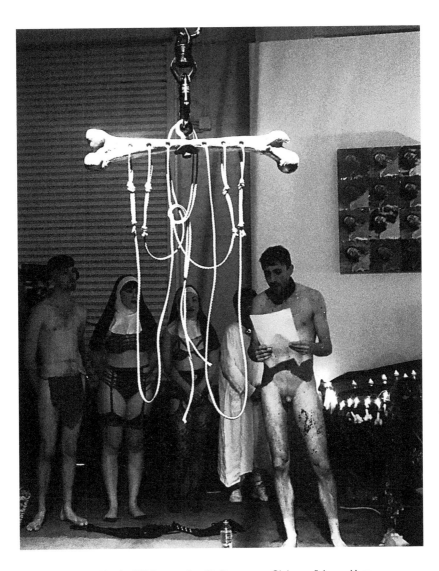

15.3. Martin O'Brien reading "A Sermon on Sickness." Jason Vass
Gallery, Los Angeles (2017). Photo by Yetta Howard.

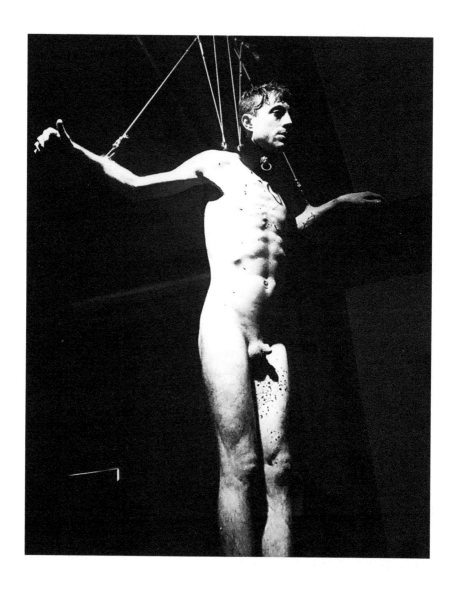

15.4. Martin O'Brien hook suspension. Jason Vass Gallery,
Los Angeles (2017). Photo by Yetta Howard.

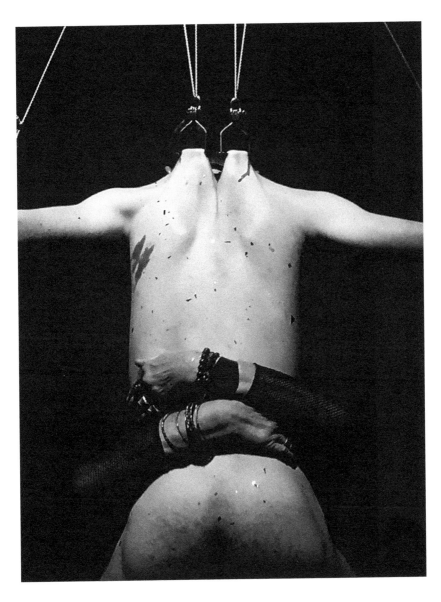

15.5. Sheree Rose embracing Martin O'Brien after being lowered from hook suspension. Jason Vass Gallery, Los Angeles (2017). Photo by Yetta Howard.

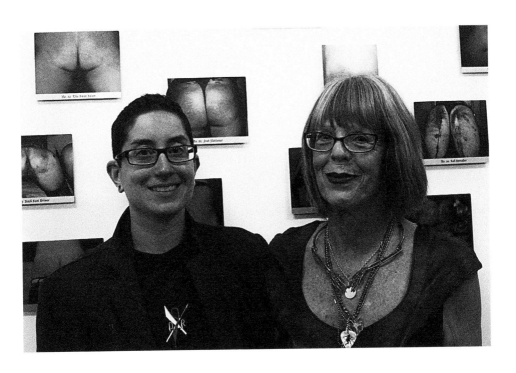

16.1. Yetta Howard and Sheree Rose at *100 Reasons*. Coagula Curatorial, Los Angeles, CA (2014). Photo by Judy Ornelas Sisneros.

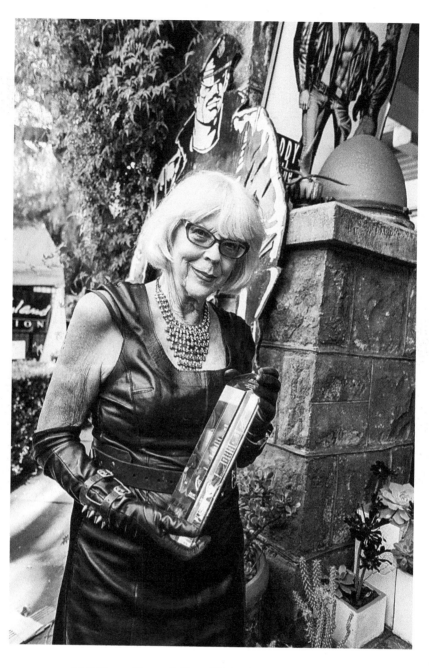

16.2. Sheree Rose with Tom of Finland Lifetime Achievement
Award (2018). Photo by Amanda Majors.

SECTION 3

APPENDICES

Out-of-Print Publications about
Sheree Rose by Bob Flanagan

Slave Sonnets

(1986)

BOB FLANAGAN

COVER BY MIKE KELLEY

Some of these poems have appeared in the following publications: Barney, Beyond Baroque Magazine, Nude Erections, OINK!, Poetry Loves Poetry, and the record album Voices of the Angels.

Very special thanks to Amy Gerstler, Mike Kelley, Michael Silverblatt, and David Trinidad.

Originally published by Cold Clam Press, Los Angeles. Courtesy of ONE Archives at the USC Libraries.

For Sheree

I've been a shit and I hate fucking you now
because I love fucking you too much;
what good's the head of my cock inside you
when my other head, the one with the brains,
keeps thinking how fucked up everything is,
how fucked I am to be fucking you and thinking
these things which take me away from you
when all I want is to be close to you
but fuck you for letting me fuck you now
when all that connects us is this fucking cock
which is as lost inside you as I am, here,
in the dark, fucking you and thinking—fuck,
the wallpaper behind you had a name,
what was it? You called it what? Herringbone?

Everything in the world is all fucked up,
and there's no fucking, but who the hell cares?
The overriding feeling is **fuck you.**
I need you now like a hole in the head.
Not that I gave a fuck about fucking
in the first place. With or without my cock
inside you I was yours, your property,
and I existed only to please you.
But if it pleases you to make the world
a hell-hole, then you're a fucking asshole
and I'll never stop the shit, nor reach you
no matter how deeply I penetrate.
Everything's fucked up alright; there are holes
for everything, and you're just one of them.

What does it matter, fucking? I don't know.
In the grand scheme this big cock will be chopped
liver. Lover? Fucker? I'm a human
dildo, you said so. What am I thinking?
How fucked up everything is? The world is?
Well, fuck that. I'm fucking. To fuck: that's fucked
I suppose, given the fact that we live
in terrible times, precariously
teetering on the brink of extinction,
I should speak up, write a fucking letter,
or at least (God forbid) a fucking poem,
something about something else, not fucking.
But what's the point? My throbbing cock, that's what.
I'm a dildo. What the fuck do you want?

I was the walking dead, blood-splattered shirt
and a knife in the back the night we met.
You were dead, too, but beautiful, alive
again, Jayne Mansfield, and with a good head
on your shoulders, which turned surprisingly
toward me: your humble and obedient
zombie ever since. "It's fun to be dead,"
someone once said, and we're the living proof.
I'm the sick skeleton in your closet;
you're my reason for living: it's real life
and it scares us to death. Some big bruiser
we know just dies, no reason. How 'bout me?
Let's make it Halloween. Get out your knife,
carve me like a pumpkin, and then let's fuck.

Death-games and kidnapping scenarios—
now that's the way to fuck, as if your life
depended on it. Fuck life anyway,
just shut up and fuck until the blood comes
or you come, or both. The heart is a pump
but it pumps more than blood into the head
–an idea? No ideas but in this thing
pumping away like there's no tomorrow;
and there isn't. Ask those few thousand sperm
what it's all about as they bash their heads
against your walls or swim furiously
away, as if they had some destination.

What do they think, we're making babies?
We're not even making love.

You can't be an Indian giver when
what you're giving is the family jewels,
more personal than a sack of beads:
the balls it takes to love some people
(the balls it takes to take some people's balls,
tokens of affection: two glistening pearls).
Her veterinarian friend knows how
(dogs and horses). "Men are a piece of cake!"
With our bitter-sweet romance on the rocks
she can talk like this and take for granted
my reaction: hard as a rock, a lust
for something permanent more than brutal.

Any way you slice it it comes out love;
without that—who cares what else is missing?

I'm an instrument. I'm a clarinet.
Maestro, I'm an oboe if you say so.
An animal if music's not enough.
Dog on command, shepherd or Chihuahua.
Eat when the dinner bells chime: Ms. Pavlov,
these experiments you've unleashed on me
hurt and strip me of everything human;
even dogs live better lives than I do.
Confession: truth is my life's a picnic.
Here I am, the ant you're about to squash.
"Ow!"—Make that "Ooo."—My lips the letter "O."
I'm a zero: nothing lower than I.

Confine me or crush me—but like magic
each reduction makes me all the more huge.

She could have been a lesbian but loves
hot dick, except what's often connected
to the prick is another prick trying
to run her life, so now she's got the keys.
Like a tethered animal: so it feels
when he gets these restricted erections.
He's up again, pissing to get it down,
make it small again and manageable.
For her that's it: MANAGEMENT OF THE MALE
ORGAN (and the asshole it's attached to),
a symbolic gesture, as political
in nature as it is against nature.

He's wild for her but he can't get near her
til the sight of his padlocked prick makes her wet.

Ay Chihuahua! The shit heaped onto my
devoted carcass. It's love—and it's hell.
Our particular brand makes my cock swell.
I'm not swell now, though, cause I've been set free.
Endurance is my middle name, but—hey!
KABOOM! The bomb drops when you feel shitty.
Why not just beat me to a pulp? (Know why?
Obedient me, I'd love every blow.)
You've got a face longer than my dick, you
arch enemy of my groveling ardor.
Peon, servant, slave: and still I'm useless;
I, who wanted to please you, can't—ouch.

Asshole me for complaining. Didn't I
ask for this shit—your shit—my cup of tea?

The name stamped onto the lock says, "Master."
But the keys are yours, Mistress. My body,
wrapped in this neat little package, is yours.
Do I dare to call myself a present?
I'm the one who's on the receiving end.
You took me on, taking in my stiff prick
and swelling my head with your compliments,
your complaints, even out and out neglect.
Nothing—when it comes from you—is a gift;
wrapped in your aura of authority
even shit tastes sweet, and the void you leave
leaves me full.

It's Christmas whenever you put your foot down,
and the stars I'm seeing must be heaven.

Bob Flanagan was born December 26, 1952, in New York City, but has spent most of his life in Southern California and now lives in Los Angeles. His poems have appeared in numerous publications, including *Coming Attractions, Little Caesar, Washington Review, Barney*, and *OINK!* He is the author of two previous books of poetry: *The Kid Is the Man* (Bombshelter Press, 1978) and *The Wedding of Everything* (Sherwood Press, 1983). Besides writing poetry, he also sings and performs.

Fuck Journal

(1982)

BOB FLANAGAN

January

Fucking on acid. It lasts forever. I am so deep inside her I feel like I'm inside out.

Still flying. I can barely feel my penis but it's hard and we're fucking while over the stereo speakers comes the sound of an exercise record: "Up, down, up, down."

She lets me fuck her and sleep in her bed as well. We fuck with me on top, and sometimes on our sides.

Tied up, face down, spread-eagled on bed, blind-folded and whipped, butt vibrator up my ass. Turned over, spread eagled, fucked, and whipped some more.

Courtesy of ONE Archives at the USC Libraries. Hanuman Press in India first published it in 1987. *Fuck Journal* is included in its entirety here, which is a transcription of Bob Flanagan's typed-out monograph of one year of sex he had with Rose in 1982. According to Rose, 5,000 copies got confiscated at customs but approximately 500 copies got through.

To preserve a sense of authenticity and the spontaneity of journal-writing, the occasional grammatical, spelling, and punctuation errors have been left intact and missing words, though infrequent, have not been filled in.

We fuck again, slow and steady, me on top, no bondage.

We fuck after a terrible day of nothingness. Me on top, her hands around my neck, choking me into a shaking, quivering come.

Tim's birthday. Drinks and presents. I show off my pierced nipples and later lick her nipples and eat her under the covers and we fuck. She chokes me. We come.

We fuck with her on top of me, spontaneously in the afternoon. Her face looks so intense and scary when we fuck sometimes that I think she's going to rip me apart.

Yeah, we fuck again, me on top, after and while she whips my ass with a studded leather bracelet. Close to coming a few times but slow down and wait until she's ready.

Nice, slow fuck after being up all night on speed writing a poem called "Available Light."

Turns out to be an awful speed-come-down, depression-filled weekend. I rape her, but she doesn't resist in earnest.

My face is hot from being slapped silly. My ass is hot from whacks with the riding crop. My dick is soft after she allows me to fuck.

February

I get to fuck my Mistress again—with a cock-ring squeezing my balls. I'm submissive again! She's dominant again!

More fucking. Lots of licking and sucking. She's all over me. Purple squeezed cock gets to come again.

Fast furious fuck in the morning.

We fuck again; she chokes me; we both come at the same time; and I wonder if I'm still alive.

Overwhelmed with feelings of submission for her. I want to explode because I can't seem to demonstrate my submissiveness enough. Tonight I eat her; she uses two vibrators, one in her vagina, and one on her clit. She comes, and we fuck. I come and she grabs my skin all over, causing me to squeal.

Wrote an impassioned letter to her, again declaring my submission. She lets me eat her and we fuck with her on her belly, me entering from behind, all the time declaring my submission again and again.

Valentines Day fuck in spite of being tired after dinner with Ann and Peter.

I ask her to touch my dick and I get a hard-on so we fuck, me on top, her on top, choking, coming.

After a night of torture, whipping, and bondage from her and Scott, she releases me from the bed in the back room and lets me fuck her. Wow! I'm her slave again!

A few smacks with the crop; choked with a tie; eating my Mistress; fucking.

After three hours of writing, I ask for and receive permission to come back to bed where we suck and lick each other's assholes, and I get spanked and bleed a little, and we fuck—oh, boy, do we fuck!

Slow fuck in the morning.

March

A day of punishment for my distant and shitty attitude on Monday. The pain was not as bad as promised and I am relieved but at the same time disappointed. But the suffering ends with a beautiful, blind-folded, tied spread-eagled fuck in which I am beaten, bit, choked, and pinched into a wonderful come by my most competent Mistress. Now, blissful sleep. More punishment is promised and I am thrilled and terrified. Help.

Spontaneous fuck after she gets out of the shower.

Biting fuck.

Fucking in the living room on the orange chair. She comes twice.

I drink her pee without spilling a drop. Another fuck. We can't get out of the house for all the fucking.

She whips my ass with a studded strap until blood comes and then we fuck.

Wild, spontaneous fuck on the black vinyl couch while watching "Network" on tv. What a come!

First fuck after a long, distant, and horrible week. It feels good to have my dick inside her. I come, pleading to be her slave again, and she says, yes, oh yes!

I suck her nipple; my tongue is in her ass; my cock is in her cunt; her hands around my neck, squeezing harder; we come.

Supposed to run errands but we fuck instead: me with handcuffs behind my back; she even sucks my cock. I sit in the chair and she rides me while I pound into her until my legs are weak and we come.

She's asleep but I secretly rub KY on my morning hardon and turn her over and wake her up by sticking in into her. No resistance. She loves it and so do I.

Reading the last few days' fucks to her while she's getting ready for work makes us want to fuck again, so we do. She masturbates while I remain hard and still inside her; then I pound to a climax myself.

Penis in bondage all day; I drink her piss from a baby bottle; I lick her nipples and clitoris; she gets hot and wet, unlocks my penis, and we fuck with slaps, biting and choking; we come, and afterwards I'm spanked.

We fuck, even though she said she didn't want to give me the pleasure of fucking too much, and even though I was an unsubmissive crazy bastard last night. She's on her period and I come out all bloody.

She gets out of the shower to watch the space shuttle land. It does and we fuck on the black couch.

April

Feeling dominant, I turn her over and fuck her with her arms pinned against her sides.

Real quick fuck before she gets ready for work.

I don't say anything. She's just out of the shower. I start eating her and sucking on her clitoris. Every time I suck her clit into my mouth I can feel her thighs jerk. We fuck on the black couch. She tries to bite my shoulder but I pull away.

Our first night in New York; the Chelsea Hotel. We fuck, and we feel tender and gentle with each other; the first tenderness we've been able to express in weeks.

Another fuck. It feels good to be inside her. But I still crave to be her slave.

I read an SM newspaper and get hot and fuck her dominantly; some spanks on her white ass which bruises easily.

The Chelsea Hotel after an all night party. She wants to piss and shit on my but I feel rushed and chicken out; but still we fuck.

Back at the hotel; after a visit to the Hellfire Club, and before her "client" shows up, we fuck. I want to submit entirely to her.

Post-client fuck after he licks and sucks her for $100 and hour.

Talking about the Hellfire Club and our new contract (which I will sign sight-unseen): we fuck again.

Staying in bed most of the day in New York City, we fuck, and then we fight about staying in bed most of the day in New York City.

We fuck after she ties my hands and feet and beats me with a hair brush and slaps my face and carves the word "SLAVE" into my chest with a razor blade.

Our first fuck since coming back from New York. I tell her there's a message she has to hear on the answering machine in the back room. When she gets there I lock the door behind her, take her pants down, and fuck her on the wooden bed.

May

Discuss the possibilities of her being my slave for a week. I get hard and she gets wet and we fuck before she leaves for her son's baseball game.

She's blindfolded and handcuffed to a post in the closet for half an hour as punishment for being in a bad mood. Afterward we fuck.

We fuck again because I'm so excited being her master.

Before going to work with Scott, I lie down, nude on the floor beside the bed and order her to get on top, and we fuck.

We fuck again after I bite her nipples and demand that she not yell out in pain.

I'm in the shower when she comes home. As ordered, she is nude and on her knees when I get out. I stick my finger in her cunt and ass. I enter her cunt from the rear and we fuck as I scratch and pull the skin on her back.

I tell her she's going to be in bondage for two or three hours while I'm out. She pleads with my to let her be free but I fuck her and then tie her up.

She is tie up and spanked, partly for breaking one hand free from her bondage, but mainly for her bad attitude about the whole thing. She is crying uncontrollably. I don't like this but follow through anyway and give her fourteen whacks on the ass with a leather shoe sole. Then I put her to bed where she continues to cry. She is distant from me. I fuck her to see if I can calm her down and bring her back, but she doesn't calm down and she won't come back.

I spite of last night she says submissive. I fuck her on the floor in front of the tv.

Mother's Day. I'm hard. I tell her to get on me and she does and we fuck.

An intense, moving fuck after a long night of fighting and screaming which started on Sunset Boulevard and ended here, in bed, surprisingly close and sexual.

I'm not feeling well, but I'm hard anyway and she has just shaved her legs and looks real sexy in her white skirt and tank top so we fuck, side by side in bed.

Long, slow fuck in spite of the fact that I worked all day and i'm dead tired.

Traditional fuck.

She's sick with a cold or the flu, but I start licking her clit and it miraculously brings her back to life and we fuck while she slaps my face. I think I may be her slave again real soon.

June

I am once again tied up in the back room, my face covered with a latex hood. I am spanked and whipped with a shoe sole, the riding crop, and a four foot cat-or-nine-tails. Then we fuck. I am immobile. She is moving up and down on my wildly, choking me until we come.

Back in bed, I ask for and receive permission to lick her asshole and then her clit. She's hot. I get hot. And we fuck again.

After a little bondage and whipping, and some television, we go to bed. She's dead tired but she lets me eat her and she eats me, 69 style. I go under the covers and eat her. I can get a better angle on her clitoris when I'm down there with my head squeezed between her legs. She turns over and masturbates while I work my tongue in and out and around her asshole. She comes a couple of times and then she brings me up and we fuck with me on top and a cock ring on my cock so it really hurts and I love it and I come and she comes again and we sleep a really wonderful sleep.

We're taking a shower together when I start sticking my finger inside her and licking her cunt with water running in my nose, and pretty soon I'm sitting on the floor of the shower, water still running, and she's crouched on top of me and we're fucking, getting wetter and wetter, and coming.

Fucking again after nearly a week of not being allowed to because I masturbated once. I start by kissing her feet, then slowly work my lips and tongue all the way up to her mouth and ears. I remove her bra and panties and dig my tongue as deeply into her asshole as I can get it, all the while massaging her clitoris on the other side. She turns over and I use my tongue on her clit. She does it herself with her fingers, but I keep my mouth close by. She comes. She brings me up to her breasts and then her mouth. She lets me enter. We fuck slowly. She slaps me. We fuck on our sides. I tell her how much I love being her slave. She turns me on my back and rides me. She looks mean. She slaps me hard a few times. She's riding and moaning. I'm moaning too. She's holding my wrists above my head. She lets them go and I grab her around the waist as hard as I can and we're coming. Oh!

Hell week. She decides, since I'm a slave, I should be treated as a slave. No sleeping in her bed. No fucking. No kindness. No fun. But she has been in a miserable state. We fight about that tonight and then make up with fucking after more than a week of not even a kiss, my face buried in her breasts, moaning and kissing and fucking.

Dinner's cooking. She's on the couch, watching tv. While talking to my mother on the phone I play with myself and get hard. She sees it and orders me to pull off her panties. I do. I eat her. We fuck. An assortment of positions on the couch. Her on top. Me. Her. Me. Hits. Bites. Chokes. Comes.

She has me get out the riding crop and put on the black hood in the bedroom. She takes out her tampon and makes me eat her while she lies in bed, reading a book and occasionally whacking my ass with the crop. She gets hot, puts down her book, and we fuck, me on top in heavenly darkness.

July

Too tired to fuck last night on her return from Catalina. This morning we wake up, she with sunburned face and swollen lips. I start sucking her nipples. She gets wet and then wetter when I use my tongue. We fuck with her on top.

Fuck again after she commands me to get hard and slaps me around a little. I come again and this time so does she, on top of me.

Fucking again, cockring on my bulging cock, after meeting with Tom and Mistress Victoria.

Taking a break from the mixing session with the band, we go into the bedroom and fuck, me on top, choked with a bathroom cord.

Me on top, in bed, before she goes to work.

Fucking on the couch while watching tv, even though I'm sick. She's on top and grabbing me with her nails. We talk about what it would be like to die at the moment of coming, and I come.

We fuck on the rug in front of the tv, doggie style, on our hands and knees, on the floor, while dinner cooks.

Watching tv in bed, I get a hard-on and she says stick it in and we fuck, on our sides and with me on top.

I'm tied to the bed. She spanks my thighs. I get hard. She's on me, frontwards, backwards, sideways. My hand breaks loose. I hold her. She unties the other. I hold her more. Tighter.

My legs still tied as she pumps me and I come.

We spend the night with Tom and Victoria, licking, sucking, whipping, and talking. Wow!

A hard-on and hangover just thinking about last night's adventures with Tom and Victoria. Feeling barely alive this morning but, still hot, we fuck anyway.

Watching tv in bed. Hard-on. Not breathing well. She climbs on top. I'm perfectly still as she slides up and down until coming.

Hot afternoon, black couch, naked, sticking to the vinyl, watching tv, fucking, me on top.

She handcuffs me, binds my ankles, and orders me to lick and kiss her feet. She whips the soles of my feet with the riding crop. I'm let loose, come to bed, eat her, suck her nipples, fuck, on top, come.

Whipped while humping the bed. Pleasurable pain. She makes us of my hard-on and sticks it in and pumps me as she chokes me to coming.

She's sick. Hot and sweaty afternoon, sleeping in bed. I get hard but she seems disinterested. I hump the blankets but she'd be mad if I came. She's lying there naked. I get on top of her, stick it in, and we fuck, silent and motionless except for my thrusting.

Quick whipping with the crop and cat while I hump the sheets. Then we bring our two sweaty bodies together, me on top, nothing really touching but our genitals, my dick pounding into her, bone meeting bone, sweat and come.

She's in a bad period mood, dressing for work. I'm hard all morning. If I fuck her it might help her mood. I put a towel under her, take out her tampon, rub my dick with KY, stick it in and fuck.

She visits me at my summer camp job. After lunch we go to the lodge, lock the doors, take our clothes off, and fuck. A quick one because we have to get to the pool.

Fucking again at camp, in the ranch house. On top of someone's "Peanuts" blanket and "Snoopy" pillow. Clothes off. Pants to my knees. I eat her. We fuck and it's great, her on top.

Hot tubs outside of camp with Lenny and Eve. She and I go off to our own tub. I get semi-hard and we try it outside the tub, doggie style, but are interrupted by Lenny and Eve. Soon Rick, Liz, Debra, and Denise show up. When they go back to their own tub we get back in doggie position, bare knees rubbed raw on the redwood deck as I pump into her until we come.

Home from camp. Tired. Naked. Restless. She whips me with the cat as I rub against the sheets. Hard. Inside her. Me on top. On our sides. Her slave again. Always was, but home now and coming.

August

Whipped with the cat. She's on top. Then doggie style, me grabbing the back of her neck slamming it until we come.

I lie on the bed, on my stomach, and she whips my ass several whacks as hard as she can. Big purple welt on my hip. We fuck, her on top.

I get on top of her and start poking her between the legs with my dick, which is getting harder by the minute, soon inside her, soon fucking, soon coming.

We're fucking, but I'm not breathing so well so I'm not so interested in fucking and she's just out of the shower and the smell of her soap is strong to me, but we still fuck, me on top, and we still come, or at least I do—without her permission.

I get the shit beat out of me at the club called Balls and Chains. I'm tied up in front of a room full of people as she and Victoria whip me on the thighs with riding crops. Someone named Erica asks me if I like chains. When I say yes she takes out this dog chain and beats me across the chest with it. At home, alone with my Mistress, we fuck and the pain disappears as I come inside her.

Up all night on acid. Drove at 5 am. Freeway from Covina. Colors. Radio. Home in bed, fucking. Can't tell for a while if I'm hard, but I am, and it seems like I'm inside her forever. I see bats and coffins and haunted house images in front of me as we fuck and she presses into my scarred and bruised chest. I love the pain. I tell her how wonderful pain can be. How she should use it on me. I'm raving. I'm tripping. I'm coming.

Hard and inside her again, but too high to come.

Too hot to fuck, but I turn the fan on and we do it anyway, after a week of not fucking, and after a night of licking and sucking with Victoria and Tom. It sure feels good, me on top, on our sides, hands around my neck, nestled in, pumping, pushing . . . there.

She has sympathy for my hard-on and we fuck, quietly, in bed, me on top.

Getting ready to leave the house, she's in her white slip and i can't resist it and can't resist giving her a few whacks on the ass. It turns red and I get hard and we fuck quickly with her on top as her son pounds on the bedroom door. "Coming," we say—and we are.

September

I get hard as she leaves to take her mother to the doctor. She pulls up her skirt and slip and slides onto my hard dick and we have a short fuck.

High on mushrooms. In the bathroom. I bite her nipples real hard. Not submissive anymore. Tell her to lie down on the floor. Stick it in her. Fuck hard.

She's wearing her crotchless panties, garter belt, stockings, and fringe top. High heels. I'm sad because I can't submit. But hard because of how she looks. She's sitting in a chair, her feet up on a table. I kneel on the table and slide into her. Knees hurt as I pump and it feels good. Good unconscious come.

Not sure of the time of day or the type of fuck. I was choked with a bathrobe cord, and that always feels good.

She doesn't want to. I was up all night in the nude, in the rain, trying to figure out what went wrong with us. Feel sexy. Lick her nipples. She's in the mood now. I lick her clit. We're fucking, me on top, with her digging her nails into my skin.

Another hard-on, another fuck, her on top.

She's on her stomach. I get hard, rub up against her ass and enter her from behind.

An unremembered fuck.

October

Morning after acid. She says no fucking but I grab her wrists, hold her down and stick it in. Then she's on top, slapping, fucking, and choking me until we come.

Tied spread-eagled to the bed. Lightly spanked on thighs, kissed on lips. She's all over me, frontwards, backwards, up and down on my dick. I'm licking her clit and then her ass hole. She's back on my, riding me until we come.

Snuggling in bed. Sucking and biting her nipples. Rough with her. Hard-on. Tampax out. Me in. On top. On our sides. Holding her down. Pulling hair. Pumping. Her on top. Light choking. Come.

Fucking in the middle of awful fights, tiredness, and depression. We need it.

Motel in Berkeley after an S&M party with Tom and Victoria. Light whipping while I eat her, then fuck, me on top.

She's on top with the cat-of-nine-tails wrapped around my neck, choking me as we fuck.

Off to the side of the road on Interstate 5 after she sucks, bites, and pinches my dick as I drive, or try to. We pull over, put her seat down, pants down, and I climb on, over the gear shift, onto her, into her, pumping, imagining cops, coming.

November

A little spanking over her lap, on the couch, as we watch tv, gets me hard, her wet, so we fuck.

Eating her after cleaning the house all day. Hard dick inside cockring. Hard and purple. She's wet. We fuck as she whips me with the cat.

Cockring. Purple cock. Whipped on ass and across back with the cat. Enter her from the rear. Watching my dick slide in and out and listening to her moan each time it does.

Warm, snuggling in bed. Hot for pain. Hard. Rubbing against her, licking her asshole while she fingers herself. I turn her over and lick her cunt. But all this is afterwards—first we fuck. Her on top, choking me with the bathrobe cord. Harder. I want to be choked harder. Don't want to come.

But the choking squeezes it out of me and then it's over—and then I suck and lick.

Some nipple licking. Some 69. I'm inside. On top. Harder and harder. "Hurt me." And she digs her nails into my already bruised ass. And I come much sooner than I want to because I never want to, it feels so good to fuck.

Dead tired. Trying to rest. Up all night, two nights. Both of us nude now, alone in bed. Too tired to sleep. I get on top and kiss her. Talk about drinking her piss and taking anything that comes out of her, even her shit. Hard-on. Slip inside her. Deep thrusts. Slow. Feeling every stroke. Both of us coming together.

Kissing and hugging and rough treatment by her: fingernails in my ass, back and balls. Hurt. Hard-on. Fucking, her on top. Choked with her hands and made to come sooner than I wanted.

Not feeling well, I finger her clit, and she my dick. Both of us hot and primed for fucking, which we do.

Thanksgiving Day fuck on the couch with "Mighty Joe Young" on the tv and the turkey in the oven.

Sucking her nipples gets her real hot this morning, and me too, so we fuck.

Fast but intense two minute fuck before she phones her kids in France. One of those great fucks where I can feel the sperm shooting out of the tip of my dick; and from her reaction I guess she can feel it likewise, splashing against her insides.

First I'm not allowed to touch her and then I'm lightly stoking her vagina and clit with my fingers. It feels softer than usual and I'm really hot to eat her but I'm not allowed. Then I am. I'm down under the blankets between her and she's getting wetter and hotter and I'm harder. She comes twice and then I'm allowed up from under the covers and my dick's inside her at last and she comes again and so do I, but I'm still licking her nipple and she's fingering herself until she comes again.

December

A really nice fuck after days of hurt feelings and distance from one another due to strange times in the art scene. But tonight I'm allowed close and then inside. She squeezes my balls with her nails and I love it. I miss it—pain. And I miss fucking. She tightens a rope around my neck, lets go, and tightens again, repeatedly until I come.

Lots to do today. But we're on our sides, in bed, her back to me, my dick nosing around in her ass crack and between her legs. Hard to find her opening from this angle, but she guides me in and we're fucking fast and hard, me grabbing her tits and squeezing as I pump, and she's moaning with every jab until we both come.

Groggy morning hard-on from her touch. She says a quick little fuck. I could take it or leave it, I feel so bad this morning. But it's good to be inside her. And then it's wonderful. Under the blankets, sliding in and out. It's not so quick after all.

I'm touching myself, and she's touching me, and I'm hard but not breathing so well so she climbs on top and I'm in. She's already wet. The bathrobe's beside me so she takes off the cord and slips it around my neck, slow and steady squeeze, steady rhythm, strong come.

Fucking after a terrible night of fighting because I'm no longer submissive. Don't feel much better this morning but she touches my dick and I'm hard and she wants to fuck, her on top because I'm not breathing so well.

More touching. More hard-ons. She wants more. So I'm sliding in. This time I'm on top and we're fucking again.

We fuck before we go out Christmas shopping. Fuck with all our clothes on, hers all the way down around her ankles. Me on top, in between her legs.

She's lying on her stomach. I'm on top of her, lying against her back, getting hard. I ask her to help me get it in. She does and I'm in and it feels good. Fucking.

My thirtieth birthday fuck, at my mother's after a night of speed and abuse. I'm her slave, but only for the day—rats!

I'm blind folded with smelly socks and undies and burnt with a red hot pin on my throbbing nipples. Then I'm tied ankles to wrists with some ribbon and I sleep for a while, until 6 a.m., then allowed to use our new vibrator on my penis; semi-hard (speed), but once inside her I'm real hard. Then she's on top and choking me hard and constantly with the bathrobe cord. Finally I come, but she keeps choking me and I come again—in my brain. Happy birthday.

She gives my thirty birthday whacks with the cat after a Japanese birthday dinner with David, Gail, Chris, Scott, and Dennis. I lick her cunt as she watches us in the mirror in her daughter's bedroom. I'm sucking and biting her nipples as she uses the vibrator and watches and comes several times. Then the beating. And then I'm fucking her as she's stretched out across her daughter's bed, her head hanging over the side, me holding her neck so the doesn't hit the floor.

Pumping, easy. All I can see is the underside of her chin, her head closer to the floor. Then we come, sliding completely off the bed as we do, laughing.